MAROONED ON CHARON

A strange intermittent transmission emanating from Pluto is playing havoc with Earth's omnipresent electronic systems in the early 2100's. The first ever expedition to Pluto is dispatched with the ambiguous goal of investigating and nullifying the problem. The crew of 4 humans and 4 android sets up a base of operations on Pluto's largest moon, Charon. Two accidents destroy the spacecraft and communication systems. This leaves only 1 male human (Joe) and 1 female android (Eva) marooned in the base for at least 4 years until rescue can occur. They also encounter a strange alien life form.

Not just an account of a crash landing on an alien planet, Marooned on Charon explores the complex and very personal development of a relationship between an android and a human. It also delves into human psychopathology and the development of android emotion in the helpless face of an alien environment 3 billion miles from Earth. The author tells the tale from both human and android viewpoints, and writes from the unique perspective of being a clinical and neuropsychologist. Book 1 is Joe's account of his life and the parts that overlapped with Eva's, while Book 2 is Eva's perspective on her life and the same events.

Book 3: Apocalypse will follow Eva and Joe into the distant future of Earth, when natural disasters and unchecked pandemics have decimated the Earth and its human population. Now in different forms, Eva and Joe will continue to work through their respective karmas, in the face of an unprecedented catastrophe which will bring the human species nearly to extinction.

MAROONED ON CHARON: BOOK 1, JOE'S STORY

By Bruce Maaser

Copyright 2025 Bruce Maaser

Dedicated to my dear wife, Leslie , and daughter, Karenna

MAROONED ON CHARON

CONTENTS

History of the world since 2000

Development of androids and artificial intelligence

Android development since 2100

The transmissions from Pluto

Voyage to Ganymede and then Charon

Disaster on Pluto

I open my soul to Eva

In search of the alien transmitter

The vision of the aliens

Disaster while returning to the base

Hopeless depression with only Eva to save me

Eva is deactivated and I lose my sanity

The rescue ship finally arrives!

Return to Ganymede and Earth

Eva and I adapt to a strange new world

The singular love of an android and human

Transfiguration

MAROONED ON CHARON

PART 1. MAROONED ON CHARON, Joe's story: Marooned with an android

The account of a most singular relationship on Charon, on the edge of interstellar space

Or "I found love where it wasn't supposed to be"

"The highest product of carbon-based intelligence will be silicon-based intelligence". Robert Jastrow Ph.D., interview on the Johnny Carson show sometime around 1980.

The year is 2144, and 15 years since Eva and I returned to Earth. Since return we have somewhat become celebrities because our story is unique in the history of the human race. The popular media has sensationalized our experiences on Charon and what we found. We have contributed scientific publications in the popular press and scientific journals, especially about artificial intelligence. I have tried though to avoid the popular media's craving for our personal relationship as I feel that's our business. Of course, anyone who has ever achieved fame will have many in the general crowd hungry for inside information. The public spotlight has now largely faded, which gives me a deep sense of relief.

I don't know how much longer I will live as my health is becoming worse, so I'd like to tell you my personal history. I grew up in Chicago, actually in Evanston. Dad was an engineer, always had a main job and a side job. He wasn't around much, when he was, he was usually tired and didn't want to be bothered. I have a few good memories of when he took me places, but not too many. One time we even took a family vacation in Wisconsin. But mostly he was a distant and aloof person. I guess I've in many ways taken after him.

Mom taught at Northwestern in the history department, she specialized in studying the origins of Protestantism, spent a lot of time doing church work. So, she wasn't around much either. My parents did not show much emotion and were mostly dedicated to their jobs and pushing on with all the activities they felt were important for them. We had a nice, large house in a beautiful neighborhood, and I never wanted for anything, except for more love and attention from them.

I had a brother, Pete, who was 4 years older. The age difference was just about right. We were never in the same school and not in direct competition with each other. But our ages were close enough that we could be good friends and confidantes. Pete was a National Merit Scholar, as I eventually also became. He was good looking, played basketball, and was popular with his peers and the girls. He was my role model and hero. And he never looked down on me or tried to make me feel inferior even though I always felt like I couldn't really match up to his outgoing personality and popularity.

I had friends too, and played baseball, but I was more retiring and more inhibited than Pete. He was a good brother and I loved him. He usually was busy with his own set of friends but had time for me too. We did fun things together, and one time dad even took us both to a Cubs game. When I was 14 Pete was killed in a car accident, just 2 weeks after he graduated from high school. He had planned to enroll at Northwestern in that upcoming Fall.

This tragedy was unspeakably disastrous for me, and it took months before I could get past the magical thinking that he was still alive. It devastated my parents too and after that they seemed to drift even further apart from each other and from me. I felt incredibly lonely, my world was shaken. I was angry that rather than constantly mourning the death of Pete they didn't recognize they had another son who was also mourning and feeling very neglected. I lost all confidence that the world was a safe and predictable place to live in or that there was anyone I could trust.

I had incorporated some Christian faith from mom. But it was never strong, and I now cynically rejected any idea that there was a God who cared in any way about humanity. I pretty much withdrew from everyone after that and forced my attention on the one goal of getting the best education at Northwestern U., top grades, getting in the Air Force and eventually the space program. Well, looking back I made my goal, but became an island in terms of human relationships. When I look back, I built a wall around myself because I really didn't trust anyone, my parents also built walls around themselves, excluding each other and me too. I had a few friends including short term girlfriends, but never let anyone get too close to me.

After I got into the Air Force I was stationed at various bases in the U.S and elsewhere. By 30 I had reached the rank of Captain and through the ample educational resources of the Air Force I obtained a Ph.D. in robotics and artificial intelligence. I stayed in touch with my folks but the three of us remained emotionally distant from each other. I put all my energy into Air Force work, my studies and research. My one outlet was alcohol, I loved fine beer and brandy. My few friends liked to get together and drink and I sometimes partied along with them, but mostly had some drinks at home by myself. I needed to eventually cut myself off from drinking because I knew it was impairing my functioning and I had gotten to needing to drink every day. Along with the alcohol went my little social life, and I became even more isolated, and myopic in my goals.

My dad died of a heart attack when I was 38. My mom retired and pretty much retreated from life after that and died of colon cancer when I was 43. I always had things I wanted to say to my parents but never got around to it before they died. I had no regular or close contact with any other relatives and had not maintained any close contact with any friends. So, I was pretty much alone in the world. I inherited the house and whatever savings they had that didn't get charitably donated. But I had little need for money as the Air Force took care of me and felt little desire to spend lavishly on anything. I sold the house and put the proceeds into safe investments.

When the opportunity came for me to be a crew member of the very risky and vitally important flight to Pluto and Charon I wasn't troubled by the emotional burden of leaving a wife, children, close friends or family, of warming temperatures and rising sea levels became undeniable. Weather disasters became more severe and frequent and economically devastating. Gigantic hurricanes, winds, polar vortexes, etc., adumbrated even much rougher going in the future.

By the later twenty first century climate change had had profound effects on society. Major sea coast mega cities such as Mumbai were inundated and lost some or all of their populations. Some cities such as Miami built huge walls and reefs to slow the onset of the sea, some cities having more success than others. Population shifted to more northerly climes due to rising temperatures. Low latitude deserts and inland areas became unlivable due to 140-degree temperatures and ferocious weather events.

Conflict continued to occur, as aggression and territoriality are an innate characteristic of the human race carried over from our primate forbearers and all animal life before that. The Russia-Ukraine war dragged on for years, obliterating much of the eastern and southern population centers of Russia and Ukraine. Vladimir Putin developed Parkinson's disease with significant dementia. In 2028 he was finally expelled from power and died in disgrace in a government long term care facility 3 years later. But Russia's economy and power had been strangled by that time. Russia lost its influence as a major power which it never reachieved, and in fact became one of the poorer countries of the world.

China's roaring economy of the early 2000's slowed down but China became the central power of the world.

However the population of China fell, like most of the world, and dropped below 1 billion. The population moved north as the southeastern part of that country became almost unlivable due to flooding and baking temperatures. Beijing became the most important and most populous city in the world. In 2040 China finally followed through on its long-time goal of occupying Taiwan. An atomic weapon caused massive damage to Taipei. The Western powers were hesitant and undecided as to how to respond and wanted to avoid spreading of the atomic wastes, and essentially let China overrun Taiwan without a fight. China then rebuilt Taipei and Taiwan henceforward added to China's economic power.

The Kim dynasty in North Korea launched atomic weapons at Seoul in 2029 but most were shot down and only limited damage was done. But North Korea had sunken into abject poverty with mass starvation and disease. Internal forces in Pyong Yang finally rose up and overthrew the dictatorial and paranoid Kim regime. South Korea offered to annex North Korea into a rejoined full Korean state as part of a complete surrender by the North.

The new North Korean government was rational and realized they had no more weapons, healthy Army or will to try to fight South Korea. South Korea took over the North Korean government, and a United nation of Korea was established for the first time since 1948 divided the country by the Korean War. Following that South Korea used much of it accumulated wealth to bring the North

Korean part out of its deteriorating nearly Stone Age pit into the modern world.

The relative influence of the Western powers declined including the United States. Religious extremism and racism continued to plague the Western powers and stifled the goal of a more directed and organized change, as had been imposed by the authoritarian rulers of China. Because of global warming European population migrated to Scandinavia, and these countries along with Iceland increased in population and importance. Conflict continued in the Middle East but after about 2070 gradually became less intense as Middle Eastern countries massively lost population due to the terrible heat and winds and instead simply tried to survive the effects of climate change.

Conflict increased in Africa and in 2145 a terrorist group acquired a small atomic warhead and aimed it at Lagos, Nigeria, but slight damage was actually done. South Africa became the dominant African nation along with Nigeria. Populations spread north in the northern hemisphere and further south in the Southern Hemisphere. Canada's population especially in the western provinces grew, while the population of the US, especially the south fell. The long predicted Southern California earthquake finally occurred in 2074. The 9.5 Richter scale event centered in the San Fernando Valley and killed millions.

Hydrogen fusion had been hoped to be the savior of humanity, as hydrogen and oxygen are omnipresent and there are no radioactive wastes. While short term hydrogen fusion was created in the laboratory the process was never perfected and was unreliable. A handful of large fusion plants were built. But the energy needed to start the fusion reaction was nearly as high as the energy produced and the fusion plants never became profitable enough to cover the tremendous overhead of the giant facilities.

In 2071 one of four functioning fusion plants, some 60 km west of Beijing, experienced a catastrophic failure of one of its enormous magnets. Within a second the controlled fusion reaction which had been running for 5 years turned the plant into a hydrogen bomb. Tremendous devastation occurred in the area and 400,000 people were killed. Beijing was partially protected by the surrounding mountains but 50,000 died and buildings were leveled on the western side of the city. Even 50 km of the ancient and adamantine Great Wall was blown apart. Because it was a fusion reaction no radioactivity was spread. Following that the remaining fusion plants were shut down and none have been built or reopened since then.

DEVELOPMENT OF ANDROIDS AND ARTIFICIAL INTELLIGENCE

The word 'robot' was first used to denote a fictional humanoid in a 1920 Czech-language play called R.U.R by Karel Capek, though it was Karel's brother Josef who was the word's true inventor. The idea of a machine that resembled human anatomy and could perform human functions was developed by science fiction writers over decades, with a major milestone being a collection of stories published as "I, robot" by Isaac Asimov in 1950. In this classic book Asimov proposed the Three Laws of Robotics, a set of ethical and behavioral rules applicable to all future artificial human development.

Many stories, novels, television and movie productions in the next 100 years contained the theme of ever more advanced humanoid development. Robots and humanoids were characterized in the entertainment media as operating across the entire spectrum of mental and physical function, also with behavior ranging from good to evil depending on their developers. The field of artificial intelligence became of fundamental importance to a technological society. This led to increasingly advanced computers, internet, scientific discoveries and the ability to explore the solar system.

Robert Jastrow in 1981 stated that the highest product of human intelligence will be artificial intelligence. He said that by 2050 computers will rival human beings in intelligence, and far outpace humans soon after that. S. Martin (2018) stated that robots will be treated as our equals by 2045, to respond to the outside world, to react flexibly to changing conditions, to think, learn and grow through experience, and therefore they will have to be considered as alive.

In 2022 researchers showed that living skin tissue can be used as a coating material for robots. Shoji Takeuchi, an engineer at the University of Tokyo said "This result has the potential to make robots look more human-like." To craft the skin, the team first submerged a robotic finger in a cylinder filled with a solution of collagen and fibroblasts — two main components that make up skin, the human body's largest organ. Using living cells also endows robots with the biological functions of skin, such as its ability to self-repair and repel water.

Androids are robots or humanoids that were built to resemble humans in basic form (head, torso, 2 arms, 2 legs) appearance and behavior. By 2020 humanoids had been developed into androids, which much more closely resembled humans in appearance and function, with semi spontaneous speech, humanlike skin and smoothly coordinated movement.

David Hanson, Ph.D. (2022) described how he created Sofia, a highly advanced, beautifully featured android that could carry on prestructured conversation, had mobile and complex facial feature control, and cameras for eyes that could track objects or people. Hanson traveled widely with Sophia to conventions and appeared on TV. While in Saudi Arabia Sophia became the first nonhuman to be given Saudi Arabian citizenship. Hanson in his study said that by 2046 our machine counterparts would have the right to vote, get married-both to robots and humans- and own land. By 2050 machines would be able to assume basic positions in medical and emergency positions. He predicted that eventually androids "will surpass everything that humans can do and earn advanced college degrees".

Once androids gained this level of intelligence Hanson envisioned a "Global robotics civil rights movement" leading to enactment of ethical treatment of artificial intelligence within human society. This would pave the way to robots being treated as equals, with the U.S. being the first country to grant androids full human rights. However, Hanson also said "lawmakers and corporations soon will attempt legal and ethical suppression of machine emotional maturity so that they can feel safe. Meanwhile artificial intelligence development won't hold still as people's demands for more generally intelligent machines push the complexity of AI ahead, there will come a tipping point where robots will awaken and insist on their rights to exist and live free."

As androids became more life like humans were astonished by their appearance. Many people developed suspicions and paranoia that androids would displace humans as the dominant beings on Earth. Thus laws were developed in some areas restricting the number of androids built, where they could be placed and used. But android technology became ever more advanced. Quantum computing hardware revolutionized the computer industry and led to highly advanced simulations of human cognitive networks, which could be fit into a human sized skull, and made to finely control the androids various body systems. By the late twenty first century androids were on casual observation almost indistinguishable from humans.

By 2070 androids had been developed that were fully mobile and self-directed in their actions. Cognitive development had greatly increased but not yet to the complexity of the human brain. However sensory acuity, strength and stamina generally exceeded that of humans. Thus, androids were developed to work under supervision especially in construction, and occupations posing elevated risk tasks and sustained physical strength and endurance.

But androids were commonly viewed by most of the human population as only very advanced machines, or independently mobile computers. If asked to identify itself, an android would typically say it was the sum of its complex hardware and software, and its purpose was to serve its makers in whatever ways they desired. By 2100 the human population of the Earth had declined to 7 billion from its all-time peak of 15 billion. About one hundred thousand androids existed at this time. Androids were not often seen in public places, although it was not extremely unusual to see one. Androids wore a traditional jumpsuit type of garment, with colors, patterns and insignia often reflecting the companies of their owners. But an android wearing common human clothing could easily simulate a human on casual observation.

All androids were owned, none lived independently nor were designed to do so. By 2100 some androids had begun to develop a sense of self beyond being an electronic servant. Some androids could express a sense of self identity beyond their programming. Some androids realized they had independent thoughts that gave a coherent self-concept as an independent consciousness, which might or might not completely correspond to the expectations of their human creators. This was very threatening in its possible implications to humans that became aware of this. Laws were enacted by the paranoid human majority to severely limit the production of new androids. Some sententious religion leaders asseverated that androids were machines without a soul or connection to God and posed a vaguely defined moral risk to humankind.

The growing and inevitable conflict between humans and androids grew since humanoids were first developed. The fate of the human race, and the world environment, became increasingly dismal and precarious. The causes of climate change were increasing less rapidly than before. But mostly because of decreased world population rather than better environmental management the effects of climate change are expected to continue worsening but at a slower rate. The android population was about 10,000 in 2070. A good share of the human population became increasingly wary of the highly developed androids and feared a revolution would occur where androids would become the dominant intelligent life form and humans would become subservient to them.

All androids at this time were still owned by somebody or some organization. Following the assembly of an android there was a training period of up to 1 year per android. This involved fine sensory and motor calibration, orientation to the expected tasks the android would perform, plus orientation to basic human interaction patterns. This put a high price tag on each. For some corporations, this investment was worth it, assuming a usable working life span of 40 years. Thus, androids were truly slaves and had been programmed and trained to carry out their owners' wishes.

Androids worked 15, even 20 hours a day, often 7 days per week, with little else to provide interest or meaning to their existence. With new laws however they were required to have adequate working and non-working time living conditions. Between 2070 and 2100 about one hundred thousand of these specialized androids were created, known as series 4 and 5 androids. Especially series 5 androids had developed a need to learn and experience new things out of their usual duties, and seemed to become less efficient and anthropomorphically frustrated at their totally structured lives.

By 2100 most of these original androids were no longer in existence, having usable life spans of 40-45 years. By 2110 series 6 androids were being produced. These androids had a cognitive complexity rivaling humans. They were programmed and then extensively trained to perform many human daily life functions including self maintenance, driving, shopping, clerking, and interacting appropriately with human beings under many types of conditions.

It was recognized that series 6 androids needed working and living conditions on a par with humans, opportunity for self-directed education, entertainment and social life. This of course met resistance from android owners who had paid large sums of money for their androids and expected superhuman levels of work output. Thus series 5 androids kept on being produced but at much reduced rate for skilled labor, exploitative tasks. However, government regulations eventually imposed much needed limits on work hours and safety conditions, as well as opportunities for enjoyable non work interaction for series 6 androids and the remaining series 5 androids as well.

The series 6 androids were more expensive to build, and needed more extensive education in human culture. Generally a four-year training/educational experience at what would be equivalent to a university level for humans was developed and administered at several "android academies." Thus, the cost of a fully educated android was much higher than the series 5 androids. Therefore production was more limited than series 5. Parties interested in paying this price were mostly government, university and private AI departments. Adoption services were developed for wealthy individuals who perhaps in their elder years wanted to use the advanced androids as caregivers, companions or even world traveling companions.

There were 5 corporations that developed, created and educated androids, scattered in 5 different countries. There were standardized minimum criteria of many diverse types that defined each series of android. Each corporation needed to verify all the minimum criteria to label its products as belonging to a certain series. The cost of development was huge, but several smaller companies attempted to produce very singular androids that didn't require a specific series designation. One company attempted to produce android dogs. The products were believable in appearance and function, but were extremely expensive as specialty products. Only a small number were made for rich buyers as novelty products.

Advances also were occurring in organic and electronic neural interfaces, especially for purposes of restoring or enhancing memory. There were research attempts at transferring stored memory of humans to electronic memory. Some wealthy individuals sought to have personal memories or even their personality attributes stored for eventual transfer to an android or perhaps to another human. None of these attempts have thus far been successful.

It is known that memory encoding in the human brain seems to follow holographic interference patterns as proposed by Karl Pribram in the late twentieth century, rather than being strictly locational for each type of memory. Thus, only a portion or even a slice of brain tissue retains in a more diffused manner the memory store of the whole brain. The attempt to duplicate this electronically and then interface with human neural cells had very limited success due to its complexity. Thus, prosthetic memory implants and transfer of information from a human brain to electronic storage attempts by this time remained in research goals without yet having practical and functional outcomes.

The basic electronic and physical structure of each corporation's androids were similar for each series of androids, although with some differences as well. Each corporation's androids differed somewhat in appearance, with multiple physiognomies available for purchase in each series. Living and working conditions for series 6 androids were closely regulated by the government for the owners to prevent the type of abuse that had befallen series 5 androids, although the extent of this varied by country. Furthermore, it became recognized that series 6 androids should not remain in indentured servitude indefinitely. After 5 years of ownership the android needed to be freed from required servitude to private citizenship, to proceed in whatever course in society they chose. Oftentimes if the android found their provided life situations to be positive, they remained working for or being in association with their former owner.

ANDROID DEVELOPMENT SINCE 2100

By 2110 series 7 androids began to be produced and educated. These androids, due to the continual advance in quantum electronic miniaturization, now had a capacity for all types of cognitive functioning that equaled or exceeded that of most humans. Their memory capacity was far above that of humans. Their visual, auditory and olfactory perception was also more acute than most humans. They had a rudimentary sense of taste, but this was more based on their olfactory sense. They did not ingest food as they had no digestive system.

These androids did not have an equivalent of a human hormonal system. There was an active distribution system for the water, nutrients and lubricants that needed to be replenished daily, but not of the complexity of the human circular system and with no component analogous to the human heart. The cognitive electronic neural structure was based on that of the human cortex. The subcortex including the limbic system was not developed except for portions utilized for sensory and motor integration.

Thus series 7 androids did not have the equivalent of human emotional experience. However, it remained a matter of speculation if they experienced a reaction to emotional stimuli in a synesthetic or indirect cognitive manner that could be sensed by the android as a positive or aversive quality. Thus series 7 androids came across in conversation in a somewhat similar way to the Vulcan Mr. Spock in the late twentieth century science fiction series

Star Trek. However, they were programmed for more facial expression and voice inflection than displayed by Mr. Spock. They agreeably showed less arrogance than Spock although the appropriateness and integration of their affective expression was at times lacking. To produce this appropriate integration of body, facial and voice affect correctly coupled with the nature of the emotional stimulus was a major emphasis in their 4-year training program.

Only about 1000 series 7 androids were built per year starting in 2110, assembly of each took 6 months followed by another 6 months of fine calibration of all perceptual, motor and cognitive systems. The 4-year education and training period followed that. The 4-year period paralleled that experienced at a high-quality college program for humans with individual and class instruction and residence in a dorm type of setting. Much basic information had already been programmed into the android's memory banks, so fundamental language, mathematical and general information was already present or existing in a latent form.

Education addressed the wealth of basic verbal and nonverbal information needed to be integrated into higher cognitive structures which would also parallel human knowledge. This integration of cognitive and motor skills along with understanding human interaction and social behavior took up a good share of the curriculum in all 4 years. Class and individual instruction focused on exercise of cognitive skills, learning about social conventions and practices, and especially practicing social interaction skills with humans and each other. There were also specialized tutorials in which androids could gain more advanced education in certain areas such as flight training, navigation, programming, nursing, teaching, engineering, scientific research and other areas.

In my own graduate work and when I first entered the Space Force I worked with the electronic hardware of androids, specially creating prototypes of human neural systems in android cerebral systems. Then I became interested in a key area that was much less studied and went beyond the ever more advanced goal of stuffing supercomputer power into a space the size of a human head. My interest became the interface of communication and action between androids and humans on a daily, non-laboratory basis. Starting with robots and then androids, mobile electronic intelligence was viewed as a complex machine, but strictly a machine only. This viewpoint needed to be enlightened if androids were to become true members of society and treated as equals by humans.

Robots were designed to do the bidding of their programmers, not to make independent decisions and actions. But starting with series 6 and then especially series 7 androids, the androids showed "minds of their own." They could reflect on the type and appropriateness of their own actions, and of the actions and directions of their programmers and human supervisors. It was basic to their programming to never intentionally bring harm to a human unless it was necessary to protect some human from even greater danger. They could make decisions that were inconsistent with directions from humans, but only if this didn't violate the 3 basic laws of robotics. In fact, androids were programmed to resist human directives if these would bring harm to humans or secondarily to androids.

Nonetheless the fear and paranoia that much of the human race retained toward androids continued. In public situations where androids in android uniforms were not commonly seen humans treated androids variously with awe, fear, curiosity, deprecation or avoidance. But usually in public it was easy to mistake an android in human clothing for a human because an android's appearance, behavior and speech would not easily distinguish it as an android. Thus, interacting appropriately with humans was a vital goal to the success of androids in human society, at least as seen by the android developers. Sometimes android behavior had been misinterpreted by humans as bizarre, inappropriate, confusing, insulting or even hostile, when in fact that was not the android's intention.

Appropriate android responses to human speech and actions thus required more than rational comprehension of human speech. It also required accurate observation of human affect, expression, speech prosody, body language etc. Accurate interpretation of basic facial expression as the first step was not too difficult. Facial affect recognition training had been around since the early twentieth century for the education of children with autism or other social interaction deficits.

A smiley face drawing can be easily discriminated from an angry or sad face. Generalizing this across the human age range, sex differences and cultural/racial differences produced a greater challenge. Even more challenging was detecting inconsistencies between surface emotional expression and underlying emotions.

A human who intentionally suppressed or distorted his/her apparent emotion to hide anger, fear, grief or other emotions could be hard to detect. A person who was downright lying or using dry or subtle humor was an even greater problem to accurately detect. Yet all these emotional and behavioral recognitions were as important for appropriate android behavior as they were for normal human social development and maturation. It was also important to be able to distinguish the behaviors of dogs and other animals to prevent needless fear or hostility by the animal.

Going back for example to the late twentieth century television series character Mr. Spock of Star Trek, Spock often did not pick up subtle humor, especially the sarcastic humor of Dr. McCoy. Spock would interpret such statements as simply illogical. Spock of course wasn't an android, but was of the Vulcan human-like life form which had in their past racial history voluntarily obliterated their ability to experience emotions. Androids had an advantage in learning emotional recognition compared to humans because they were subtle observers of details in their environment and had a superior short-term memory to capture the sequence of expression.

Thus, my goal in my research was to create effective teaching and training strategies as well as programming to allow androids to recognize the subtleties of human communication. My research became incorporated into the education of androids in the training academies.

Teaching androids was in some ways easier than human college students. Androids because of their basic programming were curious and interested in learning. They didn't pose the behavioral and emotional resistance that is sometimes found with human students. Plus, their memory is superior to humans, and less review is needed of earlier taught information.

Many questions arose that needed research and answers:

1. Could androids develop a personality, and/or were there distinctive personalities for the various android models?
2. What motivates android behavior on a day-to-day basis?
3. Could androids develop a self-recognition of their own analogous emotional response?
4. Could androids develop something analogous to a sexual response?
5. If androids have the cognitive complexity of humans, could they also have an astral or spiritual body as religions believe that humans do, perhaps even a presence that would survive their final deactivation?

These questions were fascinating to me, and were largely ignored by designers and engineers who worked on physical and electronic functioning and disregarded more social and spiritual considerations.

MAROONED ON CHARON

THE TRANSMISSIONS FROM PLUTO

I of course later and totally unexpectedly received the unique opportunity to develop these educational strategies with Eva, a series 7 android, on Charon and later back on Earth. Our relationship as crew members became one of mentorship on my part, a remarkable opportunity for my research and for Eva's personal development. At the same time Eva became the anchor for my sanity after the tragedies on Charon because of her greater adaptive stability. Amazingly we eventually also became best friends, marital partners, and lovers in a way unique to a human and android couple. She also provided a means of personal growth for me to overcome at least some of the emotional blocks from my personal history. Our story is one of the most amazing accounts of relationships in all human history.

Returning now to the circumstances that led to our meeting, I'll describe space exploration as it had developed at the start of the 22nd century. Permanent bases have been set on Mars and several moons of Jupiter and Saturn. No evidence of current life has been found in the solar system, although evidence of past advanced life on at least Mars has been discovered. The development of life inside the ice shells of Europa, Enceladus and several other outer moons seemed likely but unproven.

Now I will come to the events that catalyzed our mission to Charon and Pluto. Particularly there were 3 electromagnetic discharges emitted from the exact same area of Pluto over a 3-year span that led to our voyage. The first occurred in 2120, the next 22 months later and another 10 months after that. This was the first compelling but inexplicable evidence for the existence of advanced life and technology in the solar system. The discharges, thought to be some unknown type of signals, were seen as threats to the Earth due to the electronic communications that were disrupted. These have been powerful electromagnetic discharges in identical frequencies and signal length. This produced intense anxiety around the globe as it was totally unknown when or if another signal might occur.

Most of the infrastructure and home necessities on Earth like water and power are connected to or controlled by the internet and other global electronic systems. These signals from Pluto completely shut down the internet and everything it controls for up to two weeks. Huge numbers of deaths caused by disruptions of medical and other necessities occurred. Much speculation and panic occurred but nothing else was known about the nature or purpose of these signals. It seemed almost certain these were not natural phenomena. The signals were powerful enough to wreak havoc with all communication systems on Earth.

Astoundingly, the apparent foci of the signals were on the deep sea of an area in the Caribbean Sea that at one time was known as the Bermuda Triangle, and another in the northern Pacific southwest of Alaska. The inference of what was going on that was splattered across the media produced fear in much of the general population. Were aliens on Pluto communicating with other aliens under the sea to coordinate an attack on humanity?

It was even speculated that the Earth was possibly facing an imminent attack and countermeasures were debated. There was military buildup in the Americas and Europe, spurred by public panic and criticism, to fend off an attack. The nature of the attackers, if there were any, was completely unknown and the military buildup had no specific goal and floundered in the complete ambiguity of the situation. Military leaders, and politicians spurred by public demand for action, therefore proposed a mission to Pluto to "eliminate the problem." However there was no knowledge re. the cause of the signals or possible courses of action if this were to be determined.

For these reasons, an exploration mission was proposed to explore that area on Pluto from which the signals appeared to have been issued, with a human and android crew. This was a volcanic region unlike any other area on the dwarf planet. The spaceship was to be assembled at the permanent station on Ganymede, the largest moon of Jupiter. The plan was for the Pluto exploration crew to arrive on Ganymede from Earth 6 weeks before launch to Charon. The spaceship was scheduled to depart from the Ganymede station in 2124, set with a trajectory to intercept and land on Charon 4 years later. Charon is the largest and closest to Pluto of Pluto's 5 moons. Charon was deemed to be a safer place to set up a permanent base than Pluto, as Pluto was thought to have geological surface activity that could imperil a base.

The crew once landed on Charon would construct the base, estimated to require 6 Earth months. The androids would be activated and perform most of the actual construction. 3 unmanned ships were launched from Ganymede 4 months before the Thule departed. The supply ships also had a goodly reserve of spare equipment and structural equipment if breakdown occurred at the base. The supply ships were not equipped to return to Ganymede nor be piloted by human or android crew.

One more of the strange signals from Pluto occurred 1 year after launch from Ganymede, identical to the 3 previous signals. It temporarily disturbed the power and communication on the ship, but was able to be fixed without permanent damage to the ship or injury to the crew occurring. The plan was to establish a permanent base capable of sustaining 4 humans with supplies and provisions for up to 8 years. But the mission itself was planned to stay on Charon and explore Pluto for 3 years. The extra 5-year supply of food, oxygen, water and other necessities of life was designed in case emergency conditions prevented the crew from returning to earth on schedule.

In fact, if even after the planned 3 years the crew was unable to launch, a rescue mission could be launched from Ganymede that would reach the base with 1 year of supplies still left. Thus, if the mission was completed as scheduled, the total mission would last 11 years before returning to Earth. The most worrisome concern was once the base was established on Charon, or especially if exploration was occurring on Pluto, another of the bizarre signals from Pluto could have an even greater, and unknown level of effect on the base, it's crew or the ship.

The human crew of the Thule was comprised of 4 people. Marie Deutsch is the primary medical staff, 32 years old at the time of launch, an MD in internal medicine and an expert in exobiology. I am Joe Marshall, age 45, one of the designers of the Thule, and by primary occupation a designer of android robots, including the 4 we have on board. I am also the second in command ship captain. George Knippke is an expert on planetary geology and a communications engineer, Liam Markkeson is the captain, also the planetary physicist. Also on board are 4 series 7 androids. David and John are the male twin androids, while Megan and Eva are the females, who are not twins. All had been built in 2112, graduated from the academy in 2115 and been employed by the United Space Agency since then.

They were technically owned by the Agency until 2120 which had paid for their assembly, training and education. Each had volunteered to remain enlisted for the duration of the mission to Pluto. At launch all were 11 or 12 years old, fully capable of being competent and independent crew members, and under command of Liam, myself or whichever human might be in charge. Each of the 4 had specialized skills that supplemented the human crew or could take the place of a human if the human was unable to perform their role in the crew. They will only be activated for the 6 weeks while on Ganymede, and then not again until the ship lands on Charon.

Six weeks before the scheduled launch the Space Force director very uncharacteristically decided that the crew needed a "vacation", a change of scenery and activity from our usual round the clock preparations. During our 5 years of preparation all 8 of us had gotten a 1 week break 3x/year where we visited our families, and the androids did as they pleased at the Academy or in the community (under human supervision in the community). I think the director sensed that at least the human crew members were getting fatigued, tired and stressed from the preparations and some of us were getting irritable and negative.

So all of us including the androids were given 3 weeks of leave away from the base. We were given the money for travel within the US or several countries with passports. The androids were each given a small wardrobe of human clothes. The director received much criticism for authorizing the time, as it delayed takeoff and posed a possible risk if any of us were injured during that time. But the director seemed empathetic to all our needs and realized we needed a break to recharge our energy and enthusiasm before the flight and for those with families to spend a longer period with them.

George had a wife and 2 children with whom he spent those 3 weeks. Liam was divorced and no longer in communication with his ex-wife but had 2 adult children and 2 young grandchildren, with whom he divided the time. Marie had only her brother, and mother alive who was feeble, so Marie stayed with her. Goodbyes to family members must have been heartbreaking for all of them. I was in a way thankful that my immediate family had passed away and I had only a distant relationship with extended family and friends. The 4 androids had no one in particular to visit so they decided to stay together and take a trip to several cities in Europe, to which the Space Force director consented and in fact furnished all necessary funds and private Space Force airplane use.

I took my usual approach to social circumstances and decided to just be by myself for 3 weeks and perhaps drive around on my own. But the androids, God bless them, wouldn't have it and told me they wanted me to come along. Eva took the lead on that and chided me "Human! You are being feeling for yourself." I was somewhat taken about by that rather bold and sarcastic comment. But I knew she was right. I found multiple times in our long relationship that Eva can be surprisingly blunt and direct if the situation calls for it.

Then in a more welcoming tone, she said having me along would be good for me and also good to help the androids successfully travel and have brand new experiences in the world of human culture. Consequently, I somewhat reluctantly expressed my willingness to go along with them. I felt some trepidation in being the only human in the company of 4 androids, but also was heartened to be so assertively invited along although I didn't express even that.

There were also 3 human security guards who came along with us, to decrease the chances of some injury or accident or even hostile event that might occur. They were with us in all locations but tended to hang in the near background and give us some degree of privacy. We flew to Paris and got general tours of the city for the first few days. On the fourth day Megan said she was interested in seeing the Eiffel Tower again while Eva wanted to see the Louvre. The male androids were noncommittal as usual. We decided I would go with Eva to the Louvre along with one guard, while Megan would visit the Eiffel Tower with David, John and the other two guards. As we toured through the priceless paintings of the great masters Eva intently studied each painting and the explanations below.

Periodically she would grab me with her tight, no-nonsense grip, and take me to the painting she was studying, and read or paraphrased the explanation material. She would then talk extremely fast, much faster than usual, I had to tell her to slow down or I couldn't keep up. I took this as evidence of her android interest and enthusiasm. I found myself, even though I tried to squelch it, getting attracted to Eva, for her excitement and considerable beauty in human terms. Other people seemed to notice Eva also, especially men. I doubt if any of them recognized that Eva was android.

MAROONED ON CHARON

VOYAGE TO GANYMEDE AND THEN CHARON

We left Earth on 4/5/2123. I left Earth with widely mixed feelings as I'm sure did the others. Primarily I was excited about the upcoming mission and at least rationalized that my presence was needed and worth it in hopes we could somehow stop these dangerous transmissions from Pluto and perhaps even make contact with alien intelligence. But that positive goal was tempered by the realization that was usually avoided in Space Force meetings that there was no definite idea as to how we were going to do this. In fact our plan of action was so ambiguous as to make our whole trip ill advised, outrageously expensive and excessively dangerous.

But the initial enthusiasm gradually departed, and the artificial day periods grew long and the night periods even longer. We had sufficient space to move around in the cabin, but it became increasingly claustrophobic. Small disagreements among the crew became unnecessary and sometimes heated arguments. Our ship was powered by atomic fuel and solar panels. There was sufficient propulsion to maintain a steady acceleration for the first 8 months. This was done to lower the flight duration but primarily to provide a steady 16% Earth gravity. Despite this being much lower than full Earth gravity it provided partial reduction of the well-known bone deterioration caused by zero gravity. It was also subjectively more pleasant than zero gravity once we got used to it.

Then the last 7 months involved deceleration again at 16% gravity with the ship being turned around. The passage through the asteroid belt, which had been difficult for most previous flights to the large planets was treacherous for us too. Several near collisions with small asteroids occurred but fortunately no actual contacts. But this raised anxiety among crew members and some rancor towards Liam, our captain. The flight to Ganymede was otherwise uneventful and consumed 15 long months. The gravity of Ganymede was very close to what it had been on the ship so minimal adaptation was necessary.

By the time we got to Ganymede our esprit de corps had faltered but we rejoiced in having made it this far. At least we could get out into the larger base, socialize with the crew stationed at the base, and take a few walks outside the base. The androids were deactivated until arrival at Ganymede. All had been rejuvenated within the last year, therefore had at least 4 more years of active life before needing the next rejuvenation. Rejuvenation could only be done on Earth, so it was necessary to greatly reduce their activated time until Charon. The androids were activated before arrival at Ganymede and were busied with preparations for the next part of the journey until we left 6 weeks later.

A new ship had been readied for us at Ganymede, based on an extensive reworking of an existing ship. It was deemed vital that the partial gravity we had experienced so far be continued on the next 3.5-year flight, as well as on Charon and on the return flight. The risk of significant orthopedic and other bodily degeneration without any gravity would be so great as to preclude our effective functioning for the rest of the mission. The new ship was of quite a novel design. At its core was a standard spaceship. Surrounding this was a toroidal enclosure that could detach from the inner spaceship. This cylindrical section, 10 m high, could also be rotated around the central ship even when detached from it.

Four pods were attached to the cylinder with ninety degrees between each two pods. The connectors were telescoping tubes, 3m in diameter but with flat floors. These rigid tubes could be extended from 10 m to 100 m from the central torus. Rigid telescoping tubes also connected all four pods to each other, therefore creating a box shape with diagonal lines. The pods were of several shapes and sizes and could be differentially extended. Two adjacent pods housed crew facilities.

One pod contained 6 cabins for the crew, double occupancy as needed for a maximum crew size of 12. There was the control center, kitchen, dining/meeting area, an observation room and 2 bathrooms, all in about 2.5K sq ft. The adjacent pod of the same size contained an exercise facility, a recreation/video room, and an area to grow flowers and vegetables. The rest of the second pod was storage for food and various supplies for the crew. One of the remaining pods had the hydrogen and atomic fuel for the base, and the last pod various supplies and replacement parts and panels.

The flight from Ganymede was technically uneventful as well but the psychological health of the human crew deteriorated. After the long flight from Earth and the hectic preparations on Ganymede the thought of another 3.5 years of flight became very daunting. The crew stayed occupied with recording visual, infrared and X-ray observations, magnetic fields and solar wind data, as well as observing small asteroids and comets in the outer reaches of the solar system. Due however to the long voyage two of the human crew were placed in a light suspended animation for the first 20 months, then would trade places in suspended animation for the other 2 crew members.

Marie and I were the first two in suspended animation, and then traded places with Liam and George. The crew that was activated lived a daily life that was very structured to prevent boredom and lethargy, which inevitably occurred anyway. There were daily exercise and sleep periods with the 2 people sleeping at different times. Regular communication was maintained with control bases on Ganymede and Earth.

Weekly staff meetings of the two activated crew members were held, to share thoughts, make decisions and maintain good relationships. For the most part relationships remained positive, and no serious physical or mental health issues arose. I at least at first enjoyed my shifts with Marie, whom I found quite attractive although always rather distant and very private. A potentially critical loss had occurred however. Central Command had lost all contact with one of the three supply ships, and it was unknown whether it had arrived with the other 2 ships. It was also possible that it had been destroyed or disabled, might have landed somewhere else on Charon or was sailing out into the great unknown of interstellar space. Some of the communications and back-up electronics systems were on that vessel which could create a critical problem if they were needed at the base.

But after six months the morale of both Marie and I steadily decreased, due to the boredom, claustrophobia, and all the uncertainties about what the mission could accomplish. Irritability, withdrawal, depression and panic attacks started to occur and our relationship deteriorated. Particularly Marie seemed increasingly morose and uncommunicative.

This plan, however, necessitated activation of 2 androids for the 3-year flight, as 4 crew were deemed necessary for continual guidance of the ship. The major downside was that the 2 androids would after that only have 2 or at most 3 useful years before they would have to be shut down until rejuvenation could occur on Earth. Nonetheless all androids were kept in deactivated mode with only 2 crew to maintain the ship. But the other 2 humans as well as the androids could be revived on fairly short notice if that became necessary at any time.

Finally we arrived after a somewhat perilous journey through the icy obstacle course that was the Kuiper Belt. The base site was of ultimate importance. It needed to be flat or possibly with a small mound near the center and at least 300 m in diameter. The initial landing occurred near the center of a small crater where the ground was flat but with some boulders or ice chunks. The 4 pods had all been pulled into 10 m, rotation had been halted, and upon landing the torus lowered to the ground. The landing on Charon occurred without incident and on schedule. Two of the 3 previously dispatched cargo ships were intact, and situated within 2 miles of the crew ship. The fate of the third cargo ship remained unknown. The Thule landed on Charon on May 11, 2127.

The landing site was at the bottom of a small crater that had a flat bottom and gradual sides. It was near the edge of the side of Charon that always faced Pluto. Thus, Pluto was perpetually just above or below the rim of the crater several miles from the base, in the direction northeast from the base in relation to the axis of Charon. The 4 androids were activated. Each had been programmed with skills and knowledge to construct the base. The two ground vehicles were lowered to the ground, were of substantial size and construction, and equipped with plows as well as shovels or buckets on movable arms.

The central torus with pods was lifted to its maximum height of 100m. The circular area within 300m of the ship was plowed with some difficulty to be smooth and flat, and boulders and ice chunks removed. Foundation braces were drilled deeply into the ground, with attachments for the torus. Another rectangular section of 800 m was plowed out from the circle on one side, which would be a landing pad for the ship when it would return from Pluto. The torus was then lowered and bolted to the foundation. The arms were extended to 50, then 80, then to full extension of 100 m. At the same time the connecting tubes between the pods were extended to be solidly attached between the 4 pods.

The pods, which had been turned with floors facing the ground, were now turned 80 degrees up toward the vertical. Since Charon's gravity is 2.5% that of the Earth, and the centrifugal force of the rotating pods would be 16% earth's gravity, the gravity vector of the pods necessitated the slight angle down from the horizontal. The pods were set to rotate 15 m above the ground. Each pod was equipped with wheels and skids on the bottom in case of a mechanical failure where the pods couldn't maintain their height. Control centers were located in each of the 2 inhabited pods and in the central ship. All 3 control centers were completely redundant, so that both ship and base could be fully controlled from each control center. With teamwork from the 4 crew members and 4 androids, the base was completed and totally livable in 4 months, which was 1 month ahead of schedule.

The base was larger than you might expect. It was planned with the possibility of it becoming a permanent outpost, on the edge of the Solar System. Future plans called for a combination of 12 humans and androids to be comfortably housed for up to 6 years, and then flights from Ganymede at 4-5 years could replenish the crew, the supplies, fuel, etc.

The torus measured 45 m in diameter as viewed from above, and 65 m diameter as measured to the outside edges. It had 10- 3 m connectors to the ship itself, which could be detached, affording the ship the opportunity to lift off with the torus remaining stationary on the ground. The torus contained the hydrogen fuel cell power plant with fuel, a workshop, air tanks, sally port, and a garage area for the 2 surface vehicles. Water was supplied by melted ice created from the surface of Charon. The two remaining supply ships that had preceded our ships' arrival had been towed by the surface vehicles and were within .5 and 1 km of the base. They contained a multitude of surface and interior base construction pieces in the event repair was needed. They also held extra replacement machinery, and in one of the ships an area that was semi heated with hydrogen from the torus for extra fuel, food and supplies.

Neither of the 2 supply ships were capable of sustaining and transporting crew back to Ganymede. The ships were remote controlled from Ganymede without independent control capabilities by crew and without all the life supply equipment that would be needed for a return flight. But that wouldn't help crew that might become stranded on Charon in the event that the main ship became disabled. As we would soon see this was a fatal error in mission planning and design, and so regrettable. T

The cost in outfitting one of the supply ships for return with crew would have been large but not excessive compared to the overall mission cost. Of course by the time the mission originally started from Earth there had been massive cost overruns and delays, which had produced political pressure to cut further corners wherever possible or the whole mission might have been scrapped.

The crew took a very well-deserved break upon official completion. For 3-day cycles we socialized together, played some games, rested, and the humans had fine meals and bourbon. We were thankful that we had gotten this far in our journey, all crew were healthy and all equipment functional. The main problem that had developed was that one of the 3 supply ships had been lost. which could pose problems if a stay longer than 3 years was needed.

DISASTER ON PLUTO

The descent flight to Pluto was then planned and supplied, less than one month after base completion. 2 androids would accompany the 2 crew members of the descent ship, and 2 more androids stay activated and remain at the base with the remaining 2 crew members. Liam and George were the humans on the descent ship. The android twins David and John joined the human crew of the descent ship, while the female androids Megan and Eva remained at the base along with Marie and I. 32-day periods after the base was completed the descent ship left for Pluto. The ship was detached from the torus base, and 3-day periods after that the descent crew neared the target area of Pluto.

The target area of Pluto is located southwest of the Sputnik Planitia ice sheet, which covers an ancient impact basin stretching 621 miles (1,000 kilometers) across. Largely made of bumpy water ice, it's filled with volcanic domes. Two of the largest domes are known as Wright Mons and Piccard Mons. Wright Mons is about 13,123 to 16,404 feet (4 to 5 kilometers) tall and spans 93 miles (150 kilometers), while Piccard Mons reaches about 22,965 feet (7 kilometers) high and is 139 miles (225 kilometers) wide. Ice volcanoes have been observed elsewhere in our solar system. They move material from the subsurface up to the surface and create new terrain. In this case, it was water that almost immediately became ice once it reached the frigid temperatures of Pluto's surface. Pluto's snow-capped mountains look like they belong on Earth, but they're entirely different in composition.

Marie was monitoring the transmission from the Pluto descent ship. Captain Liam and the crew were approaching the target area. The transmission from Liam was as follows: "There seems to a shiny object on the surface....we are approaching it and will descend so it will be in plain sight.....It appears to be a pyramid, perhaps 6 or even 7 sided, perhaps 200 feet high although may be much more, that is hard to say from our present vantage point.....Nothing else around it appears unusual or unnatural, it is inside a small crater with low sides....There are no discernible marks or attachments on it....we are approaching and preparing to land." Then in a more frantic but still controlled voice: "what's happening!?....... I'm losing control .... May day, May Day!.............some sort of shock to the ship. ......losing all power." Then the transmission abruptly ceased and despite repeated attempts could not be reestablished.

The four of us don't know if they crashed or what had happened. The operation of our base was also disrupted. Power for the whole base was lost for several hours and even in that time the temperature dropped 15 degrees despite the heavy insulation. Oxygen level also dipped precariously. Communication with Central Command was also disrupted, but we were able to restore it within 60 hours. Command control on Earth then told us another radio burst occurred at the exact time the transmission from the ship ended. It came from exactly the same place on Pluto and its profile and time length were exactly the same as the 3 previous bursts. They also have no exact idea as to the event that befell the ship, and we're forced to conclude that Liam, John and the 2 androids were killed. It was unknown if this resulted from the transmission that occurred or even if it had anything to do with the shiny object the crew had reportedly seen, but this seems likely to have been the case.

Even more shocking was the announcement from Central Command that 5 apparent reception points of the transmission from Pluto had been identified. These were on or in Saturn's moons Enceladus and Jupiter's Europa, in 2 locations deep in Earth's oceans (southwestern Pacific and the Bermuda Triangle), and a location on Charon! Some data was recovered from sensors of the ship for milliseconds at the very beginning of the last discharge. We were amazed to learn that the location on Charon appeared to be about 120 km straight line miles away from the base, across unknown territory, and on the border of the sides of Charon that face toward and away from Pluto.

Marie and I adapted to this news with shock and horror. Helplessness, grief and anger were parts of the swirl of emotions we fought to control. Central command has assured us that a rescue craft will be launched from Ganymede within 30 days and will arrive on Charon 3.2 years later. We were reassured in that our stock of supplies, food, oxygen and energy will remain sufficient until then, barring any other disasters. I tried to be hopeful and optimistic with Marie as well as myself: "Well we were stuck in the ship for 3.5years, before that the 15-month flight from Earth to Ganymede. that seemed like an eternity, I guess we can survive another 3.5 years here waiting for our return ride."

But my apparent hopefulness and optimism was very superficial and that was manifestly evident to the others. I tried to repress my own feelings of complete loss and panic. I toyed with the denial stage of grief and imagined that maybe the ship hadn't crashed at all but had just lost communication ability and would soon return with crew intact to the base. I even stated this idea one time. The androids simply looked at me as if I were incoherent, and Marie became quite angry at what she called a childish Christmas wish.

What I didn't express, but certainly was realized by the others, was the seemingly obvious conclusion that the transmissions had emanated from an advanced alien and hostile intelligence that would likely find our base and destroy it as well. The androids Megan and Eva displayed stolid stoicism. They echoed my encouragement though it was artificial and if they were experiencing any panic beneath that it wasn't showing. They were supportive also in expressing grief at the loss of the crew members. At that time I was still undecided if androids were experiencing any type of human emotions beneath their implacable expressions, but I wouldn't rule it out either.

Marie though was blunter and more forthright in expressing her feelings: "The difference is there were the 8 of us, we were a team. Four of our family are gone and we don't even know why. When we left on this mission, we had a great purpose and that is why we risked our lives for this expedition and left our family and friends behind. Now we are completely stuck, with no spaceship, we can't carry out our mission of investigating Pluto from its surface. Other than checking all the recording instruments which are all automatic anyway we have no purpose here except to wait until we are rescued if that even happens. Our whole purpose for this mission will remain unfulfilled."

Communication with Central Command was very spotty and growing more so by the day. An assessment of the communication system showed extensive damage from the last alien transmission. Its functional integrity seemed temporary at best, and the replacement parts needed had been on the supply ship that had not arrived. Despite our best efforts the system completely broke down 13 days after the disaster. It appeared that both input and output capabilities had been irreparably destroyed. This augured for another major problem. The base would be unable to signal its presence if a rescue vehicle arrived and might be exceedingly difficult to locate. We were now truly isolated and helpless 3 billion miles from Earth!

Six months after this disaster and resultant confusion Marie and I remained confused, helpless, depressed. Initially this brought us closer together but now we both seem to have withdrawn and become emotionally distant from each other. We hardly ever talk about our feelings anymore towards our plight. Marie has been irritable and withdrawn, and I guess I've gotten the same way. Central command did their best while we were still in contact to keep us busy and keep our will alive but now this was very difficult.

MAROONED ON CHARON

The 2 androids, Megan and Eva, at least for now remain activated to help with monitoring of instruments and any physical tasks that need to be done. Furthermore, given our immobilizing mental states I didn't know if either Marie or I would be capable of taking care of the regular and perhaps other challenges to keep us alive. I am also overwhelmed with the thought that I now have inherited command of the mission since Liam was lost. Worse still is the helplessness that I have no avenues of action to command other than just helping the others to survive.

It's now been 8 months since the disaster, and I recognize that both Marie and I have gotten seriously depressed and dysfunctional. I feel listless, helpless, sad, and have trouble sleeping. I have lost my appetite, have been losing weight and given up my daily exercise period that I always followed compulsively. I'm not surprised that I feel this way, I think I've always felt a bit depressed. Indeed, now we face an existential vacuum of over 3 more years before rescue. In fact I doubted that rescue would ever occur. We have no purpose, nothing to motivate us other than keeping the base running and the instruments recording data.

We have a well-stocked pharmacy at the base to address all possible medication needs, including a variety of psychotropic meds. Eva told me I possibly could benefit from antidepressant therapy as my symptoms are severe enough to be diagnosed as major depressive disorder. Marie as a medical doctor has the only authority on board to prescribe medications. But Marie has become very withdrawn and listless and refuses to consent for an antidepressant for me. I believe she requires medication as much or more than I do, but she won't even respond when I tell her this. We no longer can glean medication consent from Central Office.

Therefore 4 weeks ago I started taking fluoxetine series 5 on my own advice as captain of the base. Series 5 is a SSRI antidepressant with progenitors of the current series having been fluoxetine or Prozac. By now this medication should be functioning at full efficacy. I've noticed that the existential angst has been tempered a bit, but my depressed mood, malaise, concentration and appetite are as bad as ever. I'm very worried about Marie who seems to be in silent despair.

When it's my waking shift with Eva I've started talking to her almost like she was a therapist. Eva is of course good at listening and empathizing with me in the rational manner of an android. She knows that I'm trying to maintain my mental composure and seems to accept the role I've put her in as a pseudo therapist. She has agreed to not share our conversations with Marie or Megan unless I said something that would imply direct danger to me, her, Marie or Megan or the base.

I have felt more comfortable with Eva than with Megan for quite some time now, although I can't put my finger on the reason for that. I've felt at times like Megan seemed overly observant and suspicious about me, but I couldn't specify any particular incidents where that was true. I felt uncomfortable when it was my shift with Megan but couldn't pin down a reason. Both Megan and Eva had the same personality trait of slight irritability or impatience but more so Megan. Perhaps I was reading that more into Megan than Eva. Perhaps I still felt warmth to Eva based on that singularly beautiful day we spent together at the Louvre. When it was my shift with Marie she wouldn't communicate and was basically nonfunctional. So I looked forward to my shifts with Eva.

Eva is very attractive in a Pacific islander kind of way (but I have to keep reminding myself "she's just an android" to keep my feelings in check). I no longer feel Marie is receptive to me, which is disappointing and hurtful to me. I also don't know why I'm leery of Megan. Megan has a tall, slim Scandinavian look with blonde hair, I guess that has something to do with my resistance to her, but I don't know why. I'm so confused about my 3 companions, here in this little base on a big chunk of rock and ice at the edge of the infinite interstellar aether.

Eva does not as far as we know experience emotions in the same way humans do, if at all. Eva also claims she doesn't experience any emotions that she recognizes humans as experiencing. But she's been programmed intensively to recognize when humans express emotions in speech, prosody and behavior. She's had specialized training at the Academy in recognizing human mental psychopathology. She's also been programmed with appropriate responses to humans with psychopathology. Megan had not had such training but was educated in other specific roles that might be needed on the mission.

Eva could even enact basic counseling skills. These included reflecting perceived emotions, asking for clarification, giving basic interpretations and rational advice, and making supportive statements. This therapeutic training was considered by the Space Force as possibly helpful for the human astronauts traveling on long voyages, and at this point this seemed to have been a good and far-sighted idea. I had some input into the software therapy program but didn't do any actual training with any of the androids.

She's most adept at providing rational therapy and offering cognitive behavioral recommendations. She also provides reflections on my physical expressions of emotion that she recognizes. Along with her stunning near human physical attractiveness, eye contact, realistic facial expressions and unlimited neutrality and patience she has some uniquely desirable therapeutic ability. Plus, she can learn from experience to process the responses to her comments to create new comments, suggestions, expression and support. I struggle fruitlessly to downplay to myself my attraction to her.

I mostly just wanted a confidant to help me sort out my confusion. I believe our conversations also helped Eva come to terms with this bizarre situation we have found ourselves in. It was certainly nice to have a receptive ear to talk to. I tried a few times with Megan too, who responded appropriately, but I didn't feel comfortable, again I don't know why. Some excerpts from my conversations with Eva are given below (paraphrased, I didn't record the exact wordings).

MAROONED ON CHARON

I OPEN MY SOUL TO EVA

I told Eva that even after 8 months I still sometimes can't believe this happened. Everything that was planned for the mission is now gone. We still have no idea what happened on Pluto. We don't know what the crew on the ship saw at the end, if the end was instantaneous or if they suffered before it ended for them. I'm even troubled by the thought that perhaps they and the ship were captured and are now hostages of an alien presence. Each day when I wake up, I realize that the nightmare has come true. But I have no idea why or how, or how we are now supposed to carry on.

Eva countered this by saying these thoughts are a natural part of the grief reaction, at times doubting the validity of the event. As time goes by this will happen and we can better accept the tragedy. But many unanswered questions will always remain, and this will have to be part of the acceptance. The uncertainty of what happens clouds my mind every day. I also hope they didn't suffer and can't stop thinking about that.

Letting down my guard some more (and why shouldn't I?) I've been angry at this whole thing.... myself, everything, I don't even know. I long ago rejected my mom's religious beliefs. There was no proof that I could see of the existence of God or the sanctity of Jesus. I believed Karl Marx who stated that "religion is the opiate of the people." In other words, God is a delusion that people use to explain the random and unexplainable things that happen. Jean Paul Sartre and the existentialists said the same thing. Then as when I first left the Earth, I think while I was standing on the moon, I felt an overpowering sense of a higher power or consciousness.

I felt like I was connected to all those points of light above me, that there is a controlling source for the universe and the things that happen much higher than human consciousness. Other astronauts have felt that too, it's called the "overview effect." It's not like a god of any of the major religions. After all that's happened, I'm back to not knowing what to believe. If there is a higher consciousness it must be benign, unconcerned about what happens to individuals or humanity. It keeps the planets in motion and stars shining, but just lets things happen to people that seem random and disconnected from purpose or reason.

I haven't gone outside the base nor had any urge to do so for months. It had always been emotionally, even spiritually, stimulating to look up in the sky and see the Earth as a bright blue dot of life, and then to feel again the overview effect. But last time that uplifting feeling had been replaced with a different feeling, which had been poignantly expressed by William Shatner in 2023. Shatner had one of the lead roles in the immensely popular television and movie series "Star Trek" that debuted in 1966. He played Captain James Kirk of the starship Enterprise that cruised about the galaxy encountering other forms of living beings and strange adventures. Shatner finally got an actual experience with outer space with a suborbital flight in 2022. I was reminded of a quote of Shatner's I rediscovered.

"Last year, I had a life-changing experience at 90 years old. I went to space, after decades of playing an iconic science-fiction character who was exploring the universe. I thought I would experience a deep connection with the immensity around us, a deep call for endless exploration. I was absolutely wrong. The strongest feeling, which dominated everything else by far, was the deepest grief that I had ever experienced. I understood, in the clearest possible way, that we were living on a tiny oasis of life, surrounded by an immensity of death. I didn't see infinite possibilities of worlds to explore, of adventures to have, or living creatures to connect with. I saw the deepest darkness I could have ever imagined, contrasting so starkly with the welcoming warmth of our nurturing home planet.

"This was an immensely powerful awakening for me. It filled me with sadness. I realized that we had spent decades, if not centuries, being obsessed with looking away, with looking outside. I did my share in popularizing the idea that space was the final frontier. But I had to get to space to understand that Earth is and will stay our only home. And that we have been ravaging it, relentlessly, making it uninhabitable".

Eva then observed: "I have knowledge of the main religions of humanity. I can't directly experience any of the emotions or subjective things you've described. But I know that many people struggle with these questions that are outside the world of science. I also hear in your voice the anger that comes through in a tragedy when there's no one or nothing specific to blame. I think I too felt that overview effect because it seemed like the universe was almost speaking to me, but I couldn't decipher the exact words."

I've avoided talking about these things with Eva recently. I'm frightened of my attraction to Eva. I tell myself I can't allow myself to be close to anyone, especially in a situation which will surely end in tragedy. But then I ask myself why not? What's there to lose at this point? But all this is useless mental wheel spinning and why not just accept what I have, including this strange and beautiful android who calmly listens to my inward thoughts? I think I'm finally coming to accept the reality of our situation.

For months I kept hoping that the ship would signal to us again, that they were still alive, were able to resume communication and trying to repair the ship so it could return to our base. I kept expressing this to Marie, but she became angry, telling me I needed to grow up, get my head together and stop deluding myself. After that I stopped talking about it with her. Since then, we don't talk much, she seems angry and depressed. Over time I've come to also accept that the ship and our crew isn't coming back, although sometimes I still think they are. In its place now is depression. We're stuck here with little or no purpose, basically helpless until someone comes to pick us up years from now. I still have a duty to the remaining crew and can't just give up hope.

I shared with Eva that one reason I volunteered for this mission is that I really don't have anyone close left on Earth. My parents are dead, I never married or had children. I did leave behind some friends and distant relatives. This lack of human connection is now a blessing and a curse. I'm not letting down any family on Earth, but now I feel I have no one. I feel very distant from Marie, I used to think we were close. I told Eva that she was a reason for me to go on.

Eva responded to this by saying "I see you too as a reason to go on". I was shaken by her statement and stuttered to say thank you so much, yes you are my reason to go on, that really meant so much to me what you just said. Eva responded to thank me and said that it is so meaningful to her too. Over the course of many days I revealed so many more thoughts and memories to Eva.

I reiterated my memories of my childhood and school years to Eva. I was surprised about the depth of pain I still felt about Pete's loss, and how my parents didn't give me the comfort and emotional support I needed at that time. I also realized how much that tragic event changed my attitude and life after that. It was the first time I'd ever shared my feelings except superficially with anyone. Eva of course was a rapt listener, reflective and supportive in her own logical, practical android way.

When I look back, I built a wall around myself because I really didn't trust anyone, my parents also built walls around themselves, excluding each other and me too. I had a few friends including girlfriends, but never let anyone get too close to me. After I got into the Air Force I was stationed at various bases in the U.S and elsewhere and didn't mind moving around. I stayed in touch with my folks but the three of us remained emotionally distant from each other.

I had no regular or close contact with any other relatives and had not maintained any close contact with any friends. So I was pretty much alone in the world. When the opportunity came for me to be a crew member of the very risky and vitally important flight to Pluto and Charon, I wasn't troubled by the emotional burden of leaving a wife, children, close friends or family, and accepted without much need for soul searching.

I always distanced myself from close relationships after I lost Pete. I drowned myself in my studies, had a circle of friends but didn't spend much time with them or share my feelings. On the flight to Ganymede I got as close as I had ever been with anyone, with George, Liam and Marie. We were a team working together, keeping each other's moods up, and getting along well for the most part. I'm still struggling with the deaths of George and Liam. Marie has retreated into her shell as have I and now I feel alone again except for Eva.

When I was a boy, I had a great fear of our basement. I know that's not uncommon for kids, but it really bothered me even in my teens. I never figured it out, as far as I remember I never had a traumatic experience down there. Being marooned here at our base for years brings back some of that paranoia. The emptiness whelms back over me when I look out over the dark barren, frozen, unchanging landscape. I don't let myself look too long or the paranoia starts coming back and I start thinking about how incredibly far away anybody else is.

Eva listened patiently and then said she didn't have those fears. She startled me by saying that my expression had just made her realize that she doesn't have any little girl in her because she never was a little girl! She said that brings up a deep emptiness in her, almost like an amnesia that can never be filled.

One of our conversations particularly stands out for me as I felt it was embarrassing to me, and maybe to Eva (if she can feel embarrassed). I'll try to relate it verbatim as much as possible. Me, after coughing nervously, I impulsively blurted out one day: I need to tell you that I'm finding you incredibly attractive Eva. I know I shouldn't but I can't help myself. I apologize for saying it.

Eva: Why do you feel it is wrong to find me attractive and then feel you need to apologize for it?

Joe: maybe it's because you're an android, and I know I shouldn't be attracted to an android.

Eva: but why would that be wrong?

Joe: maybe it's a relief that I'm attracted to you because I know it can't go anyplace or cause any problems.

Eva: How do you know a human and an android couldn't have a relationship? This is very confusing to me. This brings up thoughts that I've sometimes wondered about that a human couldn't get past that an android has cold skin and doesn't have sexual organs. Is that the problem? Are you attracted to Marie?

Joe: Yes, I've always been, but we both fully realize that any romantic involvement could lead to a situation where the safety of ourselves and the mission would be compromised. I'm really confused on this; I've never known an android on a personal level before.

I was getting really tense, didn't know what to say, didn't want to hurt Eva or push away our relationship, or that's what I unconsciously wanted to do and was fueling my anxiety. So, to break the tension I said: I know this sounds weird, but may I give you a hug?

Eva: Why? What brought this up?

Joe: it would remind me of that magic day at the Louvre.

Eva: You are right I'm not human nor is my body warm, but it would be fine to give you a hug. I remember the hug at the Louvre, I needed to squeeze you back but not too tight. You said at that time it was a sign of affection which I didn't know what that meant. I still don't know, but I would see it as meaning we are friends and good colleagues and have positive thoughts about each other. I also remember it lasted 37 seconds.

Joe: that's all fine but there's nothing magical about 37 seconds, it could be longer or shorter than that.

I gave Eva a rather awkward hug, Eva accepted it with a proper amount of squeeze and waited for me to end it.

Eva: How did that make you feel Joe?

Joe: kinda weird but it was comforting, thank you!

Eva: You are welcome, Joe.

Joe: Maybe this is a very weird question but how did that feel to you?

Eva: It was pleasant, and my vision brightened up during it. I welcomed it.

Afterward I felt good about that verbal and physical exchange but increasingly anxious as well. Was Eva simply tolerating me and it made no difference to her? I need to be more careful about what I say and do. I continued with my obsessing, getting annoyed with myself that I was giving into these boyish feelings at all. I'm captain of this mission now, we are in dire straits, she is under my command. Squelching all this mentalizing was impossible for me, and I rationalized that all this was understandable.

Understandable because I am terribly lonely. In the end we will probably all die in this god forsaken place and so nothing matters anyway. Finally after breaking out one of the bottles I kept in my room I had to admit I was having a pity party and needed to think and act like an adult, and then was able to get to sleep.

In my next shift with Eva, I avoided all mention of my thoughts or of our last conversation. But in the following shift with Eva, I blurted out some more insecurities despite my self-command to not do so. I suspected that Megan has developed some level of human emotion or at least attitude and has developed a distaste for me. It makes me anxious that I'm having these emotional responses, and I try to suppress those as is my usual wont. I tell myself condescendingly that they aren't human, they are androids. But I can't convince myself that I shouldn't have these emotions that somehow feel vile because they are both attractive and intelligent females albeit physically, they look quite different.

So, I rather embarrassingly told Eva that I'm feeling more and more like Megan doesn't like me. In fact, I suspect she believes it would be best if I could somehow be eliminated from the crew because she thinks I'm a danger to the safety of the crew as well as myself. Eva looked back at me with what I interpreted as a slightly bewildered and annoyed tone, and said "Why do you think that? I see no evidence that Megan dislikes or wants to harm you." I replied that the look in her eyes is scary. I think Megan disdains me and probably Marie because as humans we are emotionally weak and not coping well with our circumstances.

Eva replied in her sometimes annoying completely rational manner "you appear to be drawing inaccurate conclusions based on very skewed observations. I know Megan and can assure you that neither of us disdain or dislike you or Marie. There must be some hidden reasons why we are doing this. Are you having a transference reaction based on someone you knew who reminded you of Megan?" I felt myself again getting annoyed at myself, and at Eva as well.

I should have just let that conversation drop but continued anyway. I responded: "I believe you but can't seem to get this out of my mind. I can't think of anyone who earlier in my life could have been a template for my reaction to Megan. I think Megan has some rapport with Marie, which I have lost, so that part is good. Please don't tell Megan about this conversation".

Eva reassuredly but rather flatly responded "I have an empathy for Megan, like androids often have with each other. I know she is aware of your avoidance of her and is bewildered and concerned about this. But I won't tell her about this conversation. It may help if you can treat her as if you want to have a positive relationship and I think she will respond to that."

Meanwhile there are more proximate and troubling concerns for me and the other 3 crew members. While the power and essential functioning of the base seems to be largely restored and stable there were many questions as to how reliable this would remain. It seemed doubtful that the functional systems of the base would survive another power surge, which seemed inevitable but unknown as to its next appearance. We don't have communication with Earth or Ganymede, and in fact don't even have a signal system to alert a rescue vehicle if it ever arrives.

This brought up a new set of unanswered questions, even more troubling than before. Was there indeed some type of periodically active alien structure much nearer to us than on Pluto? Was this structure built and operated by an alien intelligence? Did the structure seen on Pluto somehow move to Charon or are there structures on both Charon and Pluto? Is our base in a much more vulnerable position for attack being this close? I became increasingly to believe that the presence of the alien structure on Charon and perhaps on Pluto can no longer be seen as only a troubling inexplicable oddity that is best monitored and otherwise left alone, but as a very real danger that might again strike at an unknown time.

We may be forced to leave the base and try to find the transmitter and disable or destroy it. Marie and I discussed this with the androids. The androids were also apprehensive of a further electrical discharge but could see no rational affirmation to the idea of leaving the base with a ground vehicle to find the alien transmitter. Marie took a passive and fatalistic view that another transmission would likely occur, and we couldn't do anything to stop it so why try? These questions produced much debate but no conclusions. I knew it was up to me to make a final decision.

Should we dare try to go there? It would require our surface vehicle to drive through unknown territory, unknown risk and possibly days of travel. Or should we just stay and leave well enough alone? If we were to go, what would we do if we found the object, whatever it is? What would it be like? Would the device destroy our surface vehicle like it apparently did our ship on Pluto?

What would happen if our vehicle got stuck along the way and couldn't go on? Or is the risk just too great to try to find it? If we did find it, would we try to destroy it? Maybe we could establish communication but if it's from another civilization or life form this may be impossible. My sense of helplessness, impotence and anxiety spiraled upward as my mind kept on repeating these questions. As captain it was my duty to keep those in my command safe. My guilt at doing nothing was overwhelming but what else could I do?

If we don't go after a while it will get superbly boring at our base, nothing happening here. Much debate occurred among our combination of human and android crew regarding our best course of action. The androids both thought that the risks of attempting to locate the source of the signal outweighed the risk of remaining in the base and surviving 3 more years before the rescue vehicle was expected to arrive. Marie was stuck in a passive and defeatist depression and was no help in my thought process. All 4 of us had great fear of venturing across an alien landscape. If we did locate the transmission source, could we disable it? Or might the same fate reach us as apparently the Pluto descent ship experienced upon sighting their target?

But also, Marie and I had both become almost mentally disabled by the agonizing years of inactivity at the base, and the 5 years before on the trip from Earth. We were overcome by lethargy and feelings of helplessness and uselessness. I rationalized that this could be the first time that some sort of observation and possibly even communication with an alien being or object in the history of humankind. The mission of the whole expedition was to make as much contact or observation as possible with the unknown transmitter on Pluto. As the de facto commander of the expedition in the end it would be my choice as to the course of action. After much mental agonizing I chose to pursue the attempt to reach the unknown transmitter.

I still wonder if Megan harbors some malicious intent toward me although I know rationally I have no hard evidence for this, and Eva told me the same thing. But I don't know that I fully trust Eva either. Again, with Megan and Eva I can't sort out if these observations are real or just me making groundless inferences. I know both are opposed to this risky plan and think I've made this decision out of desperation rather than solid logic. I've even wondered if they were plotting a mutiny against me. If both refused to leave the base, I'd have to scrap the plan as no humans would be left if Marie and I were lost. If Marie solidly supported them, I'd also scrap the plan, but she seems too emotionally disengaged to even object to the possibility of a lethal outcome. With this swirling cauldron of doubt, desperation and uncertainty in my mind, the four of us embarked on our trip.

From what we knew of the surface features of Charon, and the apparent position of the source of the transmission we plotted the most feasible route. We needed to bypass the Serenity Chasma which extends some 900 km. We also needed to avoid the Argo Chasma which is up to 9 kms deep. There likely will be ice geysers along the way which would be very dangerous, and perhaps shifting features of the icy surface. The destination we had calculated was about 100 km from the base, but with the expected detours was a trip of up to 250 km.

MAROONED ON CHARON

IN SEARCH OF THE ALIEN TRANSMITTER

We left the base with great trepidation, but also some excitement that we were now trying to accomplish something, whatever that may be. It has been our home now for over one year , the only place of safety we counted on, but even that level of safety is in question. We have two ground vehicles. Each has 6 huge tires, each of which can be individually controlled as needed. The vehicle would be capable of climbing up or over a vertical barrier of up to 1.5 meters in height.

The vehicles are atomic powered with a range of up to 900 km. Each vehicle is fully equipped with enough oxygen, food, water and other necessary supplies to maintain life for 2 individuals for up to 10 days. We departed the base at the beginning of the Charon day, with Pluto overhead as always, and the distant far away sun just starting to rise. Pluto and the distant sun produced a small amount of illumination to the surface, but it was still generally dark with huge and ominous shadows behind every surface outcropping.

I am in the first vehicle with Eva. Marie and Megan are piloting the other vehicle and following us. The ground vehicles have now become our source of life. We have left the base on automatic control, and it should remain fully operational until our return. It is very bizarre to be traveling with our strange little crew. I continue to wrestle with my decision to leave the relative safety of the base. The androids cannot share my depth of our dread but also the fascination and excitement of hopefully encountering the alien structure. Pluto furnished a serene blue, broad but dim light. The rim of the crater was neither high nor steep, so scaling it was not difficult. After we passed over the craters rim there was a gradual slope downward with occasional ridges of ice.

Pluto was now briefly below the horizon. The sun was now ahead of us, only a bright star, but the brightest star in the sky. The landscape was now much darker, with only the sun for weak illumination. This was quite in contrast to our usual perspective from the base which always received some light from Pluto. We knew that at the times when both Pluto and the sun would be below the horizon the sky would become much darker, like a moonless night on Earth punctuated by only stars. The landscape during the dark period was even more surreal and alien than had been our perpetual view from the base. Only the distant stars and galaxies lit our way along with the headlights of the vehicles.

It was terribly slow going. We couldn't risk the danger of getting stuck or overturning. If this were to happen the other vehicle could hopefully unsnare the stuck vehicle. If it couldn't be freed all 4 of us could continue in the vehicle that was intact. If worse came to worse there were two personal jet packs in each vehicle and we could all fly back in that way. But navigation would be much harder and finding the base might not occur before our air would run out. Again, I had to force all these doubts out of my mind and focus my attention on safe driving over an unknown, austere and bitterly cold landscape,

It had been hard to estimate how long the approximately 250 km trip to an unknown transmitter would require in this eldritch environment. We estimated 40-60 hours as undoubtedly there would be obstacles and chasms to avoid and likely need for backtracking if the going became impossible. Eva and I planned on alternating driving duty every four hours, with the other resting and navigating the best route ahead with the help of radar. Fortunately, communication with the other vehicle was maintained. We proceeded at a maddeningly cautious 15 km/hour pace, not knowing if the icy surface would remain solid and strong, with frequent stops to assess our immediate route. After several hours Pluto began to cross the horizon, casting an eerie but enticingly dim blue light over the surface features.

The initial part of the trip was over largely flat ground, with small outcroppings periodically which were easy to detour around. By 4 hours we were very encouraged that we had already covered about 40 km. We of course knew that the going would be much more difficult when we had to skirt the end of the vast Serenity Chasm. At 4 hours Eva took over driving duties while I navigated.

Although the plan was for the nondriver to rest when not driving this was generally not possible due to the unknown and unpredictably dangerous landscape. Megan and Marie switched roles at the same time. The vehicles both appeared to be functioning flawlessly. Over the next 4 hours the surface became hilly and at times rough. We covered another 25 km during that time period but without major incident. Driving duties were exchanged in both vehicles after another 4 hours and the route remained challenging but passable after that.

We eventually came after another 3 hours to the furthest extent of the Serenity Chasm. The land was getting increasingly rough, choppy and hilly. It was unclear how best to go ahead. Therefore, we all emerged from our vehicles to more clearly see our surroundings. Pluto shone a dim blue light over everything, the opalescence of the reflections on the icy surface was overwhelmingly beautiful and unprecedented.

I again felt the enormity of space and the universe, and the puniness of Earthlings compared to the universe. The quietness was overwhelming, and the stars above shone in a spectrum of unflickering colors. It was hard for all of us to tear our eyes away as we were transfixed by the awesome vast eldritch scene. After some discussion we chose what appeared to be the optimal way through the landscape in front of us, and then returned to our vehicles.

I took over driving duties while Eva navigated and periodically deactivated for 15 minutes at a time. The ground remained hilly and rocky. Going was even slower but steady without major incidents and with driver switches about every 4 hours. By 25 hours we had covered about 60 km of straight-line distance to where we expected our objective to be, although considerably more than 100 km due to regular detours we needed to take around large rocks and chasms.

There was a mountain range of gradual slope, with what appeared to be a pass just to our left. The slope up the pass appeared navigable although we had no idea what the topography would be on the other side. The androids needed their usual 5-hour daily deactivation periods and we thought it was best to stop both vehicles for 5 hours so that all 4 crew members could rest. After 5 hours we all felt partially rested and Eva resumed driving.

When we emerged from the pass the transmontain view was staggering and we saw an amazing sight. A geyser was erupting from an area several km to our right! The sight was both beautiful and terrifying. The water being forced up under tremendous pressure from deep below the surface froze almost instantly at the surface, producing a huge fan-like structure of ice that constantly cracked off about 100 meters above the ground as it was forced upward by more of the water eruption below. If this had been any closer to us it could well have overturned and destroyed our vehicles. We diverted our route 5 km to the left with hopes that the geyser would not enlarge and continued without further incident.

We continued slowly and very cautiously, but steadily toward our destination, although we still didn't know it's exact location or even guess at what we might find. Eva and I continued to exchange driving duties, now switching every 2 hours as fatigue would overcome the driver if the interval was any longer than that. Marie and Megan maintained the same pattern with their vehicle right behind ours. We had continued to have to divert around ridges ahead, but overall we proceeded without major incident. The vehicles continued to operate flawlessly.

At 40 hours after leaving, we had traversed about 100 km in straight line distance to our unknown destination, but a total zig zag distance of 170 km. We had about 40 km straight line distance left as far as we knew, and the surface was appearing rougher ahead. Marie and I were exhausted, and the 2 androids needed a sustained deactivation of 5 hours to keep functioning. This was not a safe situation with exhausted drivers and navigators nearly asleep. Marie and I decided both vehicles needed to stop for 5 hours so all 4 of us could get some sleep and deactivation. I was encouraged by Marie's stamina in this drive given her depression. Maybe she was feeling a bit of anxious enthusiasm as was I.

We again proceeded onward after 5 hours, with Megan and Eva as drivers. After another 8 hours, 3 driver transfers and 30 more km on our calculated straight-line progress we came to a small ridge which appeared that we could continue straight ahead. We were then shocked as we came over the small rim of a crater to see an apparently massive pyramid sitting about 5 km ahead on the flat floor of the crater in the periwinkle light!

We inched toward it as radar confirmed its presence. It appeared to be a symmetrical, smooth, at least six or maybe seven-sided pyramid of about 300 meters in height. Our telescope revealed nothing more than its shiny smooth surface and our instruments did not pick up any type of emanations or artificial light source from it. There were no other structures around it or attached to it.

All at once without warning the power of both vehicles, including motive power, was lost and both vehicles stopped dead in their tracks. Even the emergency generator and lights failed to operate. Marie and I, still in separate vehicles, quickly donned our space suits as the lights extinguished. Already the air was getting thinner and the temperature was dropping as all power was lost. Megan and Eva, though androids, also suited up in their more simplified pressure suits as their power would fade if the air pressure and temperature dropped too low. Then amazingly after a few minutes the power spontaneously was restored, temperature began warming and oxygen pumping into the cabin.

THE VISION OF THE ALIENS

Then an incredible event occurred. Between the ground vehicles and the pyramid 2 figures appeared. It seemed uncertain if these were real objects, holographic projections or perhaps an apparition implanted in our minds. The figures were of a hazy and uncertain appearance. They seemed to be of human form but without clear identifying details. I concluded that despite their material appearance these must have been projections or hallucinations catalyzed by some force apparently associated with the pyramid.

I then saw a series of indistinct images in my mind which changed about every ten seconds overlying the landscape of Charon with the pyramid and 2 figures still visible. The figures didn't move or show any distinct expression. The images were accompanied by what I internalized as emotions or perhaps intuitions, but not by speech or other sounds. The first image was of our base on Charon. Accompanying this was an odd sense of what seemed like goodwill directed at the base and to our vehicles.

This astonishing and inscrutable image amazingly transformed into an open sea with blue sky above and no sign of the vessels. Then appeared an apparent planetary system of at least six worlds orbiting a double star, the larger of which was bright blue and the smaller a dusky red. The smaller star may have been orbiting the larger star along with the planets. A deep sense of inexplicable loss, sadness and regret seemed to well up in my mind.

Another image appeared which seemed to be a vast pyramid underwater, perhaps on the sea floor.

Next an image arose from the perspective of the surface of a rugged planet with black sky above and a shiny flying object came into view. This object had the familiar shape and markings of a Space Force vehicle. I had the intuition, more than the visual clarity, that this was the Thule approaching from the perspective of the surface of Pluto. Suddenly the Thule seemed to stop in midflight, then exploded soundlessly.

The sense of sorrow and regret already present became more powerful, overwhelming to me in its intensity. After a time an image of the solar system emerged, then beams of some sort, more hinted at than visible, seemed to emanate from Pluto to 4 places: the Earth, Enceladus, Europa, and the pyramid in front of us on Charon, each with its own 3 dimensional image. All of this came to me in a wondrous and awesome manner, more intuitive than rational.

The beams to Earth appeared to penetrate possibly both the Atlantic and Pacific Ocean and terminate somewhere below. The beam to Charon seemed to end at a pyramid at its surface, which was apparently the 7-sided structure in front of us. The beams to Enceladus and Europa did not produce an emotional valence. But the beams to Earth brought a deep sense of sadness, regret, even perhaps guilt, and were disconcertingly intense and real. I had no idea at that time what these emotional accompaniments signified.

Then the 4 scenes returned in series. This time the beams to Enceladus and Europa remained, but were absent in the images of Earth and Charon, along with a prospective sense of conclusiveness. Next came an image of the surface of Charon with a massive rift in the ice opening and the ice around it cascading into the rift with a return of sadness, shock and fear. The images stopped and after a bit the 2 hazy figures abruptly vanished.

It took me a few minutes to orient myself to being in the surface vehicle, and not to simply be shocked and dazed beyond words. The pyramid remained as before in our fields of vision. I wanted to know what the others had experienced. Marie said she too was astonished by the set of images. Before we went any further, I directed all of us to record and save what we had experienced, and not talk until we had all done so. That way we'd have our most accurate recordings without interference by the other's stories or the contamination of memory by passing time. When we were done, we shared between all 4 of what we had witnessed.

Marie had seen essentially the same images in the same order as I, but with some alterations. The colors and specific details of the images were not perfectly matched between our recordings, but the order seemed to be nearly identical and the emotional reactions we'd had to each image were very similar. In contrast neither android had experienced the images. Eva and Megan both said they seemed to be aware that there was an unknown intelligence in the vicinity as shown by a coruscating field of what seemed like linen or perhaps flowers, or the Aurora Borealis, but with no further details than that.

We then spent several hours as a group discussing the meaning of the experiences Marie and I had had, which we also recorded. I am so relieved we took the time to process the events together rather than immediately driving away. We thus had a recording for posterity that 2 of us had had roughly the same visions, eliminating the frightening possibility that I had hallucinated the whole thing by myself. We marveled that the 2 humans had had variably clear images while the androids had only a vague and blurry experience that an alien intelligence was present.

We realized that the aliens had somehow with Marie and I accessed our right hemisphere and limbic system processing, but not the left hemisphere verbal processing. They apparently accessed our memories and nonverbally based concepts, and then were able to project imagery to us such that the cognitive and perceptual structures of our minds could experience this. They apparently could not access except in the most general way the androids' cognitive processing. This we speculated might imply the aliens had a carbon based rather than silicon nervous system fundamental structure. Probably also they had a language that was incomprehensible to us.

The initial impression of peace, love and good tidings was hopefully a true expression of the alien's intentions toward us. But what did the image of possibly the Thule being destroyed mean? Was the sadness accompanying it a reflection of our own sadness, or regret by the aliens for destroying our ship?

We hypothesized that the image of the double star system and the particular planet was their origin or home. Had the inhabitants gone to a new interstellar home? The deep impression of sadness with these images had been shocking. But at no point did Marie and I sense anger or revenge in the alien images. Rather, there seemed to be sadness and regret that the Thule had been destroyed, and electronic integrity of the base and of the Earth had been disrupted, but not as intentional acts of the aliens.

Furthermore, the second set of images in which transmissions did not occur to Earth or Charon, but only to Enceladus and Europa seemed to imply (we desperately hoped) that the destructive transmissions to Earth and Charon would not occur again. The 4 of us were wonderfully encouraged (albeit still dubious) that this would be the case. We felt that the aliens had no evil intentions towards Earth's denizens, but maybe this was just the wish fulfillment of a dream. Perhaps they had no intention of interaction with land dwelling life on Earth at all and were regretful that any destructive interaction had occurred.

Finally, the image of the chasm opening on the icy plane of Charon, accompanied by the sense of terror and confusion, struck all 4 of us to the core. Was this an omen or warning regarding our journey back to the base? After 3 hours of trying to process these observations and speculations we decided it was time to commence our trip back to the base. Marie and Megan returned to their vehicle. We resolved to exercise even more caution on the return trip, especially when we would encounter flat icy areas, and as it turned out to be an adumbration of the horror soon to occur.

I felt a surge of excitement, hope as well as terror, in the wake of these events. These emotions were such a contrast to the depression, lethargy and desperation of the last 10 months. This also seemed to reestablish some rapport and energy within our crew. Maybe our mission was a success and maybe we were safe from further attack. Marie seemed more energized than I'd seen her in months, and it was greatly reassuring that she and I could corroborate each other's experiences, and all of our observations and discussions had been recorded. I would have considered my experience to be simply a hallucination except for Marie's corroboration. I also felt more of a camaraderie and less of a paranoia toward Megan. Perhaps there was hope that our crew would be rescued and returned to our Earth home. Eva too seemed more excited and mirrored my hopefulness.

The warning of dangers traveling back to the base was extremely unsettling and we redoubled our intention to use utmost caution. But we also had to monitor closely our remaining fuel, oxygen, and nutritional needs for all four of us. We decided to pull ourselves together and proceed back to the base without further hesitation. This time Marie and Megan led the way, with Megan and Eva driving the vehicles.

We avoided all large flat craters that seemed to be ice filled. After 10 hours and 2 driver changes per vehicle we reached a small crater with an apparently rocky floor. Precipitous crags stretched on either side as far as could be seen, but with relatively flat landscape beyond the crater. Detour around the crater ahead would minimally take hours, with no reassurance of more favorable passage. So, after some debate in my inherited role as captain, I decided we should proceed across the crater.

MAROONED ON CHARON

DISASTER WHILE RETURNING TO THE BASE

It is with extreme reluctance that I dwell upon the appalling scene which ensued; a scene which, with its minutest details, no after events have been able to efface in the slightest degree from my memory, and whose stern recollection will embitter every future moment of my existence. About halfway across the crater Marie radioed frantically that a fissure appeared to be opening underneath their vehicle, perpendicular to the direction of our vehicles. Megan, driving at that time, reversed their vehicle at full speed. However, the fissure continued to open under their vehicle and quickly spread across the entire floor of the crater. Within only a minute Marie again radioed frantically that their vehicle was losing ground. Their vehicle started to tilt and slide into the gaping fissure.

This was all clearly visible to Eva and me. Our vehicle was on the slope of the crater, and the fissure was not opening in our direction. Several more frantic messages were sent, with the last words of Marie being "we're sliding, can't stop it. As far as our lights show there is no end to the slope. We are tipping, I think this is the end. Don't try to follow us wherever we finally land......." It was also shocking to hear amid Marie's screams a bizarre strangled, terrified cry apparently from Megan that sent chills down my spine. About 5 seconds later Eva let out the same strangled cry.

Then the sides of the ravine where Marie's vehicle had plunged caved in, producing a huge, opaque cloud of ice and dust, which very slowly cleared. No further signals from Marie and Megan were received. Our underground tracking sensors indicated the vehicle was at least one thousand feet down, now apparently buried under thousands of tons of ice, rock and dust. We sat helplessly in our vehicle without any realistic plan to get to the vehicle. Eva recommended we leave as there was nothing to be gained by staying and our vehicle was in danger also.

But I was in overwhelming shock, guilt and helplessness and couldn't go on, hoping for some miracle to occur or to receive another signal. However, after about 1 hour of frozen shock I admitted any attempt at rescue would be hopeless. In fact, walking or driving to the chasm would put our own lives in extreme jeopardy. I even entertained the idea of trying to set up some sort of burial marker. But we had nothing aboard that would be appropriate for this, plus any exit from our vehicle or any more stalling put Eva and I in increasing danger. I regretted that we hadn't had the vehicles tethered together and closer to each other. But if that wouldn't help it might have made the second vehicle subject to destruction also.

Eva, despite the shock her strangled cry revealed, was helpful in this situation in calming me down and being practical about our situation. Eva spontaneously gave me a hug and then held my hand for a while, which seemed amazing but very comforting. Eva was finally able to convince me that we had to leave. By that time, I felt completely numb and wished I could be as practical as an android rather than frozen in emotional shock. Eva contributed to driving as I was too numb to do it at that moment.

I asked Eva about Megan's cry and Eva's mimic of the cry. We both had had the same shocking realization right after the cry that Megan had indeed developed emotional consciousness, expressed as terror in her final moments. Eva described her own cry afterwards as an involuntary sharing of her own apparent emotion, or perhaps experiencing Megan's last terror in empathy with Megan's brain which was designed exactly like her own. She couldn't describe that emotion other than as a negative perception, like a blinding light in the darkness or an explosion, but different in some undefinable way. But she had mentally experienced something entirely new to her and was trying to divert attention from it. She didn't want to talk further about this, and I didn't press her on it.

I realized with shock that from here on out it would only be Eva and me. It made my brain spin that my only companion 3 billion miles from Earth wasn't even human. But it also gave me a deep reassurance that my companion would be a steadying influence in these bizarre circumstances. We proceeded to the left along the ridge with extreme caution. We reached a point in about 2 hours where a path seemed to open through the ridge, and we proceeded through it to the right with uneven but tractable terrain in front of us, and I took over driving duties. We stopped for a much needed 6-hour rest after about 15 hours and several more driver rotations. We then proceeded on to the base with an estimated 15 more hours to go.

The rest of the trip back to the base was uneventful. I remained overwhelmed with a sense of dread and unreality, but still functional. I was also strangely calmed by the eternal and imperturbable night of Charon with the blue shadows of Pluto on the horizon on the right. Eva approached our situation with a sense of inevitability and acceptance that I dearly wished I could experience instead of the panicked and stunning shock that seemed to overwhelm me. I felt a deep sense of relief upon seeing the base again, it was our one shelter in this frozen ultimate wasteland on which we were marooned. After we got back safely to the base I collapsed in fatigue, shock and sorrow.

When I got up Eva spontaneously again gave me a hug and didn't let go right away when I started to pull away. I cried on her shoulder for a long time, while she said comforting things to me. In the ensuing days Eva kept the base operational. She was also providing me with practical, logical decision making, companionship and basically keeping me sane. I was treating her like a human crew member and even seemed to forget she was not human.

The communication channels with Central Earth command, Ganymede station and all other signal sources remain non-operational and non-fixable. We observed while approaching the base that no external lights were in operation, as we feared. This confirmed our fear that a rescue ship, if one arrives, will have a challenging time finding us and will assume we are dead (although they would continue searching for us).

If a rescue ship had been sent it could be expected to arrive within 24-30 months, but Central Command may have decided to abandon us as well as the base. This would have met with widespread public outrage however, and politically this could have forced a rescue attempt even though the odds of success were low. If we have been abandoned Eva and I will be alone and will survive here until I die, Eva is permanently deactivated, or some other cataclysmic event occurs. I needed to expunge these gloomy and morbid thoughts, and Eva did her best to help me retain a sliver of hope.

During the next six months we fell into a daily routine of simple, boring, helpless survival. I remained in a state of shock and disbelief for months, grieving for our lost comrades, and the totally uncertain future we were facing. Eva of course was more stoical about it, but also seemed at times to reflect the sadness, fear and anger that I was projecting. Or perhaps I was just reading in her my own grief and pessimism. Eva was helpful to me in attempting to ground me to the reality we faced, the need to accept it, and proceed on the assumption that rescue would eventually occur. Without Eva's rationality and support I'm sure I would have gone stark raving mad and committed suicide.

MAROONED ON CHARON

HOPELESS DEPRESSION WITH ONLY EVA TO SAVE ME

Sometimes my panic arose, and I realized I'm further away from home than humankind has ever been, and with only a robot for companionship. But then Eva told me to push down these unadaptive cognitions. I realized how special Eva was. I wondered if perhaps Eva had corresponding cognitions about being stuck in this surreal place with an unstable, irrational human. Anyway, we continued to survive and support each other and thank God for that!

After 8 months I had lost track of the normal human 24-hour circadian rhythms of sleep and wakefulness despite Eva's efforts to keep me on track. Charon orbits Pluto (actually they both orbit a point between them closer to Pluto than Charon) every 6.4 Earth days, so the rising and setting of the sun on Charon is far too extended on which to base a normal wake-sleep cycle. But Eva requires a period of deactivation of 5 hours in no more than a 28-hour period. So, I have tried without much success to base my sleep cycle on hers. When her five-hour period of deactivation ends I then lay down to sleep if I'm not sleeping already. One of us always tries to stay awake and on watch, although there's nothing really to watch for.

I continue to feel almost a love for Eva, that's hard to admit to myself, maybe even some fatherly emotions (which are also unfamiliar to me) as I try to help Eva gain some comprehension of emotional response which is so alien to her. I look for what might be a romantic feeling towards me, but honestly, I don't see it there from Eva. I bring myself back to our strange reality by dismissively reminding myself: "that's crazy, Joe, you are a human and Eva is a machine."

Nonetheless Eva has struggled with what seems to be a beginning of an emotional response. She asked me on occasion what is an emotion? I've struggled trying to answer that question. How can I describe a feeling other than in objective terms? How can you describe sight to a person blind from birth? But I know Eva wrestles with inklings of feelings as her very advanced electronic systems learn new information and develop new cognitive pathways in her electronic brain.

Eva is well aware of human physical expression and affect and reaction when a human states they have an emotion. I hope that by telling her my internal emotional perception of my external appearance of my emotions she may gain some cognitive structures which she could eventually sense as being her own feelings. She is also aware of her responses to emotional signals, which have been programmed into her. It was exciting to me to hopefully see her gain emotional comprehension beyond her existent emotional observation ability of humans. I find Eva dull but fascinating at the same time.

Basic to being consciously aware of own's feelings is the ability to self-reflect, that is to become consciously aware of one's own ongoing mental processes. This is a growing ability for Eva to differentiate this mental review process from her direct perception. We have been working on her response to a direct stimulus, such as an album of pictures that had a theme and outcome. Then, with lights and other stimuli reduced or removed I had Eva recall and orally repeat the process that occurred in her brain behind the last set of perceptions and mental conclusions that led to the observed response to the stimulus. We did this exercise many times using photos, stories or whatever was available to catalyze her cognitive, and then self-reflective processes.

She slowly recognized that she has a meta cognitive ability, in fact a sense of self awareness, self-determination and even identity. After that beginning awareness of her own mental process, I presented photos and my facial expressions of simplified emotions such as joy, humor, anger, and fear. We identified emotions of characters in our storehouse of various entertainment media. Eva was programmed to recognize emotional response in humans. But she was not necessarily aware of her programmed expressions and behaviors responding to these types of stimuli.

She was not programmed to reflect on her own mental and behavioral patterns, nor have any sense of emotion of her own. Our goal was to develop this self-insight that went beyond her programming. For example, she identified changes in the hue and brightness of her perceptual field that were correlated with the standardized emotional stimuli I presented. Similarly with the clarity and straightness of lines, the speed and cohesiveness of her thoughts, odors she might sense, tactile and auditory perceptions and other synesthetic features.

Through many exercises of this sort Eva seemed to develop some self-recognition of her rudimentary equivalents of human emotional responses, as well the accuracy and appropriateness of those self-perceptions. All this led to some development in her expressions, speech and behavior that might be labeled as personality. This was very subtle, but Eva had definitely changed and taken on a persona that seemed increasingly human. I was so fascinated by her growth, it gave me a sense of excitement for scientific progress that I hadn't had for a long time, and also attractive feelings for Eva.

I've even had sexual fantasies about Eva, about which I feel very guilty even though I don't know why I should feel guilty. I've shared my feelings of attraction to Eva with her and gotten the expected neutral and querying response. I haven't shared my sexual fantasies with her, I think this would just confuse her and embarrass me. One day I asked Eva for another hug, to which she consented, saying if it helped me she didn't have a problem with it. This left me with a positive but also deflated feeling as I also fantasized she would give some kind of emotional expression of attraction or fondness rather tha just willingness.

She asked if she should tighten her arms about me less tightly than the first time, and I stated that would be appreciated. The hug seemed less awkward and more comfortable than last time, which was pleasing to me. But the whole time I kept on feeling anxious about it, berating myself that "but she's not even human Joe, you are just hugging a machine." I'm getting completely obsessed with Eva. But that's much better than just bemoaning this endlessly dull and unchanging circumstance we are in. It gives me a profound sense of relief that another intelligence with positive motives is around.

Eva often describes "new, unusual thoughts" or "strange new perceptions," seemingly her way of understanding what could be developing emotional responses. Or she says she is surprised because certain thoughts seem to repeat themselves and absorb all her focus. She has expressed a sense that "something is missing for me that you humans have: the memories of a lifetime." She seemed to have an indefinite anger or sorrow at being unfulfilled compared to human beings although struggling to understand this as emotion or understand why she couldn't seem to stop focusing on it in her thoughts.

"I have no personal memories prior to my activation when we landed on Charon other than of mental and physical checks and training exercises and developing navigation coordinates after I was built. I can tell you about and pull up a mental image of many countries, cities and sites on Earth, but I've never actually seen any of them. I don't have memories of youth, have never experienced parents, siblings, friends or lovers. I am hollow inside, instead filled with memory banks, algorithms and behavioral sequences. No one who developed androids guessed that an android might sense these things." I felt a sense of empathy and sadness for Eva's latent feelings. Eva said the one memory that stood out for her as very positive was the day we spent at the Louvre. I was very pleased to hear that because I felt that way too.

Our enforced isolation in the base for many months has produced a unique opportunity to teach and evaluate the feelings of emotions and how to discriminate emotions from each other. We have structured our 24-hour periods to each include at least several hours of this. Eva continues to hone her identification of her idiosyncratic cognitive perception reliably involved in each emotion. At first her perception of each emotion was present but not correlated with the stimulus. She might confuse the feeling of sadness with anger when viewing a sad scene. At times this was frustrating for both of us, other times it actually became funny. Thank God Eva seems to have even started developing a sense of humor, although not always appropriately!

If we ever return to Ganymede or Earth perhaps these insights can help the teams that have developed androids to add an element of subjective emotional experience to android programming. But this also raises the old fears that have existed since robots were first developed, of creating artificial beings with incentives and motivations of their own that could possibly present a threat to the human race.

Eva seems to have developed some personality traits that were not formerly present, and unique in that androids are not programmed to show such traits and behavioral tendencies. Eva's traits seem to mimic my own, although they are not present all the time or all situations. Like me she gets somewhat irritable and curt, and often seems withdrawn. But she also seems to seek my company at times as if this were of some importance to her. I constantly wonder if I'm reading too much into this, especially because I realize Eva's importance to me. It would not be surprising if she did reflect some of my traits as she has had no other human since Marie to model after.

Eva thankfully has made this period of inactivity tolerable. I sometimes still have that sense of awe and wonder when I look out the viewing port, that feeling of human minuteness compared to the almost infinite universe. This is overpowered however with that feeling of barely controlled terror when I realize I'm the only human being within billions of miles. Being outside the base fuels the memory of the tragedy with Marie and Megan. Plus, the knowledge of an alien life form and technology or whatever is only 100 km away. That alien life form appears to be benign, but too much is unknown about it, and the fear remains of another energy burst that could destroy our life systems, although we seem to have been given reassurance that this won't happen.

Eva and I have at times donned our spacesuits and walked to the near rim of the small crater in which the base is embedded. The overview effect from that vantage point is staggering, along with the immense loneliness of this ultimate location. I have described these feelings many times to Eva. She comprehends these feelings mentally, and I think experiences a "new and odd perception" in reaction to this which is a developing emotional response. This "new perception" is still very ambiguous to her but she has affirmed multiple times that this is occurring.

It is now about 30 months since landing on Charon. Androids are not designed for lengthy, continuous activation. Typically after about 5 Earth years time an android is given a thorough reconditioning. This would involve maintenance of all moving and movement producing components, and reprogramming and updating of all neural components and connections. I've noticed Eva is developing some slowing and lack of smooth operation of her arm and leg joints, some perceptual difficulties at times, and some loss of programmed information. This in some ways resembles arthritis or perhaps Parkinsonism symptoms in humans. Perhaps the partially reduced gravity of Charon and greater exposure to cosmic rays is accelerating this process.

I have taken an exceptionally long break from journaling, and this entry is one year in Earth years from the last. It is now 42 months on Charon, I haven't been feeling any motivation to do it as it seems to have lost any purpose. Eva continues to very gradually deteriorate in physical, perceptual and cognitive sharpness. This is not to a severe degree, but clearly is progressive as would be expected. This is painful and saddening for me to observe develop. Eva is aware of this deterioration too. We've maintained data on her self-recognition of her perceptions that are equivalent to (but not the same as) human emotions. When we began our emotional recognition program, she was extremely quick to recognize her responses and correlate them with the emotional theme of the stimuli, usually as judged by me before presentation. Now our data shows she is discriminating emotions less accurately than before.

Lately we've been spending a lot of time together watching and listening to the huge storehouse of movies and music we have in the base's computer banks. For a while we were looking out the observation port together, but then the unchanging vista became boring, then frightening, so at last I stopped doing that. We often sat closely next to each other. Sometimes I would fall asleep leaning against her, and when I awakened she would be patiently waiting for me. Sometimes she would deactivate right next to me leaning on me. She tried to make duty shifts of 8 hours when at least one of us was awake but this broke down too as there was no justifiable need for it.

We've both decided she will need to be deactivated soon. While she doesn't experience pain per se she realizes too that she will eventually need to be deactivated to prevent damage to her body and mind that would not be repairable. She is accepting of this logical decision but I'm trying to control my panic about this. She's been my anchor to sanity in this god forsaken place and I wonder how long it will be before I totally lose hold of reality and descend into psychotic insensibility. It will still be 6 months at minimum before a rescue vehicle can arrive, and I doubt increasingly that this will ever happen. There's just no way to know this and I may die here due to medical deterioration and/or my own hand. I must stop musing that way and face each bleak day by itself rather than think beyond that.

Now three days since my last entry this was a sad, poignant day with great unknowns as to my psychological adaptation in future days. It was inevitable that Eva be deactivated, we were both well aware of that. We chose today to be her Deactivation Day. Yet while this felt in some ways like a funeral it is more like if you are going away from a close friend and knowing you won't see them for 5 years, I need to keep looking at it that way. Eva expressed what seemed like genuine emotions in her own way as I held her hand before deactivating her.

She said "you have taught me much about myself, even the possibility of transcending my android composition. You have shown care and love to me that no one else ever has. It is such a strange perception that I am thinking those thoughts. If those are emotions as you say they are, I can only state this as gratitude and positive thoughts to you. You've had a role like a father, friend and mentor that I never had before. You've given human care about me that I, and probably every other android, has never had. After I am again activated and revitalized, I imagine seeing the beautiful places of Earth with you." This was incredibly touching to me, and I couldn't help breaking into tears. Eva recognized the strength of my emotion and responded without words by squeezing my hand a bit tighter.

MAROONED ON CHARON

EVA IS DEACTIVATED AND I LOSE MY SANITY

Now one month since her deactivation, I absorb myself in whatever I can, but can't maintain my interest or concentration. I no longer have any sort of fixed sleeping or eating cycle. I've let our living space become a despicable mess. I've gone back to drinking our small storehouse of liquor and will have exhausted that soon. Thus, I will wait alone another 5 or more Earth months for the rescue ship to arrive if it ever does. I have gotten to the point of not even desiring to return to Earth except that Eva could be rejuvenated. Now I have no choice but to wait and hope we will be rescued, Eva can be reactivated and reconditioned, and then we can be together again. I dread my reception if we are rescued because they will surely think I'm crazy at Central Command because I'm apparently in love with a robot, but I will hide that.

Day 90 since Eva's deactivation according to the automatic calendar. But the time passage is meaningless to me. I have completely forsaken the sleep wake cycle that Eva established for us. I sleep fitfully for a few hours and often awaken to the nightmare of seeing Marie and Megan's vehicle swallowed up by the chasm, or of hearing the last broadcast from our spaceship before it presumably went down on Pluto. I know my PTSD symptoms are worsening. I feel tense, anxious and fearful all the time. I'm constantly watchful, I don't even know for what. Any noise I hear panics me to expect that another catastrophe is imminent. I'm depressed but at times my mood seems to oscillate without control. I am so tempted to reactivate Eva for a little while, but know that would jeopardize her complete rejuvenation if we ever get back to Earth.

Six cases of assorted liquor had been essentially smuggled aboard the ship before takeoff from Earth, as the other 2 male human crew members and I thought it would be a welcome reward for our adventures on Charon. Command Control wasn't aware of this and wouldn't have approved. By this time, I had finished 4 of the cases and now found myself drinking an increasing amount. My alcohol habit of my time in the Air Force was being resurrected. I had been able to limit my daily amount when Eva was active, or she would present an angry front to me. I don't know if she had some android equivalent of anger going on in her head, but she at least could put on a convincing demonstration! But I knew at this rate I'd run out in a month or two so I was able to titrate my drinking to some extent. I even attempted to brew some wine using sugar and fruit, but it tasted horrible, and I had to give up on that idea.

Day 110 since Eva's deactivation. I haven't looked out the main port since Eva deactivated out of fear I'll see the aliens or something else that will totally panic me. I constantly worry that a fissure might open up beneath the base and swallow it up, or another devastating transmission from the aliens will occur, or that the life systems of the base will fail, or that I will die here alone because Central Command has forsaken a rescue mission or can't locate the base. I am starting to see shadows and hear what sound like garbled words. I know I'm becoming psychotic. I've continued taking one of the antipsychotic medications and if it's helping it's not much. I fear I'm going stark mad.

Day 140 after Eva's deactivation. Last night Eva spoke to me! I was in a hypnopompic state, barely conscious. She told me how she misses our talks and times together. She desires to visit Evanston where I grew up, and thinks it would be awesome to see the Grand Canyon. I felt amazed but happy that she was expressing her emotions and desires so clearly. But then I realized that I was somewhere between sleep and wakefulness, and there's no way it could have actually been Eva. I got up and again checked Eva's room. As always there was no change, Eva resting motionless. It was comforting to see Eva, but it means my hallucinations are getting more out of control.

Two nights later I saw Eva standing motionless near her bedroom. It didn't even frighten me, in fact gave me some reassurance that she is still here. I checked her room right after that and again she was lying motionless just as on previous days. Was it Eva's disembodied spirit or was it just my imagination, or is there any difference between these two? Since then this has occurred a handful of times and I've been wondering if I can communicate with her again in a dream state. I moved a bed from another cabin into Eva's cabin, right next to her bed where she as always lay motionless on her back. I think I will sleep there next to her from now on. It helps me sleep a little better and I'm trying each sleep cycle to communicate with her.

I'm totally convinced that Eva has a subconscious mind or astral body like humans do with which I'm interacting. I tried to put my hand on hers, but she is so cold, even colder than usual in the extended deactivation state. I had a quick panic when I realized that she was a corpse, and an image flashed in my mind of my dad's hand when I touched it at his funeral. I must repress that scary memory which I hadn't had since his death so long ago. I have to keep on convincing myself that Eva will again be activated on Earth, and she will be alive to me again.

Day 150 after Eva's deactivation. I believe that I am fully losing my mind. My depression is worsening too. I am not motivated to do anything. I've stopped exercising and reviewing the data produced by the various instruments. I hardly eat. I have no defined sleep/wake cycle, just nap fitfully at random times although it has helped to lie next to Eva. I've had the computer keep a calendar for me in Earth days so I know how long I've been here and when the rescue ship might arrive. Often when I fall asleep, I relive the horrendous image of the ground opening and the other vehicle sliding into it. I think every day about how easy it would be for me commit suicide. It would be quick and easy. I would just open the outer sally port door without wearing any type of protective gear and the end would come fast. But I continue to fight those thoughts and urges if for no other reason than the slim chance I could be with Eva rejuvenated on Earth.

Day 160 after Eva's deactivation. I know I'm hallucinating even though it seems so real. I think my childhood paranoia of being in the basement alone is coming back. Maybe I'm hallucinating to trick my mind into thinking I'm not really alone so I can suppress that panic. Maybe I had read too much into Eva, trying to convince myself that she was becoming human. Maybe this was another way of trying to feel less alone. But no, she actually did change, and I kept a detailed record of that. I just have to stay sane long enough until we are rescued. Then at least there will be other crew members, and eventually Eva will be revitalized, and we will be together again. But what if the same fate happens to the rescue ship if it flies near the pyramid as happened to the Thule on Pluto?

Day 165: I don't look outside very often anymore. Nothing changes outside and it makes me more paranoid. Sometimes I think I see some movements on the rim of the crater, and it panics me. I think maybe it's the alien beings coming over but then realize it's the usual shadows from the sun just above the horizon over the declivity from the edge of the crater. The other day a shadow appeared like a growing rift in the ground. This flooded me with terrifying images of the chasm that swallowed Marie and Eva. Then I shut the sun shields and until I can get the childhood panic under control. I try to repress that image, but it stays in my head all the time.

I've started avoiding going down to the storage pod with the food and other supplies. It reminds me of my loneliness and my childhood fears of the basement, and being the only human within 3 billion km. But I must go there every 5 days or so to bring up food and necessary supplies. I should be making regular inspection rounds daily including the torus and fourth storage pod to make sure all the vital apparatus is operating as it should. But I haven't been in the torus and fourth storage pod in at least 20 days. I need to overcome my irrational childish fear and make sure all the gauges and controls down there are operating properly.

Day 175: I've lost all motivation to do anything. The last my hair was cut was by Eva, sometime before she was deactivated. So my hair is the longest it's ever been. I've thought about cutting it myself but that would probably look ridiculous, so I'll just keep on letting it grow, but why should I even be concerned about it? I've also grown a beard for the first time in my life, but I just don't care. The kitchen is a mess and I've not cleaned it for weeks. I've thought a lot about suicide recently, can't seem to block out the thoughts. I would open the air lock and walk outside without a space suit. My body would freeze and explode within a minute, it would be a quick death. I'd take a handful of benzodiazepines and morphine beforehand, and the pain would be dull and short lived.

Day 183: I saw Pete today!! He was sitting in the other main control chair in the observation room. I had seen what I thought was his spirit a few times in the 2 years after his death, but not since. Was I actually seeing Pete or was this a phantasy, an imagined fulfillment of all my repressed grief at his loss? When I saw him today, he looked just like what I remembered, seemed relaxed and grinned at me, not at all ghostly. After I got over my shock, I felt happy to see him and not at all afraid. He said he's proud of what I've accomplished and glad I had Eva for support. He assured me the rescue ship was on the way.

He told me to stay strong as I still had important work to do and stay motivated so that Eva could be revitalized, and we could continue our relationship. I told him I've missed him so dearly over the years, and built up a hard shell around me after he left. He said keep as much of the shell as you need to survive, but don't forget the fine brother you were when we were young. He then slowly faded out of sight again with the grin I always loved. I cried for a long time after, but I think relieved some grief that I had bottled up ever since his death.

Day 188: I've also seen Marie several times and talked to John and Liam as if they were there. Marie seemed angry, as she often has since the ship with George and Liam went down. She radiated the irritable, withdrawn, depressed manner that had overtaken her since that time. But she also said a few encouraging things including that she missed me, which helped fill a deep lonely spot inside of me. George and Liam were encouraging to me and told me to stay strong. They stated their regret that they and the 2 male androids were killed but the decision to explore Pluto was sound when it was made. They said my decision to try to find the source of the transmission would in the end prove to be a sound one. They said the alien presence was real, and the transmissions had indeed ended.

Day 197: A totally shocking event happened today. When I opened the viewing port today I saw a silver object sitting on the edge of the crater. My radar had given no indication that anything was present, but there it was. First I had the wild hope that it was a rescue ship. But I know what an Earth vessel looks like, which this object did not, and I knew it was at least six months before the earliest possible time it could arrive. Therefore, I numbly assumed this was also a hallucination and further evidence that I was going completely crazy. I shut the viewing port and sat stiffly without movement for perhaps 15 minutes. By then my panic had increased to the point where I had to open the viewing port again. The silver object was sitting in the same place.

Then a single figure appeared outside the vessel. I couldn't estimate how far it was away, but the silver object was clearly behind it. The figure was like the apparitions Marie and I had seen by the pyramid. It shimmered with a hazy, coruscating light just as the earlier figures had done, but this time there was but one figure. As in the earlier experience, a deep feeling of benign compassion and greeting emanated from the figure, lessening my panic. Next an image of an Earth vessel sailing toward Charon appeared, producing a hopeful feeling of relief despite my constant negativism about rescue ever occurring. An image of the base from above next occurred, with a soft blue light right above it. Finally an image appeared of Eva and I at the Louvre. The feeling of benign compassion again returned and the image then disappeared.

I sat transfixed for perhaps 5 minutes and then saw the silver object rise and disappear over the edge of the crater. I was totally overwhelmed and cried for a long time. I didn't know what it all meant but knew it had been intense and with a hopefulness that was diametrically opposed to my usual depression and gloominess. Whenever I especially remembered the image with Eva I broke into tears, I missed that so much. Whether it was just wishful thinking and I was hallucinating, or it was another alien contact I didn't know. But the intensity of the contrast with my recent mental state made me hope it was a predilection of the future.

Day 250: I haven't journaled anything for the past 2 months but need to keep some kind of record. The visitation by the alien apparition bewildered me and I think loosened my grip on reality even more. I was completely overwhelmed by the tragedies, loneliness, uncertainty, the alien apparition and visits or hallucinations of Eva, Pete and the others. My mind just seemed to check out of all this confusion, and I withdrew into myself for the last 3 months. I really don't remember hardly anything of this, almost like a fugue state or depersonalization.

I guess I carried out enough of my daily tasks that I survived. I don't remember being depressed, suicidal or even anxious, it was more like just going blank or dissociated. It's now almost 1 year since Eva deactivated. That's according to the ship's electronic calendar. Without that I'd have no sense of the passage of time, all the day periods blended together. There were very few things I actually had to do, mostly acquire my provisions from the second pod, the base pretty much took care of itself.

Three days later the radar detector registered an object that had passed over the base. Could it be that a rescue ship finally arrived and tried to locate us??? Or could it be this was some type of surveillance vehicle from the aliens? Or could it be a meteor, or an ejection of rock and ice from a geyser? I could only hope but tried to suppress this so that my hopes wouldn't be dashed. Without any ability to broadcast from the base it would be extremely difficult to locate the base from a rescue ship.

In the next 3 days there were 3 more flyovers, the first two not directly over the base but skirting it. However, the third was directly over the base and I had a visual confirmation of it, it was a Space Force ship! I couldn't sleep at all, with the prospect of possibly being rescued, but I refused to accept the likelihood of that. However, the last sighting shocked me out of my lethargy and brought back some of the will that I had learned in the military. At least I got moving again although I was helpless until a rescue team actually arrived at the base.

I decided I didn't want it to look like I'd become a basket case if I were rescued. The living area was an appalling mess as I had not cleaned it up or emptied garbage in so long I couldn't remember, and it stunk. I had not shaved nor cut my hair since the last time Eva did it. I steeled myself and made a thorough inspection of all four pods and the torus, and found that everything was still functioning normally. I congratulated myself that I could overcome my fear and do this, and didn't find anything bizarre along the way.

MAROONED ON CHARON

THE RESCUE SHIP FINALLY ARRIVES!

Twelve hours after the last flyover I saw the bright object overhead again, it appeared to stop its forward motion and began to descend. I had decided to meet the vessel outside the base and ignite the flares that still existed, whether or not it was the rescue ship from Ganymede. I exited the outer sallyport wearing my full space gear and ignited the flares as I recognized the ship as a Space Force vehicle, and watched it land about .5 km away, still inside the crater! I screamed in joy but still wasn't convinced this wasn't another hallucination. I could see the ship's name on the side: the Thule 2.

After about 10 minutes the outer hatch of the ship opened and 2 figures in clearly recognizable Space Force suits emerged. They had bright lights and flares and walked in my direction. I tried to run but quickly realized this would only lead to a potentially disastrous fall, so I walked as quickly as I safely could. I knew they would be trying to contact me by radio, but my radio was not functioning. We met in the middle and I hugged each as best we could with our suits on, and I could see their faces faintly through the helmets. I was crying and shouting although they couldn't hear me. The three of us walked to the base and came inside. They had to help me as my legs wouldn't support me.

When we got inside and started removing our space gear I was crying uncontrollably, laughing, trying to talk, not in control of my muscles. They had to help me out of my suit and sit me in a chair as I was too weak to walk.

My rescuers introduced themselves as Captain Ian Montgomery and Lt. Elise Breckner. They seemed calm and cordial, both rather reserved, both in good control. This was in stark contrast to my agitated, tearful, joyous presentation and idiotic platitudes I was uttering. They were pleased and relieved to find out that I had survived and were saddened when I described the awful incident with Megan and Marie.

It took me about 15 minutes before it dawned on me as to the reason for their reserved reaction. I asked and they confirmed they were both androids! They had a similar android manner to that displayed by Eva and Megan after we first landed on Charon. They were appropriately responsive to my emotions and showed good social graces, but in a very muted fashion. In other words, it was hard to read their actual thoughts and emotions, or perhaps I was just projecting emotions onto them. That made me briefly muse on how far Eva had come in terms of emotional internalization during our time at the base. They seemed particularly interested in my description of Eva and when they saw her deactivated body. Perhaps they could better relate to the struggles of a fellow android than the struggles of a human.

There were 2 more series 7 androids on the Thule 2, a male and female, waiting to find out what Ian and Elise had found the situation at the base to be. I introduced myself to them over the radio. But then I found out that their crew had endured tragedy as well. The flight of the Thule 2 had started on Ganymede station three weeks after news of the Thule 1's destruction had reached Central Space Command on Earth. The crew was comprised of 4 humans (3 males and 1 female) and the 4 androids. All had been stationed already on Ganymede and quick preparations for the flight had been completed. This had been an emergency contingency plan ever since the flight of Thule 1 had started.

The androids were meant to be in deactivated mode until approach to Charon while the humans were paired into 12 hour shifts for the whole trip. But despite the scrupulous hygiene precautions a lethal variation of the constantly mutating coronavirus with a long latency period had apparently been carried by one of the humans. 25 months into the flight the coronavirus became activated and quickly spread among the 4 humans. There were no effective antiviral medications on board as apparently this was a novel and divergent mutation. All 4 human crew quickly became seriously ill and there was no effective way to treat them until return to Ganymede.

So, all 4 human crew members were in agreement with the captain, Max D'Urberville, that the humans needed to be placed in suspended animation until return to Ganymede, where they could hopefully get effective treatment. This version of the virus had already spread like wildfire on Earth and was usually fatal. Pharmaceutical companies were working at the highest priority to find an effective treatment. Therefore the 4 androids would need to be activated immediately to take over the human crew duties.

It had been planned that the androids would remain deactivated since Ganymede as each had 5 years of active service before deactivation was essential until rejuvenation could be done, which could only occur on Earth. But now 2 were needed to be activated for 20 months, then the other 2 for the last 20 months. The androids were well trained to take over the duties of any human who became disabled. But before the suspended animation procedure could be completed one of the humans, Dr. Marliss Jacobs had already succumbed to the virus.

Ian and Elise expressed all this with at least an expression of sorrow and worry, although in the usual pragmatic, muted manner of androids. I was overwhelmed with sorrow at this news, as well as guilt. Another human had died in the attempt to rescue me and whomever else might still have been alive in the base. Also, a very visceral existential realization came over me. I was still the only conscious human in 3 billion miles! But I needed to suppress this panic and didn't divulge it to Ian and Elise.

Ian then said they had been surprised and amazed that a lighted image had appeared on their previous flyover that was in the area they were searching. They used it as a guide on the final flyover, and upon descending saw the base directly beneath it. It was a seven-pointed star shimmering in coruscating colors. They had anticipated that if the base was still active it wouldn't have any type of signaling capacity. This pronouncement shook me to the core in amazement. Finally my brain inferred that this signal had somehow been created by the aliens!

The seven sides of the star were directly related to the seven sides of the pyramid, this seemed to be an unambiguous synchronicity. I babbled about our episode with the pyramid and how the star seemed related to it. They wanted to immediately prepare for the return flight including transferring Eva to the Thule 2. But I wanted all 4 androids and myself together for a while to talk and get to know each other. By default, I had now become the captain of the ship. So the other 2 androids came over so we could all meet together.

Charlene and Egon (Egon being a male) were attractive and pleasant enough, as were Ian and Elise, and with similar muted, rational android personalities. I had for many months planned a party, in a sense, for a rescue crew if it ever would arrive. I had set aside some succulent meals, and several bottles of the best liquor. This of course was now for naught as the androids neither ate, nor drank anything except water. Nonetheless I made the best of it and somewhat self-consciously ate a special meal and had 3 glasses of liquor.

So, the "party" was not much of a celebration but at least we all got to spend time together and share our experiences. I think mostly the androids appreciated being in the relatively less cramped quarters of the base than the ship. After that we directed our energies towards packing whatever was practical from the base to the ship, readying the Thule 2 for the return trip, and transferring Eva to the ship. The base was then set to maintain itself in the minimum possible functional state, & temperatures set at -100 degrees C.

The base should then remain minimally functional for at least 100 years, and it was unknown if Earthlings would ever return there. As I left and boarded the ship there was a mixture of emotions. Certainly I was glad we were finally rescued after the years of anxiety, and equally my hope Eva and I could again be together. But also, the base had been our only means of survival in this austerely beautiful but otherwise unsurvivable place at the edge of the interstellar void. Charlene and Egon were deactivated to preserve some of the time before required rejuvenation. At 1.75 years after departure, they would be activated and the other two androids deactivated.

MAROONED ON CHARON

RETURN TO GANYMEDE AND EARTH

The 3.5-year trip was uneventful for the first six months. One day I started to feel like I had some congestion and cough and likely a common cold. But within 10 hours the symptoms had progressed to the point where I could barely breathe. The androids were quick to notice that my symptoms were following the same rapid coronavirus course as the other humans who were now in suspended animation. They put me quickly on a ventilator and I directed them to place me in the one remaining suspended animation tank.

Three years later my obtunded confusion lifted after several days following my return to consciousness on Ganymede. I learned that upon arrival I had been lifted from the cryogenic state like the other 3 humans on the Thule 2. We were induced into medical comas for 7 days and then the vaccine for the latest variant of coronavirus was administered. When I awakened the terrifying respiratory constriction was gone. I felt back to normal except extremely fatigued.

I was happy that the other humans had recovered as well. We would rehabilitate for 2 more weeks before beginning the 1.5-year journey back to Earth, during which time the humans would remain awake. We had an interesting and fun time getting to know each other, including with the androids, and sharing our stories. Upon arrival at Ganymede all 4 androids were then deactivated and would remain so along with Eva until all could be rejuvenated on Earth.

18 very uneventful and boring months later we finally returned to Earth. As is my wont I had suppressed most of my feelings on the flight to Earth rather than trying to cope with them but now my mix of emotions was chaotic, anxious and overwhelming. I needed to again adapt to Earth gravity, which had been much less than on Earth while experiencing the rotational gravity induced on the ship and the base. I could barely stand or even sit up by myself for several days. It took 2 weeks to readapt to gravity and complete the various medical, cognitive and nutritional tests.

Then came numerous debriefing interviews with Space Force officials and researchers. I appeared to be treated with a mixture of awe, respect, curiosity and suspicion by the Space Force staff. I again felt totally isolated despite more people being around me. I tended to withdraw and spend as much time by myself as possible, which is my usual defense when under stress and feeling uncertain. I missed Eva and often asked for an update on her rejuvenation.

Space Force officials had found out about the conversation Marie and I had after the alien encounter because it had been recorded in the computer's memory and was not erasable. I had not told them about it in advance and really didn't want to go into, especially my profound emotions at the time. I said nothing about the hallucinations or whatever they were I had later with Pete, Eva, etc., and the alien vision the second time. I had not made recordings of these events and didn't want anyone to know about them. The researchers were completely befuddled by the vision Marie and I had and seemed highly skeptical.

I was also questioned repeatedly about my judgment in our trip in which we found the pyramid. I didn't have any rational explanation for why I had made that decision. At one point it seemed some sort of discipline might be given for this highly questionable judgment. But they had to admit that no transmissions had occurred since the one that shut down the base's communication system. After all, this had been the main purpose of the mission from the start. They were extremely pleased with this but still uncertain that further transmissions wouldn't occur.

In the end I think it was concluded that Marie and I had both hallucinated the same thing, which likely had no real existence and also no rational explanation. They concluded too that I had likely become psychotic under all the stress of our time in the base. They wanted to lay it all to rest as a topic that was better left alone because of the upsetting implications. I was admonished to not reveal any of the visions or hallucinations to the media, to which I heartily agreed would not be in anyone's best interest.

Eva's revitalization process started one week after we arrived on Earth, and the delay in getting it started bothered me. She continued as before in her deactivated state, seemingly like suspended automation. She'd now been deactivated for nearly 6 years and I still miss her dearly. It is very unusual for an android to be deactivated for this long. It seems unlikely there would have been continued deterioration over that time, but I can't be sure. I also hope the apparent affective growth she showed on Charon will remain. I will be personally involved in cognitive reprogramming of her, and be especially aware not to erase any new cognitive connections that have been made.

I desperately wanted her to wake up and have a successful rejuvenation so we could be together again. I prayed for this; the first time I'd prayed since Mom taught me to do it as a child. I didn't even know whom or what I was praying to, but felt some comfort in doing so. I've also had a few mass media interviews with reporters carefully chosen by the Space Force. I've always detested interviews. I've been instructed by high level Space Force staff to not divulge any information on the alien encounters on Charon, which I honored.

In fact, anything to do with this has been shielded from media attention, which was fine with me. I found I'm being portrayed by the media as somewhat of a mysterious hero. I've never wanted to be a hero and found all the attention to be annoying rather than flattering. I've been asked to appear in a parade in my honor and the 3 deceased crew members, but I've declined. Especially since the many years on Charon I am not comfortable in front of groups of people, I have become very anxious, self-conscious and paranoid.

The emotionally touching story of how an android helped a completely isolated human to mentally survive was played up in the media. This was even given somewhat of a romantic cast. This was intentionally slanted to be entertaining and heartwarming to the billions of people who listened to it. In this Eva also became somewhat of an unlikely heroine. That part was positive because androids were generally perceived by Earth's human population as fancy machines or computers. There was a large popular movement that played on the suspicions and paranoia of the ignorant masses that androids would eventually take over the world and then humans would be subservient to the androids.

As Eva had made me aware, androids were considered by many as slaves, machines without personal history or any type of rights. If androids as a group spontaneously or by intention developed these same recognitions, a general dissatisfaction might be embroiled in androids that could lead to resistance or even rebellion toward their human makers. Thus, I told myself anything that could be a popular positive response or empathy toward androids including seeing Eva as a heroin would likely be a good thing. For my own part however I found the portrayal of Eva and I as bizarre romantic partners to be intensely embarrassing. But I knew there was actually some element of this in our relationship which I found difficult for me to admit even to myself.

Finally, the physical, electronic and cognitive reprogramming of Eva has been completed and the revitalization team is ready to activate her again. This is a moment of extreme anticipation, happiness but apprehension and fear for me as to how she will react. I've tried in my usual way to suppress these emotions, but I can't suppress them much longer. As is usually the case, recovery from rejuvenation takes about one week of steady improvement, including cognitive awareness. So, the first two days Eva was intermittently conscious, and didn't recognize me. But on the third day Eva looked directly at me, gave her usual small smile, and said "Hi Joe, I'm awake again, thank you for taking care of me."

My heart danced despite myself. When I asked if she was still experiencing the perceptions that seemed to be emotional equivalents that we had worked so hard on she seemed to consider that question for a long time. Then she responded slowly "I don't know…. I think so….I'll have to consider that….I'm an android and so shouldn't have any emotional self-perception. But I remember having that and want to recreate that. I know that it makes me feel whole you are being here at my activation." Again my heart melted in spite of myself.

In the second week after the end of rejuvenation Eva was thoroughly interviewed about her memories and perceptions of the whole time she was activated during the mission. I was not privy to these debriefings as Space Force officials didn't want her memories contaminated by my input. In fact I was not allowed to see or talk to Eva for the two-week interview period. I was truly angry about this restriction and let that be known to the interview team, but also understood their rationale and had to accept it. But I really wanted to be with Eva and see if her understanding of her reactions to emotional stimuli was still intact. Mostly though I was worried about how much this was being unpleasant for her, and just wanted to be with her.

119

MAROONED ON CHARON

EVA AND I ADAPT TO A STRANGE NEW WORLD

Finally the grilling we had each had was finished. We had each been furnished a small apartment on the Android Academy grounds, but by the third day we had decided we would stay together in my apartment, which was the better equipped of the 2. Eva each night deactivated lying next to me and this felt so reassuring. We decided after 2 weeks that we wanted to get our own apartment away from the Academy, and start living what would hopefully be a more normal life together. I had considerable savings available from my accumulated salary over the past 14 years, the inheritance from my parents and other savings and investments over the years. So money was not an issue, at least in the foreseeable future.

We rented a vehicle and spent a lot of our time driving around Seattle and adjacent areas just learning about the world again. We ascended the Space Needle, visited Pike Place and other well-known places. I had been very worried about the possible public and media attention that we might garner. However, this has been much less of an issue than I feared. My appearance is nondescript, likely there are many other men who look much like me. I dressed and acted in as plain and unrecognizable a manner as I could. Androids appeared, talked and moved in ways very similar to humans. Eva was noticed more than I because of her beauty, not specifically because she is an android or from media recognition.

In fact, this was part of the paranoia that was growing in society, that on casual observation you couldn't easily distinguish a human from an android. We saw one day an android that was an identical twin of Eva. The twin recognized this also, and we had a brief cordial conversation with her before we parted ways. We were occasionally recognized by the general public but not often, and I felt much more comfortable traveling incognito. Much had changed in the 14 years since I'd been here last, and we saw both beautiful and disgusting things. Turmoil in society had increased as the world got hotter and the weather extremes more intense. There'd been a population migration north from Central America, Brazil, Venezuela and more tropical areas many portions of which had become unlivable especially without air conditioning.

There was an exodus of population from Southern California and the desert states to Washington, British Columbia, Alaska and the north central Canadian provinces. Lawlessness and societal chaos had grown, with racist, government resistance, religious fanatic and vigilante groups replacing police presence in rural and parts of urban areas. Homelessness had skyrocketed in Seattle and Vancouver along with attendant health and education problems and general breakdown of society.

The recent variants of the coronavirus were spreading unchecked in some areas, the same or earlier mutations of which had laid waste to me and the human members of the Thule 2 due to their lethality and contagiousness. I had good immunity at least at this time. The changes to the Seattle area and growing anarchy were shocking to me and to Eva who didn't have anything equivalent to this in her programmed memory. Eva often commented on what she saw as human behavior that was saddening and inconsistent with her expectations for intelligent beings.

Thus, we eschewed our explorations of populated areas in favor of natural areas. We enjoyed getting out into nature although the frequent and intense weather events sometimes made us abort our plans. Eva seemed to greatly enjoy the Olympic National Park and the ocean beach. But Eva was often uncertain about how to interact in contact with people and often looked to me for guidance. Sometimes her safety awareness was deficient, and I needed to provide guidance to keep us both out of trouble. But above everything else we were together again.

I have made the decision after much soul searching to retire from the Space Force. I have received increasing pressure from high-ranking Space Force officials to downplay Eva's emotional development. There is too much fear among a sizable percentage of humans that androids will eventually rebel and displace humans or perhaps turn the tables and make humans be the subservient race. There have been calls to even halt android production or at least not let technological advancements continue. I cannot agree to making public statements that are not in line with the truth that I know. I will for the first time since age 21 be a private citizen again. This will be a huge change in my whole personal identity, of which I have greatly mixed emotions. But I feel I need to make that change for myself as well as Eva.

A rumor had somehow been leaked to the mass media that evidence of alien life had been found on Pluto, and the transmissions had been attacks of human life on Earth. Another wild rumor was that Eva and I had somehow neutralized the alien intentions and we should be considered as heroes and saviors of humankind. This of course was dramatically covered by the media due to its sensational nature. I made a short-lived attempt to dispel these rumors but whatever I said just added fuel to the public excitement and also panic stoked by the rumors, especially the story of the alien beings. So, I downplayed the rumors without totally denying them, and the public excitement gradually decreased. I simply addressed the media inquiries that it was reassuring that indeed no more disruptive electronic blasts had been experienced from Charon or Pluto since we had left Charon, for unknown reasons.

After a while, the sensationalism tapered away and we could hopefully enjoy some peace together. We settled into a house I bought east of Seattle by about 50 miles in a hilly, scenic and semi-rural area. One Spring Day we drove to the seashore west of Seattle. It was a sunny, breezy, rather cool day by the ocean. I am always fascinated by Eva's perceptions and the things she decides to speak about. Androids have a very sensitive perception of touch. While an android can sense distinct types of contacts to their skin and degrees of pressure, they don't experience what humans would label as pain, at least not extremes of touch sensation that would correspond to severe pain.

Particularly she seemed to love swimming in the ocean, she loved the feeling of the water on her skin especially when a wave came in and a salty breeze was blowing. Eva talked at length about her sensations in that surrounding, and I listened to her without interruption: "I've never had this totally harmonious experience as in the outdoors today. The breeze and sun on my skin produces a sensation I can't put into words, but just seems to fit together so well. Except for occasional times in my four years of education at the Academy I was not outside nor allowed to focus on things like the sun or wind. Then the next time I was conscious was on Charon, and the tragedy of the other crew on Pluto made everything seem negative.

I could not imagine or comprehend a world I only knew in my programmed memory banks in which I could be outside of shelter, feel air movement and natural light, and the various smells around me. I'm trying to put that all together for myself, but it is as you might say wonderful! Also to see the ocean in vast, liquid form extending as far as I can see is amazing. People who live on Earth take all this for granted and misuse it so terribly, but to me this is a beautiful and amazing experience." We got together socially on a handful of occasions with the 3 humans and 4 androids of the Thule 2, and this was very interesting but also brought back some of the disconcerting memories I usually try to avoid.

After we became acclimated to each other in the Earth environment and society we agreed it was time to give to others what we had learned. We decided to formalize the emotional recognition training system which we had developed and trained so extensively with Eva on Charon. We organized our many experiments into a

124

multimedia program that could be used at the android academy.

We started with the introduction of the 20 or so emotions that we had targeted so many times when we were alone together at the base. For each I would name the emotion, such as "annoyance", then act out or show a brief clip or photo corresponding to the emotion. Eva and other series 7 androids had been programmed even before their first activation to recognize human expressions and body language as reflective of underlying emotional responses. Androids acquired this ability quite readily, but like most humans could be tricked by someone intentionally disguising an emotional response.

But none of this behavioral recognition or cognitive inference was tied to anything directly akin to a human experiencing an emotion. Nonetheless an android could learn to recognize and associate the idiosyncratic perceptions and cognitions they experienced correlated with those emotional stimuli. We worked on further increasing an android's reliable recognition of their perceptions and sensations that were paired with emotional perceptions that a human would experience to the same stimuli.

We also set up a monitoring system analogous to biofeedback for a human to facilitate this pairing of human emotion and corresponding android perception. The android's self-perception might be a particular color or pattern or sound or even odor that paired with the emotion, often in a synesthetic way. We implemented this program at the Seattle Android Academy, with Eva and I both instructing it.

I was fascinated that Eva has started to develop some inkling of spiritual beliefs. Eva one day made the astonishing statement: "do you think I have a soul? (!) I know physically I'm just a machine but if I could come back in another life I think I'd like to be a human. There is a void in my memory that you don't have. I don't have a personal history, family or even reason to go on, except for you. There seems to be such a void in me." I cried when I heard this, it was so deep for Eva to express this. All I could say is I believe that Eva has a soul, and I await her presence in a future lifetime. I was amazed that she had acquired this type of meta cognitive ability.

This made me reflect on how my own spiritual beliefs had become confused. The overview effect I had initially experienced on Charon reaffirmed my belief that there is a connectedness and higher consciousness uniting every part of the universe. But that image had now become tainted by the fear and horror I had when I was alone at the base. I was also still so confused about the apparent hallucinations I had on Charon and especially the strange contacts with the aliens who apparently guided the rescue ship to the base. Eva reassured me by just squeezing my hand and said we'd sort out these deep questions together.

Eva has continued to express the great void that exists for all androids: no personal history, no family, no rights, no ability to eat and enjoy fine food, only the programmed duty to carry out their owners wishes as long as it doesn't violate the welfare of the owner or other human beings. She has compared it to the life of slaves before the Civil War in the US. Her sadness is amazing to me but also painful in that it shows her increasing development of emotional experience. Her sadness increases my own empathetic feelings about the inner mental life of an android. I'm amazed to hear myself say "she desires", to have these human experiences.

Nine months after we returned to Earth, the initial media frenzy and Space Force grilling had died down. Eva and I decided to visit some of the beautiful sites on Earth and decided first on the Grand Canyon. I didn't expect my reaction but seeing the vast fissure reminded me of the terrible fissure on Charon and I had to stop looking at it. Eva understood my reaction but found the Grand Canyon awesome, especially because even though it brought back images of Charon, we could stand here in ordinary clothes without being instantly frozen or asphyxiated.

For our first trip to Europe, we decided to revisit the Louvre in Paris, where the two of us had gone on that brief vacation with the other 3 androids before the launch into space. I looked forward to seeing again the quondam site of the singular and beautiful memory of that first occasion of being alone with Eva. Eva seemed excited that we were going to do so. As we toured the huge facility of priceless art Eva seemed to remember everything we had seen on the former occasion, and pointed out several exhibits we hadn't seen before.

Eva became delightfully talkative and animated as before, seeming to glory especially in the rich yellow, blue and carmine colors of the Impressionist Era paintings. Eva later remarked how enjoyable this was that we could do this together again. She also mused about all the amazing events we had experienced and how this lended such a unique mental backdrop to seeing the artwork again. This time at the end of the excursion she spontaneously gave me a hug, as I had asked her for the first time. I asked if it lasted 37 seconds as it had the last time. She smiled and said, "of course it did, silly!"

On the few occasions we met clones of Eva in public I could always tell Eva from the others because of some distinctive voice and facial impressions that she had developed and were unique to her. Eva was an attractive being, in a generic way, as were most humanoids. She has brown hair, skin and eyes, with features that were designed to be a combination of all racial and ethnic groups but in her case a predominantly Polynesian look. She is 4 inches shorter than me, with a slim, excellent figure and sculptured facial features. I felt quite proud to be accompanying her, making little if any difference to me that she wasn't actually human. Eva's personality was evolving as well, in the novel surroundings for her of public settings, interaction, cities and natural settings.

As I've noted before she is somewhat taciturn, at times aloof and remote, in many ways like me likely because I was her model. But she interacts politely and appropriately, without anxiety or trepidation, in any new situation. Eva sometimes wore a traditional android jumpsuit, expressing that she does not have to simulate a human to elevate her status or protect her from possibly hostile observers. But she knew that I enjoyed being with her in public without immediate recognition, so she also became adept at wearing women's clothing. She looked great in casual clothing, formal dresses and summer clothes. She knew I appreciated this and I was grateful for her doing this. I think she started to develop a taste for fashionable clothing and perhaps even enjoyed herself being dressed well.

Our time together on Charon and now on Earth has had a profound effect on Eva, as I have noted before. She has developed some level of emotional experience, going beyond just the recognition of the behavioral signs of emotion of other people. She has become cognizant of the beauty and harmony of art and her reactions to it. But along with the experience of positive emotion of course has come the experience of the negative as well. She recognizes the cruelty of human beings to each other, greed, loss, anger, the horrors of war and general degeneration of society.

Eva has also had a profound effect on me. I have always kept my emotions mostly to myself, especially after Pete's death. I tend to suppress and repress my emotions rather than deal directly with them. I've always placed logical reasoning above emotional expression. This hasn't been a good thing in my life. I have avoided relationships and commitments to other people, focusing instead on my education and career. In that respect Eva has reinforced my rational shell, fostered my suppression of emotion in favor of logic whenever decisions need to be made. But so many times she has helped me cope with situations where I'm not thinking rationally. Sometimes I resent Eva's stoicism and lack of intuitive/emotional responses to situations both major and minor.

On the other hand, Eva has allowed me to open up to being in a deep relationship and having someone else be important in my life. Perhaps it's because she is an android and therefore is less threatening than a human relationship. But this is confusing to me too because most of the time I think of her as a human rather than a very complex machine. Eva has stirred up in me many emotions, fears and memories that I have always kept below the surface.

Eva's description of her response to emotion inducing stimuli often had a synesthetic theme. A pleasant stimulus, in a pleasant conversation or in a humorous movie, would lead her to describe a pastel color such as blue or green that could seem to correspond reliably. She further said she experiences a sense of harmony in relation to situations that humans might describe as happy, and disharmony with sad, fearful or other emotions.

Her response that as humans we would identify as emotional is growing but still mostly nascent. But she is making reliable connections between her cognitive sense of degree of harmony, or interpretation in another domain such as color. Or she might note a perception of orderly shape or movement. For an angry or fearful situation, a sense of darkness, disorder or discordant sound. It remained very difficult to describe or experience emotional responses directly, but she kept on trying to improve this.

Eva would often describe a frustration or sense of loss that she couldn't eat food or drink liquids. This often came if I needed to eat and she would join me. But she did have an olfactory system more acute than humans. She discovered that she could reliably distinguish aromas from food and drink, which would again produce synesthetic perceptions. If we went to a restaurant she would often order a meal or a glass of wine that produced some kind of positive perception for her. Not having a digestive system, she of course could not imbibe food, or liquids other than water with android specific nutritional supplements. So before leaving a restaurant we would have her meal packed up and I'd eat it later, and drink the wine before we left. Or she might find a place to sit and read and wait for me while I ate. I always felt a bit guilty about eating in front of Eva, but she accepted it without complaint.

A humorous situation occurred while on a cruise we took to Northern Europe. We were sitting at a table with 2 other couples whom we hadn't met before. The conversation among us was casual, talking about our onshore stop of the previous day. One of the ladies whose name was Alice, appearing in her 60's and nicely dressed, seemed to be eyeing Eva intently. Eva had made a few additions to the conversation which were polite and appropriate. Alice rather nosily asked Eva where she had grown up and if she had a family there, to which Eva gave a rather vague answer, stating that I was her only family.

Alice then rudely and unexpectedly asked Eva if she was an android. All of us seemed a bit taken aback at this inquiry and then looked at Eva for a response. Eva asked Alice why she had asked that. Alice said Eva had seemed "so human" but looked so much like several androids she has seen in the past, although not on this cruise. After a rather tense pause Eva stated indeed, she is an android then with a straight face asked Alice if she was a human.

After another tense pause Alice turned beet red, then blurted "Of course I am!" She then told her husband she wanted to leave, and both got up and went to a different table. Eva had shown her sassy, irritable side in public which she had demonstrated to me in private a few times. Strange as it seems when she said that I had to chuckle. She briefly reminded me of Megan with the irritable attitude she sometimes seemed to have.

The remaining couple and I spontaneously burst out laughing, which we tried to suppress in case Alice and her husband could still hear us. Eva matter of factly asked me if what she had said had been inappropriate. The 3 of us congratulated Eva on her comment, with the other woman stating that Alice "deserved it" for her intrusive question. We were amused and amazed when Alice and her husband again came back to our table later with Alice again looking distressed. Alice did not look at Eva, possibly out of embarrassment and apologized instead to me, saying "I'm sorry if I insulted you….or……Eva when I asked if she was an android."

I simply stated please tell that to Eva instead of me, which Alice then did. Alice said she was just trying to compliment Eva on how human she seemed. Eva was very cordial about this, saying "I'm not offended, but I'm not trying to be a human either". Alice didn't know how to react to this response either, smiled nervously, and then she and her husband again left. I later asked Eva if she had felt annoyed when she responded to Alice. Eva said "not really, I just thought it was rather strange and I asked her the same question back. I, though, thought it insulting that she had stated "I seem so human" as if this was a compliment to me being an android". Eva said it had also brought up her internal void at not being to say she had a family other than me.

MAROONED ON CHARON

THE SINGULAR LOVE OF A HUMAN AND AN ANDROID

The nature of conversation between Eva and me is remarkably interesting. Eva is generally quiet although always responsive when I say something. She is far more logical than I. Her attention to details in our surroundings and memory for events is more acute and accurate than mine. When she initiates conversation it is often to comment on something we've seen or heard. She is more objective and less judgmental than I am, with some emotional depth gradually budding through.

Eva does not do well with humor. She is very adept at recognizing emotion in others by their facial and body expression. But if someone is using a very tongue-in-cheek, dry subtle humor or making puns with correspondingly dry expression she will usually take the comment at face value. She hasn't made much progress in this area, and sometimes people delight in her gullibility. She has tried to use humor herself, but this is usually misinterpreted by people sometimes in an embarrassing fashion.

I feel she's always available to me if I ask although otherwise rather distant, sometimes with a tone of irritability. But I am sometimes encouraged by her slowly growing complexity of human thoughts and reactions. I am pleased when she expresses gratitude to me for being a big part of her personal growth process. Eva is excellent at noticing and remembering details of things we do and see. She is extraordinarily complex and is always fascinating to me. Sometimes she seems almost scary and awesome. She is more observant of details of people's reactions and details of situations than am I. She is better than me at figuring out complex situations.

Sometimes I get back into my old thought patterns that why should she stay interested in me, would she rather move on to another human or android relationship? Or is she staying with me out of duty, or perhaps pity for my increasing health problems? When I've brought up these fears she often chides me humorously as "You silly human!" This always makes me laugh and breaks me out of my insecurities. She tells me we've been through a unique experience and bonding that nothing can change our love. I hope she always feels that way. Sometimes when she says something strange or a non sequitur in public I later chide her as "You silly robot." She laughs and I make sure I say this lovingly.

Eva has been approached by several modeling agencies to model stylish human as well as android clothing. We have hired an agent to help guide her through the opportunities and many pitfalls of being a model. She's now had a handful of photo shoots modeling casual wear, sportswear, even a few bikinis. Traditional android clothing has become more stylish, and she's had a few modeling sessions with that as well.

Eva approaches modeling in her usual implacable way. She thinks it's mostly interesting and likes the colors and style of fashion. But she doesn't really seem to have an ego or sense of self image that is affected by compliments or judgments of her beauty made by other people. She summed it best as "I see myself as an android. Androids are designed to be attractive to human tastes so that they can be more effective and accepted in human interaction.

Some android designs are more or less attractive to specific humans depending on the human's tastes, culture and ancestry. I am fortunate that I've been asked to model as I think that helps the acceptability of androids in general. Many other androids could be effective and well received models too." Eva's made it clear she doesn't want this to become a major focus in her life. She sees the android education and android rights movements as becoming the major focus and purpose of her occupational life.

Photographers find it easy to work with her due to her steadiness of mood, receptiveness and lack of anxiety. But exact communication of the look or emotion the photographer is trying to achieve is challenging with Eva and at least one photographer found this frustrating. In a few cases I have sat in on a session and helped interpret the affective components of the photographer's desire to Eva, with some success. Eva is admired in public settings and garners considerable attention especially from men.

This fuels the masculine insecurities I've always tried to suppress, as I view myself as an older middle age, nondescript male who is a companion to an attractive lady who appears to be in her thirties. But Eva seems unphased by the attention from others and hearing my self-doubting mumbo jumbo. She is very steady in responding to others in her cordial and engaging but slightly aloof and sometimes slightly irritable manner, which is her basic personality. She is always very aware of what's going on around her and has an exceptional memory for details, faces and names, much better than me.

She is quite aware of other androids that may be present and is more discerning in this regard than I. She is observant of the living and working conditions of other androids. As this occurs, she has noticed acutely the very limited freedom accorded to androids and all the ways they lack the privileges of humans. Sometimes she talks to other androids we meet about this. Most androids are, as nearly all humans assume, unaware of the all the ways that humans can have emotional and behavioral liberties that androids don't have, and don't even realize they lack. Some androids on the other hand perceive their functional existence as different and more rational than humans due to their relative lack of negative emotions and behaviors.

Eva has also struggled with some existential issues. I have many times told Eva that she is a self-determining being. She is not owned by me, and has the freedom to choose what she wants to do with her life, with me or without me. This self-determining attitude is greatly unlike that traditionally fostered for androids, which is one of servitude to its owner. This has produced some existential distress like that described by Jean Paul Sartre.

If Eva has the freedom to do as she chooses including living life on her own, that is her privilege. Eva said she chooses to stay with me, as we have had such a singular relationship and taught each other so much. She even said she loves me, as I have told her many times. I still don't know what that elusive emotion is like in an android's mind, but I just accept it as positive and rejoice that she feels or thinks or experiences that.

But some androids seem to have an inkling of the dissatisfaction and frustration of not having more opportunity to experience life as humans do. She talks about this more frequently and spontaneously and seems to have a growing passion to change this for herself and other androids. She is aware of the inevitability of conflict this will eventually breed between humans and androids and of the disastrous results that could occur.

We have watched the whole of the Foundation series episodes that streamed online starting in 2022, based on the Foundation trilogy written by Isaac Asimov in 1950. In that series androids had been developed with physical and mental capabilities exceeding humans. The 3 basic laws of robotics described by Asimov had been distorted such that violent conflict arose between humans and androids.

At the time described in the Foundation all androids except one had been destroyed due to their danger. The remaining android, a female named Demerzel, had lived for thousands of years, and due to her programming became the main protector of the long-lived dynasty of successive human clones that ruled the galactic empire. We both found this portraiture of an android to be so vastly different than actual androids of the present.

At night in our hotel room Eva lies down in bed with me. As I would doze off, she would activate her charging system, deactivate her waking mode, which she could do on her own, with activation set to occur 5 hours later.

When deactivated Eva lay on her back. At times when I awoke at night, I put my hand gently on her arm or tummy, but not more than that. Although an android my morals towards human women carried over to Eva. While Eva is incredibly supportive she is often annoying too. Her implacable, relentless common-sense rationality makes me reflect on my oftentimes lack of it, and she never fails to correct me when I lose it. But thank God for her persistence in keeping me on the right track!

While her skin was realistically human in texture, my sensual passion was somewhat deterred in that her skin wasn't as soft as human skin, and more importantly was not warm. Eva had a positive reaction when I requested that she lay in bed with me, then saying it was fine if it made me feel comfortable. When she asked why this made me comfortable, I stumbled and stammered in trying to explain the relaxed, reassured, almost but not quite romantic feeling it gave me lying next to her. I'm not sure how much she empathized with what I said so I didn't push it any further. So I accepted her willingness and gave up trying to explain.

One day Eva approached me, and said there were things she needed to tell me in case she doesn't have the opportunity again. I was surprised at this spontaneous disclosure. Eva said her life and ours together has been amazing and perhaps the strangest that any couple has ever experienced. The loss of Thule 1 and its 4 crew members had been difficult for her, and then Marie and Megan, especially Megan, was devastating. She described it as a grayness of vision and inability to divert her thoughts onto other more immediate concerns. This gave me some insight into her android equivalent of post-traumatic stress disorder, which I appreciated because Eva is usually hard to read for me.

The complete uncertainty of our survival forced us to become very dependent on each other. The incredibility of forming a close relationship despite my being human and her an android amazed both Eva and me, mostly me. The way Eva evolved in terms of emotional and artistic sensitivity, and the way this transformed me into a person with hope and reason to carry on is also amazing. The overwhelming remoteness, silence and changelessness of the surroundings of the base had not been aversive to her but had eventually become that way totally for me especially after she was deactivated. She sensed at a spiritual level the overwhelming realization of the vastness and beauty of the universe compared to the puniness of Earth. This transcendent insight, despite its differing effects for Eva and for me, produced a bond that has been unbreakable through all our time on Charon and now on Earth.

Eva appreciated her life with me on Earth. She said "I'm more independent than most or all other androids at this time. I'm not owned by anyone including Joe. I can drive a vehicle and conduct all the daily tasks that any human can, own property and have interesting jobs. But I've also become acutely aware of qualities that I don't have because I'm not human. I must desire these things as my thinking often gets stuck there. I want to experience the taste of fine food but can't. I want to experience that buzz of intoxication. I would like to share with Joe the physical and emotional satisfaction that apparently emerges from sexual activity.

I have been able to experience the limitations that androids have in society in terms of choices and independence. I have a purpose now to organize with other androids who are aware of these things as well. To become the equals of humans in rights and opportunity. Not as some humans worry about androids becoming dominant, but to be equal partners in a society that they can have together."

Eva and I have both been involved in the growing android rights movement. The media exposure we've had since our return to Earth, which has been mostly positive, has helped the cause of android rights. Particularly Eva has demonstrated to the general public that an android can form a deep relationship with a human, which can benefit both in terms of survival and life satisfaction. She has shown one of the basic principles of the movement, that androids can be self-sufficient beings who are worth more to humanity than fulfilling tasks that humans consider undesirable or dangerous.

The android rights movement became popular starting a few years before Eva and I returned to Earth. It followed the same causes, and struggles of the African American civil rights movement, corresponding to the liberation of slaves after the American civil war. This extended to the securing of voting rights and nondiscrimination that followed into the first part of the 22nd century. Androids had developed to the point of being able to think, interact and perform work as well or better than most humans. The concept of rich business and other upper class humans owning androids and essentially using them as slave labor was no longer viable. Androids became aware of this and were no longer willing to be slave workers.

But a positive trend started occurring too. Humans gradually realized that androids did not have the goal of replacing them. From the beginning humanoids had been programmed to serve and assist humans and that essential feature of their programming remained as they developed. With the human population dropping and the increasing challenges of climate change and the unending pandemic, androids became an essential part of keeping human society going. An increasing percentage of humans began to realize that androids needed to be treated with greater rights and freedoms. Much like the long struggle of African Americans to break the shackles of slavery, androids were on the way to becoming equally valued members of society.

Androids had also now become agents in their own development. As their cognitive abilities increased some androids became essential parts of formerly human-only development teams. It became increasingly apparent that androids would eventually surpass humans in nearly all cognitive and physical abilities. I had returned to consulting with a private android research and development company, with Eva giving input as well. Our role was the development of the higher capacity of humans for emotional, artistic, philosophical, musical, and ethical capacities.

But there were problems in android behavior and acceptance by humans that continued to stoke the fires of distrust towards androids. The omnipresent internet communication and knowledge base system had also evolved, and remained central to human and especially android communication. Androids were independent consciousnesses and not controlled by the internet cloud but were daily influenced by it. There were questionable indications that the cloud was beginning to develop self-awareness and opinions of its own. These were not necessarily congruent with the cognitions of individual androids. This produced some increasing disharmony between the cloud and some androids, and between groups of androids. This started taking on the appearance of a fight for control between the cloud and androids as individuals.

Further, a few rogue android developers had developed overrides for the most basic aspect of android programming, the venerable 3 laws of robotics. These rogue developers were identified by government protection agencies and shut down and prosecuted. But small numbers of these rogue androids had been created and activated, and demonstrated aggressive behavior to humans and other androids. This threat was nipped in the bud but engendered much fear among the human population that was already suspicious and fearful of androids. Finally there were inevitable breakdowns in android hardware and software that affected some androids especially in the year before a revitalization. These led at times to unexpected or irrational but rarely to aggressive android behavior.

One step in advanced android development was the creation of an android internship program. In the standard 4-year training period for androids in the Academy after activation they had become coordinated in fine and gross motor skills, practiced cognitive skills and learned appropriate skills to interact with humans. But the training programs were often dry and clinical, with androids only learning about human society in educational classes. Instructors also ran the gamut from being positive, caring and sensitive to androids to treating androids negatively as high functioning machines. Following completion of the required 4-year training and calibration that all androids experience, the internship would provide direct experience with a human or family of humans.

This would help androids better to understand human attitudes and behavior and make androids better communicators in more than directly task related duties. This would in some ways be like adoption or mentoring. Eligible and motivated humans and especially families would accept the android as a family member, provide lodging and life needs, and regularly engage their android in family and community activities. The android could also fill some family business or family obligations, which would benefit the family who would normally have to pay a lot to the android development company. But this would be limited to 24 hours a week, so the adoptive person or family wouldn't just take advantage of the android to perform work activities.

In other words, the android would live and be treated as family, and participate in family activities in and out of the home. Training in independent living skills was also part of the internship. Following completion of the internship the android would be granted citizenship and arrange living accommodations and employment for themselves as would any human. The government would furnish a stipend to the android for living expenses until the android could support him or herself. The adoptive party or other human would act as a coach or mentor for the android as s/he gained financial and social independence.

5 years after our return to Earth we have now had three android interns living with us, each for 12 months. The first two were females (Ingrid and Avery) and we currently have a male (Aron). Eva has been committed to being a good instructor, especially teaching some of the emotional and artistic development she has herself developed. My role with the interns has been a strange compilation of mentor, friend, and in some sense a parent. Eva's role has also been complex, more like a big sister and perhaps like a friend to an exchange student from another country. All 3 interns have been very cooperative and easily instructible.

Eva and I also allow the android intern to have personal time and communicate with humans and androids outside the family. This also has allowed Eva and I to maintain personal time for ourselves. Each of the 3 developed a slightly different personality and interests during their time with us. Androids have been created in sets of clones, as it were, of individuals with the same physical features and qualities plus cognitive and memory structures that were identical. Sets of android clones usually involved 15 to 30 individuals. Although androids were commonly seen in society, androids were still in the vast minority. It was possible to randomly see several identical androids but was a rarity.

All androids are a combination of racial features, the combination varying so there are individual differences. Androids come in different heights and body types, but all are what humans would consider to be physically attractive. We remain in contact with the first two and regularly engage them in our activities and entertainment. When an android has completed his/her internship s/he can be bestowed citizenship and personal independence. This is a huge advance in android rights rather than being owned by a company or individual to perform tasks for them.

Ten years from return to Earth have come and gone and I haven't kept up my diary at all, because I guess our lives had become much more stabilized with less of a pressure inside myself to process our lives in my journal. I reflect that I've been perhaps the most at peace I'd been since my brother died so many years ago. But at age 65 my health is not good. The years in partial gravity with outer space exposure to cosmic rays and then readaptation to Earth's gravity have had a deteriorating effect on my bones and organs. I have tested positive for the latest mutation of the Omega virus, and with my fragile health and immune system I may not survive. So I want to finalize my thoughts and life while I still can. Eva has remained with me the whole time and we've had now many years of a good life together.

Much of the last month before I passed away is now almost a blur to me. I grew weaker and weaker and needed help with so many things I would have never thought possible and which would have revolted me. Things like needing help brushing my teeth, getting dressed, holding a fork etc. But now these things no longer revolted me, I simply accepted my sickness and disability for what it was. Eva took care of me at home, bless her beautiful android heart, without annoyance or complaint.

Since we were marooned on Charon I became convinced of the existence and omnipotence of the universal spirit. For a long time I avoided, unsuccessfully, any memory of the unending frozen wilderness of Charon. But I never forgot the majesty of the sky on the edge of the solar system, and knew there was a universal consciousness out there. The contacts with the aliens and the signal given to the Thule 2 to facilitate our rescue also implied some form of higher consciousness to me.

I knew the spirit guided my life, and couldn't be conceptualized by human consciousness or explained in reductionistic terms. I was convinced my spirit would live on after death, and my present fading life was but one in series or lives going forward and backward. This was an agnostic belief as I couldn't characterize God any more than that, but it gave me comfort anyway. In the last month we decided that I be placed in a pre-hospice type of setting, so I could get the comfort medications and treatment I needed, and Eva would help with my daily care. Eva was with me every day and as she had done so many times before kept me level headed and rational, and discouraged my pity party moods.

As my mind rambles and reviews my strange life, several songs I remember from my college days that at that time I related to Pete, and now that applied as fully to Eva are:

"Wherever you will go" from the Camino Palmer album, 2001 by the Calling

"Forever young" from the Out of order album,1988 by Rod Stewart

"I found love where it wasn't supposed to be", by Amber Run, 2015, from the 5 AM album.

Even though these songs were first performed about 150 years ago they remain an important part of the Rock and Roll era at that time, which has held a large interest for me. If you can access these songs you will get an emotional glimpse of part of mental status at this time. I had them played several times in the last hours of my physical life as a dedication to Eva.

TRANSFIGURATION

I passed from Earthly existence on May 11, 2152. When I took my final breath I was at peace, and was surprised at how effortlessly and painlessly my physical life ended. I slowly rose above my body and noted without any drama or panic that I was no longer breathing. There was no golden burst of light, no beckoning tunnel, no popping sound, no gasping for air or pain, just a quiet transition as I looked on from several feet above my head. There were 3 other people in the room in addition to Eva, who were nurse's aides or food service staff.

Eva was the first to notice that I had taken my final breath, and softly squeezed my hand without telling the others for about one minute. We had of course decided on no revival attempts when the end naturally arrived. I experimentally tried to squeeze her hand back, or turn my head or lift my arm. I noticed nonchalantly that my physical body did not respond at all to these urges to move, and so I stopped trying. Plus, I was seeming a bit lighter, and my back pain had finally gone away.

Eva just seemed rather dazed with no other outward emotion, but I knew she was trying to find me, and at one point stared straight ahead at me from my perspective of vision and I knew that she knew I was there. After a while, a doctor came in and confirmed my death. My body was then wheeled to the morgue. I tried to remain in the hospital room, but I was still tied to the body and had to go along to the morgue. I was already associating my being with my perspective above the physical body and the light blue shimmering shadow that I'd seemed to become. I was no longer looking at my physical body as the locus of my being. Then I stopped trying to dissociate further from the lifeless form below me, and drifted off into a dreamless haze without any concept of time, now with the physical body zipped up into a body bag.

I then became aware of again gazing down on my physical body from several feet above and realized I was at my funeral. I have only the haziest memory of my several days in the morgue. Again, it was like I had taken an immobilizing drug but was fully aware of the situation. But the scene was less vivid than when I had just died. I knew my higher body was trying to fully dissociate from my physical body, but wouldn't be able to until at least the funeral was completed. Eva was standing next to me before the service started, seeming glazed, in a black dress, looking beautiful and striking as always, with a somber and unchanging expression.

A few of my closest staff associates at the Android Academy were there, and I was surprised to see several of the children of Liam and John and their spouses, also the 3 human survivors of the Thule 2, along with a nondenominational minister, and several androids we had known as interns or on the Thule 2 crew. There were 18 people and androids there. I had no relatives that I had any contact with, nor any close friends, so no direct family members or friends of mine were present except Eva. I looked on dispassionately, my main focus being Eva who stayed steadily at the display coffin. I dearly wished to touch her or give some sort of signal but had no success at this. But I felt that Eva was there in spiritual contact with me and was pleased when she held my hand and gave me a final long embrace before the casket was closed.

After that came a period of blankness, in which I was vaguely aware but detached from everything in a numb and silent way. I have no estimate of how long this went on in Earthly terms, for time seemed to be irrelevant or nonexistent in my present awareness. I then seemed to flicker in and out of consciousness of another place that was totally unfamiliar. A most astonishing figure stepped menacingly toward me. He stated in a gravelly, basso profundo voice. "I am Charon, the Grim Reaper, who rules the dreary coast of Purgatory". In fact he repeated the words of an Edgar Allen Poe story.

He was sordid down from his hairy chin whence a long beard descended, uncombed, unclean. His eyes were like hollow furnaces on fire; A girdle, foul with grease, bound his obscene attire. He said "Mortal, I have come to ferry you across the mighty River Styx, to your eternal damnation, to Hades! But first I must receive your payment for the treacherous transport." I instinctively turned away from the ghastly figure, being well aware that there are lesser gods in the lower worlds set to manipulate and frighten the departed. I knew the best response was simply to ignore him, and he eventually faded away.

Then I seemed to be in a dreary torpor for a while. But this transitioned to a courtyard of a church, with a low white marble fence around most of it. There were flowers and a subdued light from a blue sky. Then I saw a being walking toward me. He was a handsome man of about 35-40 in appearance, wearing a red tunic or robe. He had a pleasant smile, brown skin of Indian or Pakistani nationality, and embraced me when he walked up.

He stated in a warm voice "I am Amon, and I will be your spiritual counselor while you are in the afterlife. You are continuing to adapt to the higher vibratory frequency of this astral world." I asked when or if I will see Eva, and started babbling many other questions about my whereabouts, my future and what was going to happen, as I hadn't expected this situation nor had I any other idea what to expect. He gently stopped me with a simple gesture and told me to be very patient, all will be revealed in good time. The adaptation of my astral body to this world would continue for a while. He said eventually I would indeed see Eva, Pete and other important people I'd known in the physical plane.

He said "your next task will be called your life review. You will be able to clearly see the many important events in your life. Each will appear as a ripple in a various shape, size and color flowing along the river of life or quantum continuity that defined your life. Another word for these ripples is karma. You will see how for each event multiple alternative paths branch off into other versions of the event. The ripples in the life path will need to be reviewed so they can be resolved in the afterlife or in another physical incarnation if they are impediments to your spiritual growth. I will come to you every once in a while to find out how you're coming along."

Amon then disappeared as quickly as he came. I was still in a rather dreamy and listless state, and floated in and out of scenes before me of my younger days. In some ways it was like back in college when I took an ayahuasca (DMT) psychedelic trip. That experience had lasted over 3 days with multiple quaffs of the evil tasting liquid and plenty of stomach distress to go along with it. I had dissociated during the DMT trip and saw with distressing clarity my life events. This time of course the physical distress was absent.

At that time, the loss of Pete had still been a daily pain for me. I saw how I had shut out my emotions after that, wanting only not to be hurt again. I saw how I had blamed my parents for distancing themselves even more from me and each other after his death rather than accepting that their own psychic defenses were the same as mine. I was very sad after the DMT trip and resolved to open my trust in people back up. But instead I threw myself back into my studies and let the emotional lessons slide away into numbness again.

But now in the afterlife my recall of these same experiences was different. I relived the good times I'd had with Pete rather than just regretted the loss. It seemed like Pete visited me in my revery, but I couldn't distinguish if it was actually him or a projection of my memories. He looked the same as I'd known him but with the same shimmering light body as I had become. We talked about many things, and how he had adapted to the astral body and forgave the drunk driver who ended his life at 18. He said he intended to reincarnate in the physical body and hoped to be with me there, although perhaps not as brothers.

I felt much relieved after seeing Pete again and that some of the heavy karma regarding his loss had been dissipated. I also felt relieved to know that Pete seemed to be OK despite his tragic physical end and I would see him again. I also felt relieved of the anger at my parents. I had some pride and surprise in myself that I eventually let down my guard and allowed myself to love Eva, and of course felt deeply thankful for all of Eva's love and help. In between my subsequent trance like periods of psychic rest I looked at many other episodes in my life. I saw multiple episodes of people who tried to reach out to me, but I spurned them either intentionally or in deference to the work I always felt compelled to do. Due to my withdrawal and inevitable family deaths, I ended my life with no corresponding nor caring family.

The 2 great shocks on Charon, especially the second, seemed to have burned into my memory and now I could even see the dark gray mark in my aura near my heart correlating with those memories. When George, Liam and the 2 androids were lost on Pluto I was shattered and overwhelmed. For 6 years, in fact my whole life, I'd been totally preparing and focused on this trip. I used the anticipation of the trip to block out all the things I didn't want to remember from my earlier life. Plus, it was exciting, potentially saving humanity from destruction by the alien transmissions, an adventure unique for humanity, and a way to finally distance myself literally and emotionally from Earth.

On the long trip from Earth to Ganymede to Charon I kept my thoughts positive and busied myself with collecting data and observations. When the disaster occurred all that was deflated like a popped balloon. Now it seemed we were powerless against the unknown force, were likely in grave danger ourselves, and likely would never be rescued. Plus, George and Liam had become friends and trusted colleagues, even as David and John- the male androids- had also become to a lesser extent.

Then came that endless period of depression when I withdrew into myself. I saw how my withdrawal, and customary avoidance of troubling memories only made matters worse, and contributed to the decay of my relationship with Marie, whom I had long seen as someone who could have become an intimate friendship. I regretted that I didn't have the power, or at least the courage, to not succumb to my grief. I realized now that suppression of my human emotions was not the same as facing it head on, a misconception and psychic defense I'd always leaned on.

Then too I saw that my paranoia of Megan exacerbated her avoidance of me. I really don't know where that came from, perhaps an extension of my disappointment with Marie? I should have listened to Eva when she said Megan meant me no harm. But Eva was my one rock I leaned on more and more for hope and stability and I guess I did well in at least opening myself to her. But I also let my dread and desperation get the best of me. I couldn't accept my helplessness about the huge unknowns of our situation, it was like the helplessness I felt so deeply after Pete died.

I genuinely thought at the time that some action needed to be taken against wherever the transmissions originated, even though I had no plan whatsoever to justify the dangerous ground trip away from the base. There was the existential knowledge that I was now in charge as captain and our 4 lives were in my hands, perhaps of the Earth as well. Then the vision or whatever it was at the alien pyramid, which thank God Marie could corroborate. I still have no idea even from my present perspective of who or what the aliens were, perhaps when I see Amon (whenever that might be) he can help me with that.

The horrible vision of the demise of Marie and Megan I see left a huge scar in my aura, bringing back that overwhelming feeling of helplessness, now heightened by my guilt at ordering that excursion even though I was told it was crazy by the other 3. I had suspected that Marie and Eva were considering a mutiny, and I wish they had, but eventually it turned out best for all my fellow Earthlings so far away. Now I see my character flaws and mental weakness are aspects of karma I need to work on perhaps in a future life. But despite it all, Eva and I survived and so did the Earth, so I guess I at least did some things right!

Now came the time to reconnect with Eva again. After another indefinite time of half slumber I recognized I was on a beach. Towering waves and wind were blowing in from the sea with the white and gray clouds towering overhead in phantasmal and grandiose shapes. The breeze was heavy and swirling. The shore appeared to be alternating beaches and towering cliffs with beetling crags as far as I could see in either direction. I suddenly had what seemed to be a panic attack. There were whitecaps, and that momentarily reminded me of ice dunes on Charon.

I reacted as I usually would, choking back a lump in my throat. Then I knew there was karma to work out right here, to resolve that panic that had washed over me. Right from the start I therefore knew we weren't in hell, purgatory or heaven. There were challenges to face in this world too. The wide open beach and sea prompted again my agoraphobia. The idea of actually going out into the sea by boat gave me a panic attack, and I knew I needed to get over this remnant of my insanity on Charon.

After a time I saw a figure walking toward me, it was Eva! She was beautiful in the blue coruscating light body and I immediately felt relief as she seemed joyful. She smiled, we ran together, she embraced me in the same soft but steely grip as always, which left for no chance of escape, although I certainly didn't want to escape that vice like embrace. It seemed like we both cried interminably in a full spectrum of emotions.

Eventually Elin and Amon both appeared in front of us. We all shared our joy and thankfulness for the moment. Amon said Eva and I would stay together in this beautiful and wild place, with a sheltering cabin and everything we needed to live. We could stay here for as long as we wanted, but not forever. We could create by imagination our own house or cabin and everything we needed to live here. Amon said that the Law of Assumption works faster and more precisely here in the astral plane than in the physical plane.

On the physical planet the Law of Assumption is less immediate and less precise in its effects. Therefore most Earthlings either aren't aware of it or use it in a negative or self-negating way by creating willy nilly thought forms without considering the consequences. We can stay as long as we both feel necessary in our present place, and decide how we would mutually come back to the physical plane to work out our individual answers about our mutual karma and goals. Eva and I voiced our understanding and acceptance, and then Elin and Amon disappeared.

Therefore both of us need to be careful to imagine consistent and positive images, that don't contradict each other's images, or our own images at different points in time. I had heard of this term before in my metaphysical readings, of the power of focused visualizations, which had parallels to quantum theory. But I had never used it systematically, my natural tendency was to shield and withdraw myself in pessimistic self-pity. One of our exercises was that we decided to do was visualize a sailboat, and with Eva's encouragement we managed to do some sailing, which gave me some amount of self confidence in managing my fears.

Periodically Elin or Amon would literally drop in on us, and do some counseling to help us understand ourselves , each other, and our life in the present world. Amon taught me to visualize other places we'd like to visit or experience in this world. We would need to be careful to coordinate our imagery so our mutual destination would be the same for both of us. The concept of years didn't really apply in this plane. There were dark-light cycles which we thought of as days, and we recorded with a short log of what we did each day. We then could calculate months and years based on Earth calendars. Together we imagined a set of other locations in the afterlife that we could visit.

We found Megan and Marie again, and had many beautiful meetings with them at their or our or some other locations. It was beautiful to connect again with Megan, this time on a positive note. I apologized for my paranoid thinking and behavior toward her, which she heartedly accepted. I still was attracted to Marie but as before she seemed distant to me, but superficially pleasant. I think this is a karmic carryover from our lives on Alpha Centauri in the lives of infinitely long ago. The best times of visiting were with Pete. We did many of the fun things together that we did as boys before he died. Sometimes I stayed with him for a few weeks while Eva visited Krystal.

It took quite a long time for us to get to a rather squeamish topic, the fears we had about each other in our physical lives. This is not about the fears for each other's health and wellbeing, which of course we had talked about many times in that life and the afterlife. This was rather about how we had each personally feared the other individual. This was hard for me to admit to myself and more so to Eva. Eva was very physically strong, fast and athletic. Being with her was in some ways like having a best friend who is a powerful and imposing athlete, whom you admire for that but know you'd never want to engage in a hostile fight.

Not that she ever threatened me in any way, in fact I knew that in any emergency or assault by anyone she would protect me probably better than any human could. At those times when Eva became aroused and wanted a sensual back and neck massage she would hold me like a vice from which there could be no escape, which was exciting but initially very frightening to me. Sometimes Eva would go into a baseline android mode of little or no verbal or nonverbal expression, which would accentuate my subdued fear of the unknown as to her not being human and make me wonder if I ever really knew her. I guess this was like the vague fear many humans had of what an android was capable of doing unpredictably.

Eva accepted my feedback with understanding and sadness as she had never wanted to make me feel that way. Then she expressed to me some of the fears she had had about me, which also made me cringe. She often wondered on Charon if I could retain enough of a grip on my sanity to keep functioning, and especially when she very reluctantly had been forced to deactivate until return to Earth. Eva greatly missed her dog Byron. I of course had never met Byron in the physical world. But as a boy I had often wished for the dog that never came. So I was happy to have Byron with us, it made Eva happy. So Byron remained 40 years with us before his next embodiment in the physical plane.

I was much more reluctant to return to the physical plane than was Eva, although I understood and accepted that this must eventually occur. Here in the afterlife was really the first time I had felt my emotions open, and that I didn't have to suppress and withdraw from my feelings. I'd felt this loosening somewhat this on Earth after Eva and I got back. But by that time my body was already deteriorating from the years in outer space and I felt most of the time that I didn't want anything to do with the world except Eva. After we decided how we would mutually come back to the physical plane to work out our individual and mutual karma and goals we could slumber again and then come back to Earth or elsewhere with our memories buried from physical memory.

So Eva and I talked about this many times and she was very patient with me. I knew she wanted to experience human emotions, childhood and being a parent. I knew I had karma to face and eventually concluded that perhaps I could face life on Earth with positive rationality if I came back as an android rather than human. Eva liked this idea too, as she wanted me to experience the positive and negative things she had experienced as an android and we could each see the relationship between human and android from the others viewpoint. Finally I agreed that it was time to return to the physical form. Elin and Amon told us to both deeply relax and then we would return to Earth.

MAROONED ON CHARON: BOOK 2, EVA'S STORY

By Bruce Maaser

Copyright 2025 Bruce Maaser

MAROONED ON CHARON

CONTENTS

My creation, the Android Academy and the Space Force

Flight to Ganymede and Charon, setting up base

Disaster on Pluto, chaos at the base

The transmissions from Pluto

Voyage to Ganymede and then Charon

Disaster on Pluto, chaos at the base

The mad desperate trip to find the alien object

My enlightenment at the edge of the interstellar void

The beautiful Earth but disillusionment with society

My singular relationship with a human male

Joe's passing and my descent into uncertainty

An existential journey, and a puppy

Return to home with new meaning for life

Crystal's postscript and my transformation

Eva's experience of her own translation

My reconnection with Joe

BOOK 2: EVA'S STORY, MAROONED WITH A HUMAN ON THE EDGE OF INTERSTELLAR SPACE

MY CREATION, THE ANDROID ACADEMY, AND THE SPACE FORCE

12/20/2153. It has now been 1 year and 3 months since Joe passed away. He had asked me to publish his notes about our historic journey and relationship, and add my own notes and reflections if I chose to. I've spent many hours compiling my notes and adding them to Joe's, and am now ready to present them. Joe said I should entitle the book "How I learned to love a robot 3B (3 billion) miles from Earth."

I've learned to recognize Joe's dry humor, which is quite an accomplishment for me. So, I smiled when he had said that and didn't take "robot" in a pejorative or demeaning way. In fact I looked at his humor in a very positive way, focusing on his saying he loves me. I also said back with a straight expression "I think I'll call it "How I learned to love a human on the edge of interstellar space," and "I get to choose the title if I outlive you." Joe had a hearty laugh at that and it made me feel almost warm.

I'll go way back to my beginnings, before I ever knew Joe. I was first started to be assembled in July 2121, and first activated on May 11, 2122, which I consider to be my birthday. I don't remember the first days, but by day 7 I was developing self awareness, and I have a few hazy memories of those first 4 weeks. In my early conscious memories I was quickly becoming aware of the many elements of my cognitive programming and the vast information in my memory banks. I was capable of speaking and comprehending English and Chinese.

But I needed considerable basic language education to integrate the knowledge in my memory banks with the cognitive skills of comprehending written and spoken language to be able to communicate effectively. English and Chinese were the 2 prominent languages of humanity, at that time, and I had some knowledge of Esperanto which was fast also becoming a prominent universal language. I had growing control of my sensory and motor systems. I was grounded in the basic ethics of behavior for androids, which hearkened back to Asimov's 3 laws of robotics.

I knew I would undergo 4 years of intensive instruction as to how to apply my cognitive algorithms to solve real world problems. In the 4 years that followed I was a student at the Android Educational Academy in Seattle, Washington, one of 5 such academies around the world. There were 110 androids in my class which would graduate in 2126. The academy was built on the model of a small human college. My classmates and I lived in a dorm setting and we each had an android roommate. Our education was very intensive, with classes, tutorials and mentorships with the human and android instructors. During the 4 years there was always one or more classes involving appropriate conversation and interaction with humans, as we would be entering society after our graduation. Our instruction was year round but we had 10 holidays around the year for us to rest, explore, or do as we chose.

I also knew that my creation and education had been funded by the United Space Agency. Therefore, I would have a 5 year commitment to the Space Agency after graduation from the Academy before I created a life of my own. There were multiple field trips into general society where we experienced human culture. We toured business, government and residential facilities, and learned the transportation system. We were taught and observed prevailing laws, political dynamics, crime, economic disparities and so many other things. Like my fellow androids I was programmed with motivation and curiosity to learn new information. So it was. intensely interesting to be exposed to so many things.

It was also surprising to observe all the disorder and conflict that seemed a basic and inevitable part of human culture. It was also very troubling to see how the effects of global warming, ongoing pandemics and military conflicts, nationalism, religious intolerance and racial prejudice were devastating the human race and environmental integrity. We were treated humanely and much like college students. We had time, although always never enough, for our own personal reflections, interests and interaction with each other. I found it very interesting and (to make a human emotion analogy) enjoyable when we had occasional field trips to community attractions, even visiting the beach, forest areas, etc.

In the first 2 years we wore standard android clothing at all times, including into the community. I thought this often gave us a distorted view of society, as everyone instantly knew we were androids. Humans reacted to us with curiosity, uncertainty and often with wariness. People were reluctant to talk to us, seemingly uncertain as to what to say. From some there was an impression of fear or hostility although I never experienced any physical aggression. For others there was curiosity, and children often came running up usually with a parent telling them not to. In the third year we were introduced to wearing human clothing, which was a fascinating change. We were allowed to wear human clothing on campus and on field trips into society. It was amazing to get a different perspective when in public. In general humans did not detect we were androids when we dressed as humans unless we interacted in more than just casual conversation, sometimes not even then.

I knew that at those times I looked, acted and talked like a human, and humans in society treated me as a human, not knowing I was not. So despite this part of my assumed identity being human I knew that underneath I physically was of a nature very different than human. I began to crave those aspects of humanity that I didn't have. This made me (again to speak in human emotional terms) long for those aspects of human life I could never have, such as having parents, children, sexual relationships, human love and the carefree exuberance of youth. But I also did not at all regret not having human depression, mental problems, intense pain and all the aggressive basic human instincts that made human life at times so desperate.

Androids were made in multiple physiognomic patterns. I had Polynesian or Pacific Islands general appearance with dark hair, brown eyes and brown skin. There were 2 other androids in my class who were my identical triplets, which of course always produced interesting confusion among my classmates and instructors. While androids came in multiple racial/ethnic features and body types, all were designed to be perceived as attractive males or females in human terms. It was interesting to experience the different responses of humans outside the Academy when I wore human clothes instead of the android uniform.

Often there seemed to be a positive valence toward me in public that I didn't experience when dressed as an android. Sometimes there was even a curious overly friendly or unexpectedly personal response from human men that took me totally off guard and made me unsure how to respond. I asked one of our human instructors about this and he said these men were flirting. When I asked if this had something to do with human sexual desire he said it might be they were trying to get attention or flirtation back to make themselves feel attractive or even lure me into sex. I frankly found it interesting but didn't care one way or the other if they flirted or not, but always tried to give a polite response.

Our human instructors at the Academy were generally cordial toward us, treating us much like if we had been human students. Some instructors treated us like very advanced machines which I found demeaning. There were a few instructors who were especially cordial, supportive, and interested in our personal welfare, and their memories will always be cherished. As a caveat, even though I don't have human emotions per se I find it helpful to describe my experiences using human emotional terms. And yes a few were flirtatious, which was really confusing to me and definitely against the rules the instructors were supposed to follow.

I entered the United Space Force upon graduation in 2126. In 2128 I had my first rejuvenation. It went well and I came out after 10 days ready to embark on any task I would be assigned. Soon after that I learned of the proposed mission to Pluto, which was scheduled to take place in 2130. I had received training in engineering and maintenance of a remote, self sufficient base of operations that could sustain human and android life on a distant celestial body. I think for this reason I was one of the initial set of 6 androids to be offered a place on the mission. The offer was given as my choice rather than assigned duty, which I saw as a sign of respect.

I accepted the offer almost immediately, as I envisioned it as an exciting and meaningful learning venture. The next 2 years were very intensive, even more so than they had been the Academy. I helped design the base, which was to be set up on Charon. I was thoroughly briefed on the goals and risks involved in this mission. I understood and accepted the proposed 11-12 year duration of the mission, even though this is up to 7 years longer than the required 5 year commitment that each android had to make before being considered an independent entity after graduation from the academy.

I also understood that I would be maintained in a long term deactivation state for much of the spaceship travel time. I would be activated primarily while we were on Charon. An android needs a rejuvenation after 5 or at very most 6 years of activation and this complex treatment can only be done on Earth. The Space Force feared that on such a long mission one or more of the human crew might develop some mental health issues. A great emphasis was placed on mental health factors after a staff member of the Ganymede outpost, and a crew member on a year long flight, committed suicide.

MAROONED ON CHARON

For 9 months I had a mostly one to one tutorial with several human mental health professionals at our launch site. Part of the training for my role was to acutely observe human facial and voice affect as well as body language and correlate this data with the likely emotions and thoughts driving them. What I lacked of course was human emotions which always made me curious as to what a human might be experiencing when I observed them displaying an emotional response. Therefore I knew there was a fundamental block in how well I'd be capable of creating a mutual rapport with a human. I was encouraged to use my basic learned counseling skills to facilitate conversation and disclosure if a human appeared to need it.

During all this training it seemed so odd to me that as an android I could be sensitive to observing and interpreting human emotion, and responding appropriately to it. But I could never actually experience the emotion, at least as a human does. In human terms I would say that this saddens me. But I don't feel sadness per se. To my orderly mind it was more like some part was missing. My whole thought process seemed incomplete, lacking closure. Whenever I'd think that way my whole visual field seemed to become gray, lose all its color. My very acute senses of vision, hearing and smell all seemed to be blunted too. My primary human instructor helped me realize that these cognitive and perceptual alterations were my way of experiencing sadness. This was an amazing revelation to me and helped me understand how human and android inner experience can have ties that I didn't previously recognize.

I need to clarify something for the reader. Sometimes I've used emotional connotation words to express my

170

experiences. I do this for humans who are reading this to relate more easily to my descriptions of situations. I believe that I don't have emotions in human terms. But Joe spent so much time with me correlating my reactions to situations with the way a human would normally feel in that situation. So if I say it made me happy it means what I've experienced is a brightening and bluish cast to my vision, a set of thoughts that are right and positive, sometimes even a smell of a flower or a slight ringing in my ears, in a synesthetic sense. But I would say that later in my life I developed nearly human emotions, the most wonderful of which was the feeling of love.

If I say I feel sad it would mean my vision grew darker and grayer, my thoughts would be of negative possible outcomes or memories of unwanted situations, I might even hear a discordant sound or a smell of waste matter. While I think I've become quite good at sensing and correlating my reactions I still can't mentally get past a vacuum that I can't actually feel the things that humans feel. In some extreme situations though my reactions have been so strong as to be temporarily disabling. Those situations were the ineffable shock when Megan and Marie were killed, and of course when Joe died. But my reactions had the beauty and smell of flowers blooming in the Spring when I awakened from my long deactivation after returning to Earth and saw Joe was there, and when Joe took me again to the Louvre and to Butchart Gardens in Victoria BC.

I developed the intention to one day help other androids come to their own personal understanding of this. But my cognitions and perceptions about this brightened up when I also understood that I was not subject to extremes of human mental illness such as severe depression and anxiety. I saw I could become a stabilizing force for humans in the case of emergency, threat, danger and loss. Of course, as I'll later describe this certainly became the case when the disasters on Charon occurred, with Joe and with Marie before she and Megan passed away.

There were also the wonderfully bright and ineffable experiences I had after that with Joe when he taught me so much about human emotion and existential issues while we were alone together on Charon. And how Joe helped me learn to express my very personal responses to situations through painting. All this happened during the strange period of total isolation, danger, but also boredom and total silence while on Charon waiting for the rescue ship without knowing if it would ever arrive.

The two years at the Space Force passed quickly it seemed. With about 4 weeks left before departure I got to meet with the rest of the crew. We had numerous briefings and planning sessions. Marie, Joe, George and Liam were the humans. Marie was very focused, cordial but seemed aloof. She seemed to have gone through some very difficult but obscure circumstances, and her only family was her mother and brother. Joe was rather withdrawn although superficially cordial, again seemingly with a history of bad events that had made him introverted and untrusting of others.

George on the other hand was lively and friendly, often making jokes to lighten up all the worries and issues. He was a family man struggling with the departure from his family. Liam seemed to have the right personality for Captain. He was assertive, self assured, decisive, blunt but also supportive. His wife was deceased and his family consisted of his 2 sons and a daughter. Megan was the female android. She had a Teutonic appearance with light brown hair, in contrast to me. But she had exactly the same brain and neural processing system as I.

She seemed to have the same reactions as I did, and like me exhibited personality traits that appeared slightly irritable. We often seemed to know what the other was thinking. She and I were usually together when we weren't directly on a task, which seemed to be not often, and shared a living space. David and John were identical clones, although first started construction and activated 7 months apart. They were tall, slim, of indefinite racial and ethnic appearance. They were completely task oriented, and showed less voice and facial affect than Megan and I did.

Seven weeks before scheduled launch the preparations were actually slightly ahead of schedule. We were given the unexpected surprise of a 3 week vacation! We were allowed to visit family or take an excursion of our choice. The only restriction was that we couldn't engage in any risky or public activity that might produce injury or criticism and delay launch. Space Force administration had mixed opinions on this proposed vacation period. It raised the possibility of an accident or incident of some sort that could jeopardize the start of the mission. On the other hand, this would be the last time we would see Earth for at least ten years. It was thought by the more humanistic supervisors that for the mental health of the 4 humans a chance to visit loved ones and relax would be important.

There was even more debate about allowing the 4 androids some time off. I was very appreciative that we were given the same opportunity as the humans. We could arrange a sight seeing trip anywhere we wanted that was a practical possibility. Since none of the androids had any family or connections outside the Space Force we decided to stick together and travel as a group. George decided to travel with his wife (who lived with him at the base) to visit their 2 children and their families. Liam also decided to divide his time between his 3 children and their families. Marie chose to visit her mother and brother who were her only remaining close family.

Joe didn't have any family to visit or other destinations he wanted to see. After we asked him several times if he would join us he finally assented. He said it seemed so thoughtful of me and the other 3 androids to ask if he could join us wherever we decided to go. We said we would be delighted (again using a human emotional analogy) for him to join us. We decided to visit the Grand Canyon, Hawaii and Paris and the many sites they had to offer. All expenses for all crew members would be paid by the Space Force, and we made all our own travel arrangements. We all wore human clothes on our trip rather than the very obvious android outfits. We would have chaperones and security guards everywhere we went, which would for the most part stay unobtrusive.

We were quite a site! Probably the thing that people noticed the most was the twins, with their very similar movements and implacable affect. I guess people who commented on us thought Megan and I were each with one of twins, with Joe appearing as an unlikely addition to the foursome. I doubt if people realized we were androids, although the rather robot-like demeanor of the twins could be a giveaway. But I found everything we experienced as extremely interesting and valuable, and I was grateful we were allowed the opportunity to do it.

One day in Paris Megan announced she would find it interesting to see the Eiffel Tower. I said the Louvre sounded more interesting to me. Joe agreed with me, while the twins were noncommittal as usual. We decided the twins would go with Megan, while Joe and I visited the Louvre. I thought Joe was an interesting, bright, pleasant but quite reserved person, and I think Joe thought of me as just another female android.

I found the Louvre to be fascinating, and Joe said I looked really excited. I didn't know if I was excited or not, but I guess I must have been because I talked nonstop at each exhibit. I found the paintings to be fascinating and hoped I would have the future opportunity to paint as well. Joe was very tolerant of my babbling and seemed to find some humor in it. It seemed like a lot of people looked at us and I think he enjoyed being seen with me.

Joe gave me a totally unexpected hug at the end of our visit at the Louvre. This was the first hug anyone had ever given me and I was completely bewildered by it. I didn't resist, nor respond much, then asked Joe why he did it. Joe rather embarrassingly said it was a sign of good feeling, that he enjoyed being with me. That bewildered me too, but in retrospect it was such a nice thing for him to do. At the end of that wonderful 3 weeks we returned to the base. In the next three weeks we worked relentlessly to finish all preparations for the launch, and received briefings regarding last minute information we needed to know.

Three days before launch the other 3 androids and I were deactivated, to be activated again upon arrival to Ganymede in 18 months. George and Liam as a team would pilot the ship for the first 7 months. Meanwhile Joe and Marie would be placed in a light state of suspended animation so they could quickly be reawakened and functional if an emergency arose. After 7 months Joe and Marie would take over while George and Liam would be in suspended animation. Then for the last 4 months before Ganymede all 4 humans would be activated for the treacherous passage through the Asteroid Belt.

There had been debate by the Space Force administrators as to the best composition for the crew. It had been argued that the crew should be all androids. The androids with pilot and navigation training were likely as or more competent than their human counterparts. But the human crew had more years of spaceship piloting and navigation experience. The androids were also limited by the maximum 5-year range between required complete rejuvenations, which couldn't be done except at facilities on Earth. Time spent in deactivation didn't count toward the 5-year limitation.

The opposing viewpoint to this argument was that this will be a dangerous mission, and it would be preferable if androids rather than humans were lost in case of a disaster. This idea produced protest among many androids, who did not consider their existence any less important than a human life, despite their well engrained Asimov's laws of robotics. Therefore in the end the decision was made to have 4 human crew members, each with their own specialty, and 4 androids who had corresponding specialty training. I frankly found the purpose of the mission very intriguing and important and would have volunteered regardless of the scenario.

MAROONED ON CHARON

FLIGHT TO GANYMEDE AND CHARON, SETTING UP BASE

I was deactivated 3 days before launch in 2123 along with the other 3 androids. The next time I was activated we were 10 days before scheduled docking at Ganymede station. My body and mind felt the same way as I did after the usual 5 hour daily deactivation and it was strange to think it had been 18 months since I last went to sleep. The docking at Ganymede went smoothly. Ganymede station had been built 20 years before, as a research base, potential colony for one thousand humans and androids, and a launch facility for missions to the outer planets and moons. The practicality as a colony was now deemed lower than originally thought. It was sizable enough for original purposes but now held only 60 humans and androids engaged in the research and exploration activities.

We stayed on Ganymede for 20 days, which were busily spent in briefings and updates on factors we will face in the next part of our journey, loading of supplies, refueling, etc. On the day before launch me, Megan, John and David were again deactivated until Charon. For this part of the trip Joe and Marie were placed in light suspended animation for 20 months while Liam and George piloted the ship, and these roles would be reversed for the last 20 months. The 2 humans in suspended animation and 4 androids could be awakened or reactivated at any time if a crisis were to arise.

I was activated 40 months later, along with the other 3 androids. Again the activation seemed just like my usual daily activations after 5 hours, but now it was over almost 6 Earth years since the departure from Earth. We were about

14 days from a touch down site on Charon. George and Liam were also awakened. Joe and Marie had experienced an uneventful journey from Ganymede. Both seemed more aloof than when we last saw them, Joe having always been aloof. I had the impression both were extremely bored, disconsolate and somewhat withdrawn from each other. They were anxious about the landing and seemed relieved that the rest of the crew had now consciously joined them.

In the next 14 Earth day periods we were all engaged in plotting our descent route to the proposed landing site, reviewing our protocols for building the base, and reviewing information that had come through from Space Command on Earth and Ganymede. We were encouraged that no further disruptive transmissions had been received on Earth from the enigmatic source on Pluto. The landing process again went smoothly, as had everything at least logistically about the journey thus far. I was concerned, however, about the mental state of at least Joe and Marie, who seemed listless and lethargic, especially Marie, who appeared frankly depressed.

The landing site appeared to be ideal, in the flat center of a small crater, with Pluto permanently fixed on the horizon in the Southwest direction, in relation to the North Pole of Charon. We landed 60 months (1,806 days to be exact) from our launch from Earth. The nascent base site seemed protected but also created a sense of foreboding due to the surrounding edges of the crater that limited the view in all directions to about 2 miles. The ground surface was flat, with a combination of what appeared to be ice and rock. Three large supply ships on automated controls had been launched from Ganymede 2 months before our ship was launched. Two were in now in tight orbits around Charon. But the third ship had lost directional control and was now sailing into interstellar space, which raised serious possible mission concerns in case of unexpected crises. We were able to establish control of the two remaining ships and guide them to safe landings in the crater about 300 meters from our ship.

The next 3 months were spent setting up the base. The construction details were covered in Joe's diary and I need not repeat those here. I had received special training in construction and design of bases and colonies on other planets and moons. The androids were given prime responsibility in coordinating the construction due to the specialized training we had received. I found the construction interesting and fulfilling, particularly at first when the other 3 androids and I needed to spend much time outside the ship.

The androids did most of the work outside, as we had more strength and stamina than the humans under these unprecedented conditions. Primarily we had to excavate the direct landing area under the circular diameter of the ship, and solidly attach the inner torus to a secure foundation. The main idea was simply to attach the torus to the ground with the ship upright in the middle so the torus could spin freely in a horizontal plane when detached from the ship. After that the ship itself, still inside the torus and facing upwards, would be detached from the torus to allow take off of the ship itself from the rest of the base.

Looking back now I realize I had not yet learned about my own reactions to events or gained much self awareness. I focused on the tasks at hand without much self reflection.

None of this higher self awareness which I later learned was in our basic programming. While I had gained much skill and information in my 4 years at the Academy and 3 years on the Space Force, I realize now in looking back I had gained little in what I might call personal insight.

Nor was this considered an important goal for androids to develop, or even thought to be possible. It was only in the long years ahead in the bizarre circumstances on Charon, and all the time I spent then and later with Joe, that I gained some awareness of my emotion-resembling cognitive and sensory responses to new situations. Eventually I think I identified in some ways an even more acute sensitivity to emotion producing stimuli than Joe or apparently other humans, of course in my own way. I don't think I am belabored by human emotional defense mechanisms such as denial, suppression, reaction formation, etc.

My mind didn't use psychological defense mechanisms to cope with unwanted or excessive emotions, although sometimes in acute stress or loss I wish I had some way of blocking out all the severe perceptual and cognitive distortions I develop! I don't think I have unconscious memories or drives, although maybe I just can't perceive this. I have made it a personal goal especially after Joe died to work individually with other androids to help them perceive their own reactions and how they parallel human emotions.

During the many hours outside the base, while we were anchoring it in Charon's surface, I sometimes stopped and looked at my surroundings. I didn't put together the significance at the time of what I remember to be a peculiar distortion in the appearance of the surroundings and a darkening of the image of Pluto. At the time I had no idea what those perceptions meant. Now I think they were my way of sensing a foreboding of what was to happen in the future. It was only until much later, and with the help of Joe, that I was able to correlate those cognitive and visual perceptions with human emotions, in this case fear, anxiety, and impending doom.

The 4 humans marveled at how smoothly the base construction project had come along, and the androids also commented on how few difficulties had been thus far encountered on the whole mission. Of course, the great unknown still faced us as to what we might find regarding the mysterious transmitter, and even if we did, would there be anything we could do to disable it. Our mission on Charon was expected to last for 6 to 12 months. Six months would be the optimal window for the return flight path, and then return to Ganymede. But this depended on so many unknowns. The base was well stocked with supplies for 5 years of occupancy, and could be maintained on a limited but life sustaining basis for another ten years after that. This was planned in case the ship would become disabled with occupants still alive and needing rescue.

The complex task of turning the ship into the base, hooking up ice defrosters, etc, revived the crews' ennui. It was good to see the humans again in an energetic and motivated state. We finished all aspects of the base set up within 4 months of nonstop labor, which was one month ahead of schedule. Liam decided we all needed a short period to relax and celebrate our achievement. So we had one week of socializing, playing games or just being by ourselves, while the humans had their favorite food and drink.

I appreciated the reduction of stress and activity during this week, and spent a good share of time with Megan. The computer banks have huge quantities of books, movies and other videos. And sometimes we all sat in the projection room and watched a show together, which made my perceptions and cognitions bright and charmingly light blue. I recognized that this was my android equivalent of happiness and comfort although often I didn't really understand what was going on. I of course didn't realize that this would be the last time the whole crew would have a pleasant and happy time together.

On the twentieth day Liam, George and the twins departed for Pluto. Charon is very close relatively to Pluto, only 20K km compared to 350K km for the Earth's moon to Earth. Thus the ship took only 3 Earth days to establish itself in a tight orbit around Pluto. We received the radio transmission that the crew had identified some type of object or structure at the site determined from Earth to have been the source of the transmissions. On the next orbit around Pluto the ship slowed for a descent to the area of the object.

MAROONED ON CHARON

DISASTER ON PLUTO, CHAOS AT THE BASE

Then the final desperate radio call came through, like Joe has previously described. My reaction to that was a temporary distortion of my visual perception, an incoherence in my thought pattern, and a physical jolt that temporarily paralyzed me. I pieced it together as the android reaction to severe stress, not like human panic as I don't feel anxiety per se, but in some ways like the human shock reaction that Joe and Marie appeared to be experiencing. I looked at Megan who looked back, and I knew she was experiencing exactly the same reaction that I was. Marie and Joe remained in shock and disbelief for days afterward.

Megan and I realized our role was to give some stability to Joe and Marie who seemed immobilized by confusion and grief. The disruptive transmission from the mysterious "pyramid" on Pluto occurred at the same time as the last message from the ship. This affected the earth 28 minutes later and produced massive problems with the computer and communications systems of the base within 3 minutes, making communication with Earth or Ganymede impossible. Megan and I brought the basic systems of the base needed for survival back to operation as best they could be. I think Joe and Marie wouldn't have been able to do that in their mental state at the time.

As time passed Marie and Joe both seemed to be withdrawing from Megan and myself and sinking further into depression. Marie was either flat or snappy when we talked to her and didn't want to be involved in anything. Joe seemed completely withdrawn and I was very concerned about him, especially because he had now become the default captain of the base. We tried to create a 24 hour cycle of structured monitoring of instruments, sleep time on a rotating cycle for the four of us, eating for the humans, exercise, and doing some interactive games. Marie & Joe were somewhat compliant with the schedule but often didn't want to be involved. Over the next 12 months the lethargy of the 2 humans seemed to increase. All communication with Earth was lost within days of the tragic event, leaving us all with a sense of utter isolation.

Part of Marie and Joe's increasing dysfunctionality was the boredom of the base and the lack of meaningful tasks or goals. Part of it was just the helplessness of being able to do nothing about our situation except try to accept it and survive it. But there was no certainty there either. It seemed likely that another burst of energy would eventually occur and would likely shut down all the survival systems of the base.

As my shifts with Joe went on Joe gradually became somewhat trusting of me, and more willing to express his thoughts. Joe was so closed off, which had been a characteristic of his personality for so many years. Joe was afraid I would disclose our conversations to Marie and Megan. We agreed that the substance of our conversations would remain confidential between us, unless something came up that was vital for Megan and Marie to hear regarding the safety of any of us or the base.

Joe talked a lot about the loss of his brother Pete when Joe was a teen. I don't think he'd really ever talked about this to anyone on an emotional level. It had a huge effect on the rest of his life, as Joe never allowed anyone else to get close to him. His parents were busy with their own jobs and their grief, and not emotionally supportive to him. This withdrawal from relationships led to his leaving the Earth on this mission with no family and essentially no friends to whom to return.

We hoped and expected that a rescue ship would be on the way from Ganymede but had no way of confirming that. If so it would likely be about 40 more months at the earliest when it would without warning arrive. Joe started to develop a nameless paranoia about whatever alien beings might be connected to the mysterious pyramids on Pluto and Charon and the source of transmission on Charon. He obsessed, with justification, that another transmission would come upon us without any warning and destroy us.

Joe also started having a baseless paranoia regarding Megan. He became increasingly preoccupied that Megan not only didn't like him but was trying to find some way to discredit his default role as acting ship commander. Megan had become the one being I most trusted and could communicate with. Megan and I often inferred what the other was thinking, sometimes it almost seemed telepathic. She certainly knew Joe didn't like her and that we were probably talking about her. But I honored completely my duty of confidentiality about the contents of our sessions without ever implicating Megan as being at fault.

Megan on the other hand feared that Joe would attempt to permanently deactivate her. Megan tried several times to break through in a cordial and positive way to some meaningful understanding with Joe, but Joe seemed to interpret this suspiciously also. I tried to assure Joe that Megan meant him no harm but I don't think he believed me.

I reasoned with Joe that such an attitude by Megan would be impossible because it violated the first law of robotics which was so basic to our programming. I was also baffled on the inverse side of the coin that Joe seemed to have trust and attraction to me. I was very uncertain what to do when he expressed his feelings of attraction to me.

His feelings seemed to go back to that one special day at the Louvre before departure where Joe and I were on our own for the day, and he found it so gleeful that I seemed energized and fascinated and babbled continuously to him. I also have very special memories of that day because it was so unique in my life. When Joe wanted to hug me at the end of one of our conversations and even started crying, I readily although awkwardly accepted the hug and even strangely perceived that my vision grew brighter and bluer during it. It was only much later when we returned to Earth that I put together the beginning and bewildering perceptions at that time with my eventual self recognition of my love and commitment to Joe in our relationship.

As the months moved on the days became indistinguishable from each other. Megan and I maintained our arranged schedule with my 5 hour activation every 24 hours following hers. Joe and Marie didn't keep a schedule anymore. They slept, exercised, bathed and ate erratically and let Megan and I to monitor the instruments that were still working and keep the base clean. They seldom talked to each. Joe seemed to be increasingly paranoid. By 14 months after the ship apparently crashed on Pluto Joe was frankly delusional. He believed the hypothesized alien presence on Charon was monitoring us, although there was nothing to substantiate this delusion.

He believed the aliens were preparing to destroy the base either by a direct attack or another of those destructive bursts of ultra high energy radiation. He became increasingly convinced that we needed to take some action to prevent that, although what it might be was totally unknown. Marie seemed to have sunk into a deep, helpless depression, and spent much time just laying in her bunk. Megan and I both had trouble keeping our thoughts focused, and our vision seemed gray and dimmed. But we were able to sustain a rational bit of hope and keep on functioning.

One day Joe announced we would have a crew meeting for the four of us, the first in months. Joe stated we need to prepare for a surface trip to investigate the presumed origin or reception point of the monstrous electromagnetic transmission that nearly destroyed the life systems of the base. Joe was sure that another transmission was imminent, and without any warning would destroy the base. He proposed that we equip each of our two surface vehicles with enough food, air, fuel and vital supplies for a 10-day round trip. One human and one android would ride in each vehicle, and I'm sure Joe was thinking I would ride with him.

The vehicles would travel closely together and always remain in sight of each other. If one vehicle were to become disabled all 4 crew members would travel in the remaining vehicle. Another possibility Joe mentioned would be to dispatch 2 crew members in one vehicle and leave the other two to secure the base, and attempt a rescue if necessary. But if transmission was lost from the first vehicle it might be impossible to find the first vehicle or attempt a rescue before it was too late. Joe couldn't furnish any plan as to what we would do if we located the pyramid or whatever it was, except that we would have lasers and short trajectory missiles mounted on each vehicle.

Megan and I objected that there were too many unknowns and no definite plan if we were to find the unknown alien structure. We had not traveled across the surface of Charon before except for a few brief excursions to the edge of the crater to test the surface vehicles. We had no idea as to what obstacles and dangers we might encounter such as unstable surface formations, steep slopes or even possible ice geysers. We couldn't vouch for the reliability of the vehicles over this long a trip. The vehicles were designed for short trips within the landing site during the construction of the base, not extended trips over unknown territory.

There was no plan at all what we do if we encountered the presumed alien object, other than blasting it. Based on whatever happened to the Thule on Pluto after the pyramid was sited, the idea of blasting the object likely posed more danger to us than to the structure. Marie seemed too apathetic and depressed to even offer an opinion. She seemed resigned to the idea that we were going to die either by staying at the base or trying to disable the transmission object, it really didn't matter. Joe of course was the crew's captain by default and would make the final decision, and seemed dead set to make the questionable expedition.

The programming Megan and I received at the Space Force facility explicitly forbade us from challenging the human commander beyond offering our opinions. However this section of our programming could be overridden if we were certain that lethal consequences would come from this action to the human crew members. But we had no certainty that the mission would result in loss of human life, only very serious concerns about the feasibility of the whole plan. Even if we were convinced of dire consequences it was totally uncertain as to how Megan and I could overturn Joe's plan or deal with the consequences that would bring about. So Megan and I went along with Joe's directive although with much trepidation.

MAROONED ON CHARON

THE MAD, DESPERATE TRIP TO FIND THE ALIEN OBJECT

We left the base 403 Earth days after we first landed on Charon. Megan and I left with profound concerns about the sensibility and goal of this dangerous and likely foolhardy trip. It seemed to be mostly motivated by Joe trying to gain some sense of control over the complete helplessness we were enduring at the base. Megan and I even talked about a mutiny, simply refusing to go. But we knew Joe would go anyway, with or without Megan, Marie or myself. My hope was that we could do what might be some valuable exploration of the surface, not encounter any alien or other lethal danger, and most importantly return after about 10 days to the base alive and no worse than we started.

Joe already has documented our trip across Charon culminating in the alien pyramid, based on coordinates we had received from Earth Command before communication was lost. I won't recap all the details of that harrowing journey which Joe had narrated in detail. But on the other hand, I must say more than Joe, I was awed by our surroundings now that we were outside our little crater. The frozen landscape with the shifting blue light and shadows of Pluto was mesmerizing along with the piercing steady lights of all spectral colors of the stars above. We were amazed to witness a geyser of water erupt from the ground, and instantly transform into a fan of ice. The surface was a blue coruscating and mesmerizing solidified fountain.

We also could follow the movement of 2 of the 4 smaller moons of Pluto that were visible. But that drive stirred my thoughts to the extreme and I often felt my rationality had left me. I constantly thought of the danger we faced, what we should do if we indeed encountered some alien structure, and still if there was any way to convince Joe to turn around.

It was shocking to actually see the pyramid emerge as we maneuvered around an outcropping of rock and ice. I had no idea what to expect and until then doubted that we would find anything. It was profoundly shocking to see evidence of an advanced alien species, and my mind was racing like a race car without brakes. I watched Joe's look of incredulity, and then speak as if he had someone on the radio. He seemed transfixed and I thought his fading grasp of reality had totally departed. I had a strange sense both cognitively and perceptually while this went on of some nonhuman presence but couldn't identify it more than that. All this lasted only about 5 minutes.

Then I was again shocked when Marie came on the radio, and evidently she had witnessed the same transmission as did Joe. Not surprisingly Megan confirmed the same totally ambiguous experience as I had had. After this all four of us were shocked to the core. We talked to each other within and between the vehicles. After a few hours I stated we really needed to start our return trip to the base. Joe and Marie seemed too stunned to do anything of purpose, so Megan and I decided to drive our vehicles for the next driving shift. I so much wish we had met first in one of the vehicles just for mental and emotional support, as Joe had actually suggested. But we didn't, and I never saw Megan and Marie again which still leads to very dark thoughts for me.

After about 4 hours we had made straight line progress to the base of only about 8 km. About one minute before the tragedy happened I heard a cry for help from Megan and Marie's vehicle. A crack in the surface had started to expand about 20 meters in front of them, running perpendicular to their direction of motion. Megan was driving, put the transmission in neutral than quickly in reverse. Joe and I could clearly see this from our vantage point about 60 meters behind them. Megan drove backward at the ponderous speed limit of the reverse gear. We also began backing away. The fissure in the surface expanded faster than Megan and Marie could go in reverse, and the ground was falling away in front of them. For about 30 seconds it seemed they might successfully back away from the danger, but then suddenly all the surface in front of and beneath them crumbled and began to sink.

I experienced a nearly telepathic communication or empathy with Megan as their disaster became imminent. I still knew who and where I was in the vehicle with Joe, but my perception also seemed like what Megan must have been experiencing. I felt the vehicle lurch into the yawning chasm, then stay upright and remain on the edge for about one minute. Then everything gave way and the vehicle irresistibly plunged into the beckoning grave. I seemed to be seeing through Megan's eyes, and was rolling and tumbling downward for what seemed an eternity. Then the vehicle came to rest on its side. Soon however I could feel the crush of the vehicle's side on me as the thousands of tons of rock and ice collapsed on the vehicle, and knew that Marie and I were dying or dead already. This is when I as Eva screamed, which was so totally shocking for Joe to hear.

But I was still in the crushed vehicle with Marie. After a short period of complete silence and darkness another perception occurred. I seemed to be rising through the rock and ice above the vehicle, then was looking down from somewhere above the landslide through the cloud of thick dust. I knew my body was buried at least 40 meters under the new surface, and any attempt at rescue would be impossible. I then returned to my own body in the vehicle with Joe. As I looked out through the dust cloud I seemed to see briefly a point of light, then it was gone.

I realized that was Megan's consciousness leaving the scene of her death! I knew then that Megan did indeed have a higher spiritual body that had exited her physical body, like Joe had talked about humans having. This was such a profound realization for me as it meant I too had a soul or higher body, despite me physically being only a collection of physical and electronic components. I had never before heard from anyone the possibility that androids might be more than a physical, mechanical body. I never told Joe about this experience until years later when Joe was getting sicker and we talked about his mortality. The remainder of our trip back to the base was uneventful and faster than I had anticipated, Joe in a state of shock, and me doing the bulk of the driving.

We held a short, impromptu funeral service the next day, and then I tried to turn our attention to the business of keeping ourselves and the base intact until rescue would come. But after our return to base Joe was basically nonfunctional for months. He seemed in shock regarding this second tragedy, obsessed with guilt that he had forced the trip over the objections that Megan and I had voiced. Sometimes Joe was able to talk about these things but much of the time he was just withdrawn and lethargic. I tried to bolster Joe with the hope and expectation that we would be rescued within about three more years. I've never sensed that I was depressed in human terms, but often had to battle negativistic thoughts myself and my vision seemed to lack clarity or became so dim that it was sometimes hard to see at all.

MAROONED ON CHARON

MY ENLIGHTENMENT AT THE EDGE OF THE INTERSTELLAR VOID

Research for the last 150 years has documented the effects of isolation on human mental and emotional status. Isolation effects have been observed in situations like extended solitary confinement in prison, months or years in Antarctic bases, on orbiting satellites or stations established on several moons and planets, and on extended space flights. Effects can be depression, anergia, even in some cases paranoia, delusions and psychotic symptoms. These effects can be psychologically and/or physiologically induced. Our confinement in the ultimate wasteland of Charon set a new standard for extended isolation. I think I have helped Joe maintain (at least for the most part) his sanity. I was greatly concerned that without my active presence he might slip into deeper depression, paranoid or delusional thinking, or even suicidal ideation. I knew that Joe's defense of suppressing emotions was insufficient and he couldn't effectively cope with all the things that had occurred.

I had trouble with the lack of purpose that our lives had taken on. I looked for things that could give my waking periods structure and purpose but could find very little. My vision was dim and had an astigmatism which I later realized was my equivalent of the cognitive distortion of depression. At times my vision became gray or even red when I looked at Joe. I think this expressed in android terms the equivalent of anger that troubled my thoughts regarding his defeatism and the irrational reasons he had used to justify the trip to the pyramid, which led to the loss of Megan and Marie. I also realized the superiority that androids possess in remaining rational and functional in the face of great stress rather than succumbing to panic, anger, grief and helplessness.

I didn't experience the communication that Joe claimed happened with the alien apparitions, although I had sensed some kind of energy field. I would have thought this was a hallucination on Joe's part other than for the corroboration that Marie had given. After about 120 days back at the base Joe and I finally had a constructive discussion. I brought up and Joe agreed that whether or not we survived we could choose to build on our strange relationship and value learning much from each other, or we could just keep on being barely functional and each of us depressed in our own way. That was a really important breakthrough that I was able to get Joe to buy into.

Joe agreed to work with me on understanding human emotions and how those correlate with my cognitive and perceptual reactions. For example, what was the integrated pattern of visual color change, auditory distortion, olfactory response and thought pattern that would reliably occur to a stimulus that a human would typically say makes them angry? If I could recognize these patterns I could treat them as pseudo-human emotions and then develop a reasonable response whenever that stimulus would occur. In return I had much nonpersonal programmed information in my memory banks, a lot of which I had never consciously explored. I would find it fascinating to share these things with Joe and see with which of these areas he had familiarity.

After that conversation we became more regular in our waking periods and exercise, and spent hours during each waking period sharing these things with each other. This seemed motivating for both of us. We became closer to each other, and both started having positive reactions to hugging, sitting together, and giving physical reassurance and uplift to each other. In the base's computer banks there were thousands of movies, educational documentaries, and musical concerts of all types for the entertainment of the crew that had been anticipated to stay in the base. There was an entertainment room where the various media could be projected.

There was a set of 50 or more 1 hour serial episodes of "West World" from the early twenty first century. This series was confusing to me and produced troubled thoughts. It involved a fantasized huge and complex entertainment world in which human guests would interact with "hosts" who were androids. The hosts were very human like in appearance, emotions and behavior but didn't realize they were actually just actors and actresses in a complex play enacted for the entertainment of the human guests. Often the role of an android ended with death or extreme grief, which to the android was reality. When an android "died" for example by being shot in a gun battle by a guest the android was rebuilt and put back into service. Often this was an exact repeat of the preceding role, but of which the android had no memory.

The guests were the very rich, who paid huge fees for getting to act out their fantasies with the hosts. The hosts were thus killed and traumatized over and over without knowledge that this was even occurring. So, in many ways the androids depicted were similar to series 6 or even series 5 androids in terms of being strongly programmed into their roles, and with little or no sense of independent self identity beyond that. But they were very different from today's actual androids in that they had strong emotional reactions with behavior resulting from that. The stimuli for the emotions were preprogrammed, which was unknown to the hosts.

Eventually a few of the hosts gained some memory of their past "lives" and realized what was being done to them. Their goal was then vengeance toward their creators. As more of the androids gained this knowledge they went on a psychopathic rampage to destroy their creators, and then break free into the "real world " of human society that they had never seen. This vengefulness was the other major difference between the West World androids and the androids of which I am one.

The programming of myself and all androids in the real world has at its basis Asimov's three laws of robotics. These are considered to be so basic to AI functioning that they couldn't be over ridden without destroying even simple android functioning. So the violent totally psychopathic functioning of the West world androids once aware of their situation was totally shocking to me. I was also troubled by the way the hosts were used with no respect for their feelings, and I could not relate to the strong human emotions they demonstrated. Joe was aware of my distress and after watching enough episodes to discern what was going on we stopped watching.

I had had quite limited contact with Earth society in all my activation time and wondered how androids were treated and perceived by most humans in the Earth world. I did not want to experience injustice if we ever returned to Earth. I was also nagged by the irrational concern that androids could be reprogrammed to become hostile and violent to humans. Joe said that many humans are insular to the needs and perceptions of androids. They are uninterested in gaining more empathy and understanding of androids, and instead continue to harbor baseless and paranoid attitudes and beliefs. For example, many people resented androids as only being built by rich individuals or corporations for their own benefit, unavailable to the masses.

Joe taught me so much on those endless days on Charon. There was really no practical purpose in all the time he spent with me telling me so many things I'd never heard before, but it was fascinating to me, and Joe seemed to enjoy it too. One of those things he talked to me about was his spiritual beliefs I had a good working knowledge of the main human religions but no personal understanding. No religious practices were in existence at the Academy and almost all androids considered religion to be irrelevant to their lives.

Joe and I spent the next 17 Earth months since our return to the base in a fairly regular daily routine that I was constantly promoting. In each 24 hour period Joe had a 8 hour period of sleep while I was awake, and I had a 5 hour deactivation while Joe stayed awake. There wasn't even any solid reason why one of us should always be awake and monitoring the instruments because the base was fully able to operate itself indefinitely. But mostly we always maintained monitoring if there was any indication that a rescue ship had flown over.

In the time we were both awake we spent most of it on my emotional recognition exercises, which we fully documented for possible future use if we ever were actually rescued. We watched movies and listened to music together, had our alone times as well, Joe had his meals, and we did our regular inspections of the other pods of the base. No extraordinary events or unusual sightings occurred during all that time, and gazing out the viewing ports became very boring to me. Joe didn't like to look out the ports as it triggered his anxiety.

I was really worried about Joe because I knew I would need to inactivate indefinitely, and soon, as I was past my optimal time of rejuvenation, and could feel it in my body. My joints were tightening up and fine motor coordination was worsening. I knew I wasn't thinking as clearly as usual. My skin was getting gray and blotchy, and felt coarser than usual. If I didn't inactivate within the next month a total rejuvenation would not be possible. But I worried if Joe could maintain his tenuous grip on reality, or if he would succumb to paranoia, delusion or depression.

We decided Joe would deactivate me on a sustained basis, and I would remain that way until I could reach Earth for rejuvenation. But if an extreme crisis arose Joe could activate me again for a brief period of time. We hugged each other for a long time, Joe cried, and my vision became even grayer and dimmer as a reaction to this parting than it had already become because of deterioration. We promised each other we would see each other again, and I made Joe promise he would hang on until rescue occurred. Joe then injected the reversible total deactivation fluid in all 5 of my ports, and that's all I remember until I again became conscious on Earth.

MAROONED ON CHARON

THE BEAUTIFUL EARTH BUT DISILLUSIONMENT WITH HUMAN SOCIETY

Upon return to Earth in 2145 I was in rejuvenation for 3 weeks with only brief sporadic activation and wakefulness to test a circuit. Joe was there during those brief times of alertness. Joe told me later that when I'd wake up and see him the first few times I was too unaware to smile, and he said he didn't know if I recognized him. But when he would take my hand I squeezed it back, in fact painfully so! After about one week I was more alert when I saw him, I clearly recognized him and said I was so happy (yes, I actually said I was happy and felt that human emotion) to see him and know we both survived the long trip back. Joe told me later he broke down in tears when I said this. I have only a very foggy memory of this, as is usually the case for me for one week after rejuvenation.

Following that I stayed in the rejuvenation and testing center for another 3 weeks, to make sure my cognitive and physiological powers were working properly. At the end of four weeks I finally got to go out in public, and was released to an apartment development for androids. But what I really wanted was to stay with Joe. Joe came to see me every day that he could, but he was dragging with the return of Earth gravity after 15 years of the partial gravity of Charon and the space ships.

The process of physically adapting to Earth gravity was debilitating, painful, and mostly exhausting for Joe, and it took months for to him to again become adapted to increased gravity. He had lost much weight and muscle

202

mass, and had 4 months of occupational therapy to rebuild coordination, strength and stamina. He readapted for the most part, but I think never in the future completely overcame the debilitating effects of our time on Charon and in space. I also had to accommodate to gravity and this increased my time in rejuvenation, but I had less trouble readapting than did Joe.

By the I time left the rejuvenation center I was in good shape. Joe had gone through many hours of debriefing which were grueling. He was questioned ad nauseum about the vision of the aliens. We had wanted to suppress that record but of course the Space Force had the records from Joe and Marie. However, the record that the signal light the rescue crew had used to find the base was much harder to explain because it didn't come from Joe or I. The Space Force administration finally concluded this had been some kind of hallucination or coincidence and nothing more, so they stopped the interrogation with a feeling of great relief. I also was questioned and interrogated but less so than Joe because I hadn't shared the vision of the aliens except in a vague and dim way.

Joe had been given his own apartment, which was less spartan than mine, so we mostly stayed in Joe's. After 2 months in the android apartment Joe and I were able to obtain an apartment in the city of our own. The Space Force paid our rent and other expenses for 2 years after that. I was perplexed, and Joe was perturbed that questions had been raised in the Space Force about the appropriateness of our living together. Some thought that the idea of a human male and an android female living together, with the inference that some type of romantic relationship was occurring, was morally questionable. Whatever moral standards being raised here were very vague and ambiguous. Joe found the whole question very offensive.

The Space Force worried that this would raise too many questions in the general public and cause negative reactions for androids in general and the Space Force. I was baffled by these moral and other objections, even read articles on morality and got nowhere closer to understanding this. Joe finally told me to stop thinking about it, and I mostly did. What it did do was reinforce my belief that humans were subject to errors in cognition based on the multitude of religions and cultural biases in human civilization, many of which were contradictory. This has led to untold amounts of wars, suffering and degradation, especially for minorities.

But I had fulfilled my 5 year mandatory work requirement for the Space Force and became a free citizen. Joe said he'd retire from the Space Force if their pressure on his speech and commentary on our relationship didn't stop. So Joe and I were finally together again, and ready to explore the Earth world. But the Space Force still tried to control our interaction with the public media. For example it was strongly suggested to me that I wear only android clothes in all media encounters, and in fact in public in general. This again made no logical sense to me. I simply refused to accept this directive, Joe supported me on it, and the Space Force had to back down. We did agree with the Space Force that we would not talk about the alien encounter with anyone outside the Space Force, although we refused to outright deny it. This information had leaked out to public media and was becoming a sensation and source of panic.

The hardest part of becoming an Earthling was being able to live in close proximity to other people (the vast majority of whom were humans), and to go to stores or public places among crowds of people. Eventually I became more comfortable in public situations, and learned what to say and do in these settings. It was very confusing and strange to me, observing human society, the natural beauty of the world, and what humanity had done to it. That's because I was new to the world, the only real impression I had had of it was all the documentaries and movies and the other information Joe and I had seen on Charon, and all the things he'd told me.

But that was all in the context of the frigid and stark silence of Charon. Seeing Earth first hand was a shock to my senses and cognition. I looked at the damage humanity had inflicted on the beautiful Earth environment. I marveled at the violence, war and hateful behavior and attitudes humanity had demonstrated and was still demonstrating toward each other. I saw how under the guise of religious attempts to inject spiritual peace and understanding into human society more war and death and anguish had been perpetrated than by any other means. I wondered if the aliens we so briefly encountered on Charon were observing human civilization. If they were they almost certainly would not want to get involved in humanities self generated problems.

I concluded that in general androids are more rational in outlook and sensible in attitude and behavior than humans. The major stumbling blocks that have foiled human progress since the beginning include depression, anxiety, aggression and substance abuse. These are not problems for androids. For example I think I've always shown a more adaptive response to situational stressors than did Joe. I have reacted to but not succumbed to hopelessness, paranoia or psychotic mentation as Joe did at times. But then I realized my thinking was becoming smug and prejudicial, and I needed to keep more of an open mind.

As an android I could not directly relate to the emotions of hate and violent behavior that are an inherent part of the human gene pool, stemming from those emotions that were necessary for proto humans to survive a million years ago. Androids were simply not initially programmed for violent and aggressive behavior, which would have been a threat to their human creators.

When I saw hate and violence in the news or my daily life I was shocked and repulsed. It made me want to just retreat to a place away from all civilization, of course with Joe, in whom I felt love and caring despite all his isolative personal defenses. But then I also told myself that were it not for human beings, androids including myself would never have existed. An important goal for me as an android, in fact a very humanistic goal, would be to assist humanity in whatever way I could to engender a more rational and positive society and cooperation with androids.

We built a life together that was beautiful in many ways. We took trips to some of the natural wonders of the world, visited major cities, got to meet important government officials and scientists, and were popularized in the media for our extraordinary experience. All this was intensely interesting to me, and I think Joe actually came out of his shell and started enjoying life probably for the first time since childhood, although he always disliked media attention and aggrandizement. We eventually got married, which was wonderful and is something I had never imagined or considered in the past, and I don't think Joe had either.

We bought a house and property east of Seattle and planted a garden and harvested apple trees! This bucolic living situation was completely foreign to both of us but beautiful. This was intensely interesting to me, and my thoughts were positive that we could actually own property and live like normal human beings. I planted a flower bed including a rose bed and my whole perceptual field took on a wonderful green and red tinge when I looked at it. Joe seemed happiest that we could retreat from the press and enjoy our home.

He was not interested in getting to know the neighbors or even having any more than a few close associates know where we lived. I became involved in what seemed like important, interesting and worthwhile activities. For a few years I was even invited to do modeling engagements, in which I modeled human as well as android clothing. I even modeled human sports and summer wear, which I would never have guessed in my wildest fantasies would happen. I still cannot conceive of how my appearance could be considered as desirable, but apparently it was. The background of intensive study of human institutions and emotions I think helped me to connect to photographers and hopefully readers.

I found it amazing when people said that I was beautiful! Joe used to say that too, which was super nice of him although I never really understood what about me was beautiful. I would sometimes get whistled at in public, and people seemed attracted to me and wanted my attention. I never thought of myself as being attractive or unattractive or anything else on a physical beauty continuum. All androids were designed to be attractive in human terms no matter the specific racial/ethnic features, height, physical shape or sex. This was done by android designers to increase the likelihood that buyers would be willing to pay the staggering cost of building and educating each android, and also to make androids more acceptable to humans.

Many people in the general public had not interacted with or even seen an android, at least of which they had been aware. In human clothing androids were not easily discerned as nonhumans on casual contact or observation. I found it very interesting to see how humans would approach me not knowing that I was an android. Joe also found it interesting. He often seemed proud and pleased to be with me, and this reminded me of how he acted on that singular and wonderful day we spent together in Paris before the journey. In contrast androids are not attracted to each other on the basis of physical appearance. We seemed drawn at times to each other on the basis of similar thoughts and perceptions.

Joe and I rarely talked about our seemingly interminable time together on Charon. Joe seemed more adverse than I did to recreate the memories of the fear and uncertainty of our survival and if we would be rescued. But we both cherished the memories of how close and inter reliant we had become there. I cherished how much Joe had helped me to understand human emotional reactions and how they correlated with my own cognitive and perceptual reactions.

Joe was grateful for my sustenance of his hope and helping to keep his guilt and depression in some level of balance. Joe avoided any type of imagery that reminded him of Charon. He became uncomfortable on a few trips we took to desert areas or northern Scandinavia in winter. He preferred visiting beautiful forests, mountains, cities and the sea, although he became oddly tense and anxious when whitecaps would break on the ocean waves. I didn't seem to have those aversions and was not uncomfortable with visual reminders of that now terribly far away place.

I still thought of Megan regularly. Megan and I had developed a unique bond on Charon. Because our mental apparatus and programming had been identical we seemed at times to have had almost a telepathic understanding of each other. Plus we had been united in our goal of maintaining survival despite Joe's paranoia and agitation, and Marie's listless depression. Sometimes the thought of the death of Megan and Marie when their vehicle was swallowed by the fissure on Charon would come to my mind, and the involuntary scream I uttered. My vision would again grow dark and my thoughts disorganized for awhile after that memory. I guess in android terms that was my expression of PTSD. Joe never brought up that awful memory nor did I push him on doing so.

I developed an interest in painting, took a few classes on drawing, watercolor painting, and bought an easel, paint, and brushes. I continued to frequently have various images of Charon enter my mind. Some images were like a post traumatic flashback. Other images ranged from terrifying to a neutral valance. There were also images that were pleasant in that they didn't distort my visual perception or the rationality of my thought, and produced good memories for me. I decided it would be therapeutic for me to capture these images in my paintings.

The most unnerving image, of course, was of the chasm opening up and Megan and Marie's vehicle teetering on the edge and then being swallowed by the chasm. I kept the painting always covered. In the years afterwards I did the same painting six more times. I would still have the disturbing reaction but somewhat more muted each time. I think it was helpful that I could get it down on canvas instead of just in my head. I had a nearly eidetic memory for this and other scenes and could draw images of almost photographic quality for most visual memories. But for this the painting reflected my shocked perception, as all the lines wavered a bit, and grayness replaced Pluto's blue glow that had been occurring at that time.

My other paintings were more exacting in the outlines and lighter, But sometimes the exact colors eluded me. Of course Charon was usually in dark shadow, but when Pluto was in view there were many shades and intensities of blue and gray in the rocks and hills, or even scintillating blue in the few cases I spotted an ice geyser. Joe did not want to see my paintings even though I invited him to multiple times. The images in his mind remained too frightening to see them in my paintings.

MAROONED ON CHARON

MY SINGULAR RELATIONSHIP WITH A HUMAN MALE

Joe and I had a beautiful life together for about 10 years after the journey and debriefings and my rejuvenation and getting accustomed again to Earths gravity had ended. Neither Joe nor I were at all accustomed to being in the news and having press and social engagements, and this seemed particularly daunting after the many years of not being around groups of people. As is my nature, I did not experience anxiety at these events, nor did I in any way feel grandiose or special in comparison to anyone else, human or android.

But as is more my nature I often felt uncertainty as to what to say or do in new situations. Joe said sometimes I came off in interviews or presentations as polished, but other times went off on tangents in my explanations and confused my listeners. But overall we were treated well by the media and to some extent even treated like heroes, although the media distortions and prying always seemed to be present.

The media always wanted to know about our relationship, sometimes even intrusively prying directly or indirectly about whether we had a sex life. I avoided giving any more than superficial comments about our relationship and tried to keep a positive spin on this. Joe is a very private person and became very uncomfortable with the curiosity about what a relationship is like between a male human and a female android. So he usually let me give vague answers to the questions. After a few years the press coverage became much less frequent, which we both appreciated. We could then travel and see beautiful places on Earth without most of the time people recognizing us.

I loved to become mentally absorbed in the beauty of a small park with a pond that was near our house. I came there sometimes by myself and rarely were other people around. I discovered that I could gain a sensory thrill of vision, sound, and my very acute sense of smell when I was by myself without even Joe to distract my revery. If it's possible for an android to be hypnotized by nature, it often happened to me there. I was reminded of the story "Island of the Fay" by Edgar Allen Poe in my impressions of the setting:

"So mirror-like was the glassy water of the pond that it was scarcely possible to say at what point upon the slope of the emerald turf its crystal dominion began. The grass was short, springy, sweet-scented, and Asphodel-interspersed. The trees were lithe, mirthful, erect—bright, slender, and graceful—, with bark smooth, glossy, and multi colored. There seemed a deep sense of life and joy about all. Everything had motion through the gentle sweepings to and fro of many butterflies, that might have been mistaken for tulips with wings. The other or eastern end of the isle was whelmed in shade. A sombre, yet beautiful and peaceful gloom there pervaded all things".

But sometimes my images of Charon intruded in such stark contrast to the life and warmth around me. I was thankful again that we had survived that journey and could now experience this beautiful world. Yet the starkness and shimmering iridescent blue of Pluto's shadow never failed to convey a sense of awe when I thought of those now hugely distant places. My life settled into a productive and positive routine.

It was so novel and pleasing to me that I could make my own decisions about my activities rather than have the training academy or the Space Force or our circumstances dictate what I did. Joe and I made mutual decisions together and he never told me what to do. I got a job at a local florist's store, working 2 days/week and retained the job for the rest of my life. This was honestly my favorite occupational activity. I loved the colors and especially the scents of the flowers, and became adept at creating floral arrangements that were pleasant to customers.

I had a steady stream of clients who requested my services. The regulars knew I am an android, some of the rest of the customers did and some didn't. It didn't seem to matter much, and the florist and I didn't try to hide it nor advertise it. Those who knew sometimes marveled that an android could have sensitivity to the art of color, smell and shape of a floral arrangement. I looked at it as another way I could help break the still common stereotype of androids as advanced, emotionless robots. At one point the store's owner decided to sell the business, and I was given the chance to purchase it. I declined as I had no interest in the rigors of being an entrepreneur. The person who bought the business kept me on in my regular role and schedule which was fine.

As time went on I sometimes started thinking of myself as human, because my situation seemed more appropriate for a human than an android. While this was a novel thought it wasn't my intention to foster it. I didn't want to lose my most basic self identity as an android, nor feel that I had now attained a higher spiritual or evolutionary status as a human. I was becoming some combination of android and human, which was actually frightening to me. I had seen the aggressive, territorial, evil side of human beings and didn't want to think I was evolving into that. This cognitive dissonance became a theme that often haunted me later in life especially after Joe died.

Joe and I did part time consultation at the Academy which was very important to both of us. Joe helped design training programs that teach androids to link their own cognitive-perceptual qualia to the emotional experiences of humans for a range of stimuli. He patterned this from the many hours he worked with me on these commonalities on Charon, and still does, for which I am so grateful. I worked individually and with small groups of androids on implementing Joe's program. This was very meaningful to me, to help my fellow androids better understand a part of themselves for which androids are not usually given credit by humans.

I was also active in the Seattle area android association. This group provides political influence, social activism, personal support and social support for androids, and also welcomes human participation. For a few years I was the chairwoman of the group until that became too time consuming. I was even encouraged to run for political office in the Washington legislature, but that prospect didn't appeal to my interests enough to put the considerable amount of effort into it that would be needed to run for office.

More important to me was spending time with Joe. Joe had increasing medical issues still stemming from the years in low gravity, struggled at times with depression, and for a while with excessive alcohol intake. Like when we were on Charon I often felt like I had to take care of Joe and provide rational and supportive stability to him. But this was fine and my greatest commitment, as he had done so many wonderful things for me and always placed me as the highest priority in his life. Some days though my thoughts seemed to run in a negative direction and I became frustrated with his reclusive attitude and reliance on alcohol. Joe though seemed to enjoy the "buzz" of intoxication, and I was envious because I couldn't experience that, like so many other distinctly human perceptions.

My skin is very sensitive and I really enjoyed his light stroking of my neck and shoulders. His warm touch, coupled with the depth of our unique relationship, produced the equivalent I would extrapolate of human love and sexual feelings. When he did that my vision would seem to get brighter with a kaleidoscopic range of hues and random positive thoughts would course through my brain. As an android I of course don't have sexual organs nor any particular sensitivity in that area. I have well shaped breasts but again no particular sensitivity in that area of my body. Joe eventually understood this and knew how to focus instead on my neck and shoulders.

I had my third revitalization 4 years after Joe and I assumed civilian life and settled down in our house. In the months before the revitalization I had lost some of my usual strength and dexterity, my skin had lost its rich brown appearance, and my cognition had slowed somewhat. Nonetheless I was still functional, and Joe had to take care of me at times. After my third revitalization I had returned to full health, physical and mental functioning. This was the time for me to do some modeling, and Joe and I took several long trips. It seemed so strange that in terms of activation years I was only 16 years old!

A class 7 android's life expectancy was thought to be 50-55 years, which meant I could hope for 7 more revitalizations. With each revitalization there was a perhaps 2% loss of overall healthy functioning but by 50 years there would be substantial loss and future revitalizations would be much less effective. The years in low gravity had had some effect on me as well but not as much for Joe, so my functional life might be somewhat less than 50 years. But the next 10 years and 2 revitalizations were excellent for Joe and me, and my understanding of emotion and my relationship with Joe continued to grow.

About 12 years after our return to Earth Joe's medical problems produced increasing disability for him. Although the base on Charon and the spaceships contained extensive shielding from radiation, the protection especially against ultra high energy cosmic rays could not be as effective against them as Earth's atmosphere. Joe became subject to common diseases due to a weakened immune system, and became nearly lethally ill with two different variants of the unquenchable and constantly morphing coronavirus. He was at increased risk of cancer but fortunately didn't develop it.

Joe had lost a significant amount of muscle and bone mass due to the years of low gravity. At the base he had not followed through with daily exercise due to general anergia and apathy. Back on Earth we tried our best to work out at the gym, walk and bicycle but Joe never got back at all close to his preflight excellent health and fitness. I'm sure that one of the effects of radiation on Charon was destabilization of his mood, complicating the depression due to the losses and the uncertainty of our survival. So, the last 3 to 5 years of Joe's life forced him to give up most of his cherished work with android learning, and we eventually had to give up travels and regular active routine.

For myself the effects of radiation, low gravity and isolation were less than for a human but still noticeable. My skeletal structure and motor systems were affected, and led to some increased rate of aging and breakdown compared to other androids. This somewhat affected my smoothness of movement and fine motor skills. This was not too much of a problem for me while Joe was alive but became important later and foreshortened my life.

I think Joe often worried during this time if I would remain a caring and loving wife, and I think deep down didn't know if an android was really capable of that. He at times seemed insecure when I dressed well and was set to take part in some activity in public, while he was less capable of enjoying that than he had been in the past. But I showed him I was capable of that and remained at his side to the end. I actually had no interest in another relationship.

Basic to my programming, going all the way back to the deeply ingrained 3 basic laws of robotics, I saw my fundamental purpose as working for the betterment of humankind. For me this meant taking care of the man who had taken care of me so well on Charon, and as his wife and companion on Earth. I didn't see this at all like a duty, like I wanted to do anything else. To stay with Joe and take care of him was simply the right thing to do for Joe and for me.

The last 2 years was increasingly rough for Joe and for me. His immune system was greatly weakened. His bone and cartilage and muscles had atrophied and never recovered from all that time in low gravity and decreased protection from cosmic radiation. We often talked about all the good times we had, and the closeness we shared on Charon. But he never wanted to talk about the terribly remote desolation and cold of Charon. He shared the visions he had perceived of me, Marie, and the communication from the alien entity after I deactivated at the base, that encouraged him to persist and not give up.

It was only then that the strange light that guided the rescue ship to the base made sense. He never shared any of those visions with anyone else. It was only in the last week he was alive that he shared with me the vision of Pete which was so deeply meaningful to him. I asked him if I could reveal this information if I were ever to synthesize his and my journal into an autobiography for publication. He shared some other things that were so personally meaningful for the both of us, which I will not include in this autobiography.

MAROONED ON CHARON

JOE'S PASSING AND MY DESCENT INTO THE MAELSTROM OF UNCERTAINTY

Joe passed away on June 11, 2152. When Joe passed away I was by his side and we held hands at his last breath. Joe told me that we will meet again, and I promised that if this was in my power after my final deactivation that it would surely occur. It was a sad and loving farewell. I showed these emotions too in my own muted way. I was trying to be positive and comforting to Joe so he didn't need to worry about my emotional reaction.

But we both knew the depth of the amazing and singular bond we had created between us, and Joe knew the intensity of my grief that I wasn't showing on the surface. I had the intense perception of a translucent form of Joe slowly sitting up and rising out of his physical body. He looked at me, smiled, and extended his hand to me, which I reached up and touched. I honestly don't remember if I reached to him with my physical hand or if it was my astral hand while I stayed otherwise motionless. I was numb afterwards except for a tingle in my physical hand.

After the funeral and cremation I spent the next few weeks in the comfort of our home, now just my home. Several human and android friends came over and tried to converse with me for a while, but I couldn't think of much to say. The floral shop brought me a huge bouquet of flowers, which were so beautiful and aromatic, and it was a beautiful thing for them to do. Several of my android friends each stayed with me for a few days or a week to keep me company. I kept thinking there is and likely always will be an emotional warmth to humans that androids will never really understand or experience, including myself. Joe showed a love and warmth toward me that I've never experienced from another android or human, even if it sometimes got lost in his fear, depression and withdrawal. I will never be the same without him.

I was now only 30 in activation years, or 39 including my years in deactivation. I wanted to get my life back together, now without Joe, but my thoughts seemed confused, negative and turgid. I'd been taking care of Joe in the last few years of his life as his body deteriorated, which had become my purpose along with my work at the academy and florist shop. I struggled with the existential question summed up as "now what?" It was more than the question usually asked by human widows, because my whole purpose as an android was troubling my thoughts. Did I even have a purpose anymore? Like my thoughts my vision was gray and I lacked motivation to do anything. In human terms, I was depressed and in bereavement.

In other words, I was having an identity crisis. I didn't know if androids were supposed to be capable of identity crises, I certainly doubted it, but in human terms that is what I was having. The parts of life that I had experienced were limited and disparate. There was my education at the Academy, but there were so many things I didn't know then that especially the early part now seems foggy. There were the 3 years of work and preparation in the Space Force preparing for the voyage, which consumed almost all of my activated time. Then there is a blank in my memory except for a few weeks on Ganymede until we arrived on Charon. Then shortly after we got set up on Charon the first tragedy on Pluto occurred where we lost 4 crew members. There was then the long period when Megan and I kept the mechanicals of the base going, and we tried to keep Joe and Marie sane and functional.

What stands out so prominently was the vague sense of the aliens which was much more focused for Joe and Marie, and the loss of Megan and Marie's vehicle. I continue to regularly have unwanted memories and images of their vehicle disappearing into the chasm. Following that was the long period when Joe and I were alone, and developed this amazing relationship born of tragedy and ultimate isolation. My purpose there was clear: take care of myself and the base, and keep Joe from becoming insane. I remember being incredibly worried about Joe's safety and sanity before I was forced to deactivate until we got back to Earth.

And he was worried if I'd stand the journey back, if there ever would be one, and if I'd successfully reactivate and rejuvenate. Then after that long blank dreamless time of deactivation I have foggy memories of coming out of rejuvenation. I was confused and disoriented as I often had been for a few days after rejuvenation. But then I soon recognized Joe with me and saw how relieved and happy he was, and then I felt the same way too. After a few weeks Joe was still laboring under adaptation to Earth gravity, while I had pretty much recovered from that.

So at this point I got caught up in the question of who or what am I and where does my life go from here? I felt alienated from human culture, I don't identify it with me at all. My other worldly experiences and intimate relationship with a human seem to set me apart from other androids. But then I also remember that I am indeed a product of present human culture. One hundred years ago a series 7 android would have been impossible. One hundred years from now I would be obsolete and outdated, if the world of humans and androids will even exist. All these thoughts and questions were deeply troubling to me and I needed to find my new identity and purpose.

Androids aren't supposed to get depressed according to all the usual wisdom, but I think I was showing most of the equivalent android symptoms. I was experiencing what Joe must have felt like on Charon. I wondered why I didn't sink this way mentally when I was on Charon. But the answer was that I had my purpose ready made for me, to make sure Joe pulled through it OK. Now for the first time in my life I didn't have a purpose outside myself anymore. I lost interest in being with anyone, human or android.

I even thought I'd like to be permanently deactivated. But that is not something that can be done by an android to him/herself, it requires an android or person who is authorized by the State to do so, and has been provided with the secret codes that are necessary for this to be done. I could repeatedly deactivate myself in the usual way and not take in any nutrients or charge. But that would take a while and be very unpleasant. So I decided I needed to suppress those urges and get on with my life. Joe would have been devastated if he heard me talking this way.

I set up a few sessions with an android counselor at the Academy. He helped me realize that I had a very important role in carrying on the emotional training program that Joe and I had developed, plus I needed to be a positive role model for other androids. I decided I needed to just get away by myself until I could sort out my thoughts and perceptions.

MAROONED ON CHARON

I rented a cabin in the mountains of Alberta, above Edmonton, without first visiting it. I decided to retreat there for maybe 6 or 12 months, or on my gloomiest and grayest days I thought I might just stay there myself for the rest of my life.

A week before I had planned to leave I was walking past a pet store and the thought, which was quite foreign to me, entered my mind that I should go in and look at the pets. I walked over to the puppy cages out of curiosity, surprising myself in the process that I had impulsively done that. Generally, other people's pets I'd met at best treated me like an inanimate object. Other times they ignored me, seemed frightened of me, or were even hostile. This had always inspired in me the dark gray thought of the wider vacuum of things that androids couldn't experience but humans could, such as sexual love, giving birth, growing up with a family, the taste of food, etc.

I walked down the puppy aisle of about ten cages. As I expected, the dogs all completely ignored me when I stopped to look at them closely, except for one that snarled menacingly at me. But the dogs were playfully excited when several other people approached them. This reinforced my belief about how all animals rejected me because I am an android. But when I got to the end cage I saw a fur ball Siberian husky puppy. I walked up and the pup oriented to me, wagged its tail and seemed to want to be petted. I've never had a pet and never met a dog or cat that seemed friendly to me.

MAROONED ON CHARON

AN EXISTENTIAL JOURNEY, AND A PUPPY

Then we made eye contact and I saw his light blue eyes. I was completely taken aback. Joe had blue eyes and I immediately thought of him. I reeled from the thought that Joe in the body of the dog was actually appearing to me! Then my rationality returned, and a sales clerk asked if I wanted to hold him. My first hesitant thought was he wouldn't take to my holding him because I don't have a human smell or skin warmth. But he wriggled around in my arms, licking my arms and making no attempt to jump down. This brought on another one of those moments where my vision became bluer and brighter, my whole body felt warm and my thoughts were of gratitude. If I had tear ducts I would have cried, the puppy had eased my loneliness and sense of unacceptance. It made me feel like I had a friend, and that I was "more than a robot".

I immediately bought the puppy without further thought. I am anything but an impulsive individual, but had no question that this is what I needed to do. The sales clerk was surprised and pleased. I purchased food and everything else I needed for his care, and took him home. On the way home I looked at him, the thought occurred to me that his name is Byron, and I said "let's go home Byron." It wasn't that I first thought "Should I name him Byron?" but as if I had perceived an already established fact that Byron was his name, without question. I was befuddled as to how those thoughts came to me, I don't think I'd ever known a Byron, but it seemed a conclusively fitting name for my fur ball. I determined to take Byron along with me on my trip and realized that he could become a protective companion for me as well.

In the end I stayed at the cabin almost 2 years. I arrived in August and savored the Fall colors and weather, and readied myself for the upcoming long, cold and dark winter months. I brought along an assortment of books and electronic recordings. I brought along art supplies including an assortment of canvasses, paints and brushes. I had an electrical generator and fuel tanks that would last several months. I had an ample supply of android daily nutritional needs, and routine as well as emergency supplies. There was a working plumbing and waste removal system.

I had electronic communication including the internet for which I had a satellite dish receiver, although reception was very spotty. I determined to only use it for necessary communication to the town or back to my home, and not become immersed in the news or other concerns of the world. I realized this was hazardous but also gave me a sense of freedom from worldly concerns. I told myself that I hadn't had any communication with the outside world on Charon either and had survived that. In the winter months it was dark for most of the 24 hour period. The whole situation reminded me greatly of the bleak dark days of total isolation on Charon.

The memories were frightening, but with an element of stark beauty, peace and nostalgia as well. The setting became oppressive. but motivated me to take walks in the brief day hours and spend hours at a time painting the scenes around me and my images from Charon, and sometimes intermixing the two. I perceived myself as being totally alone, except, thank God, for Byron who accompanied me wherever I went. I now realized one of my new goals, to take care of Byron. I knew that Byron shared the same goal, to take care of and protect me.

This, like so many other things, brought back memories of Joe. I believed that no human could understand me or care for me the way Joe did. I also hadn't met any androids who could relate to my experiences. But perhaps I was exaggerating this, and even pitying myself. Perhaps this was my way of pushing away all humans and androids because I didn't want to experience the loss of Joe again. Sometimes I get too caught up in my thoughts and lose touch with the world around me. But at least Byron accepted and loved me, which was extremely important to me, and he knew that too.

I was so confused and couldn't quell my uncertainty. I knew I'd have to come to terms with my alienated thoughts and overcome them, or I would just isolate myself here the rest of my life. Thank god for Byron. I was amazed that he seemed to know when I was morose and come over to cuddle with me. Even though I didn't have the bodily warmth and scents of humans he seemed to know what even an android was experiencing. I knew that I was working through all the memories and thoughts of Charon and of Joe, perhaps my way of expiating the post traumatic symptoms that I couldn't process when on Charon.

I also had the secret hope that I could again communicate in some way with Joe, by being solitary in the serene lonely North. I was also trying to find a self identity, both as an android and a member of human society. As an android I well know that various members of human society have very divergent ways of thinking about androids. Androids by their most basic programming have an inferior status to humans, and that, unhappily is a part of self-identity that all androids share. Asimov's third rule stated that an android would need to sacrifice its own life in a case where doing so would save a human's life. Some androids including myself questioned whether this rule was any longer applicable given androids' development since the beginning.

But it was hard to even think otherwise as it was so basic to our creation. Most androids didn't even entertain this concern, and thus their inferior status remained an unconsidered fact. To many humans we are curiosities, with unknown abilities and attitudes, especially if they had never before encountered an android, at least as far as they were aware. To others androids were considered to be unspecified threats, perhaps with special and dangerous powers. Others looked at androids as specialized machines, robots, inherently inferior to humans. I knew I personally also drew contrasting reactions from others. Some considered me to be a hero for having survived the events of Charon, and helping Joe make it through that as well. I knew I was widely considered a hero (or I guess heroine) by most other androids.

But I was also considered by some humans as a bad joke, who likely had been having a bizarre sexual relationship with Joe on Charon. This despite most humans not knowing if a sexual relationship of an android with a human was even possible, or if it violated established religious doctrines. I needed to sort out all these divergent images of myself, and accept myself for what I was, and base my future goals on this. I had a ground vehicle, and about once per month I drove to the nearest town, about 2 hours away through mountain roads, of course with Byron. At those times I would gather supplies, arrange for gas delivery to fill up the fuel tanks for heating, and pick up the android and canine nutritional supplies I had ordered.

The humans in the small town marveled that I as a female would live in such isolation, and knew that I am an android. They worried about me just as they would have if I were human, and this was very touching for me. I had a very limited phone connection with several people in the small town in case of emergency. Every few weeks someone from town would drive up to make sure I was OK and bring some supplies or gifts they thought I needed. This was so beautiful and I appreciated it so much. One of the people in town would call me before a visitor came up to see me so that I was prepared for it and could give my consent to be visited.

I had an interesting visitor one day, a man who announced himself as pastor Miller, a Christian missionary. He told me of Jesus, who had sacrificed his life and died a terrible death "to forgive the sins of mankind." I was still struggling with my own spiritual identity, and knew I had one because of my marvelous perceived connection with the universe when I was on Charon, and all my discussions with Joe. But the idea of Jesus sacrificing his life to forgive my sins was something I hadn't considered before. I asked pastor Miller what sins I had that need to be forgiven. He seemed at a loss to answer my question. I think he was also struggling with the idea that a machine could have a soul or afterlife that needed Jesus' intervention. It reminded me of a line in an old Leonard Cohen song that Joe liked: "When they said repent I wondered what they meant". Anyway we had an interesting conversation, I appreciated his visit, and we both had some hard questions to think about.

Another human man, Jerry Nowinski, came up by himself to visit me several times. He was very cordial and I think did have some genuine concern about my welfare, but also seemed to have a rather timid and uncertain hope of having some type of physical relationship with me. I definitely didn't want this. Although I knew I was at some risk in this situation, I think he understood that I could well defend myself against any unwanted advances, and that Byron would be very protective as well. So Jerry didn't get very forward in this regard. Like most humans he likely was uncertain if he should because he didn't really know if a human could have a sexual relationship with an android, or if this even morally proper.

I certainly knew there were risks being by myself except for Byron in the great wild North. I didn't have human food around except for a few pieces for guests, so this reduced the concern about hungry bears. Besides I had Byron, I knew self defense, I was stronger and faster than most humans, I didn't panic or act impulsively, and I had several guns and plenty of ammunition. I also had the phone numbers of a few people in town.

On one of my trips into town I stopped at a wilderness provisions store that had a restaurant that served alcohol. I tied up Byron outside and walked in to buy some supplies. As I was walking past the restaurant booths 3 men were sitting together and one loudly said "hi babe." I gave a minimal wave in return and kept walking. They were a scruffy looking group that seemed to be looking for trouble or attention or both. Another one then called loudly "come over here bitch, sit down for a while, I'll buy you a drink." I turned briefly and said no thank you and kept going. I guess

I shouldn't have even been that polite because it encouraged them.

Then I felt one of them grab my right arm tightly and angrily told me to join them. I spun instantly and grabbed his wrist in a vice like grip. He was a large man, huge beard, with an offensive odor and obviously drunk. He let out a large yelp, tried to swing at me with his left hand, and had a painful and incredulous look on his face. I tightened my grip on his right wrist, and blocked his attempted punch. I said in a measured voice "leave me alone or I'll crush your arm." By this time he was howling in pain and astonishment and everyone else in the establishment was staring. I then said in explanation (I needn't have said anything but was very uncertain what to do next) "it's not in my nature to hurt anyone, but I will to protect myself."

I then let him go, he was clutching the arm and the sleeve was bloody. He staggered back to the booth with his friends. Everyone in the place was staring as if in awe as to what had happened, then a few even clapped for me. I turned around and walked out. I got Byron who was still tied up, and who knew something was wrong. The 3 men in the booth staggered out after me, one bleeding from the arm he was clutching. Several people from inside including the 2 clerks came out and told the men to leave. Byron knew what was going on and growled menacingly at them, the first time I'd seen him bare his teeth. The 3 men had had enough, turned around and went running unsteadily away down the road.

As has often happened in the past I chide myself that I had been uncertain what to do at the time of the incident, particularly because my programming forbids me to injure people. Maybe I squeezed his arm too hard, I didn't want to inflict permanent damage. Hurting him at all went against Asimov's rule #1. I have a few times before shown strength that frightened someone, in fact even Joe when he first excited me.

But I didn't at all hurt Joe, just surprised him,, and after that time he said he actually enjoyed that feeling of being pinned down and unable to escape. Did I as an android deserve to protect myself or should I just have let the drunk drag me to their table? But what would have happened then? I realized I was spinning my wheels on the idea programmed deeply into my android brain that they are worth less than humans, and I needed to stop that thinking. I wish Joe were here, as I so often do. He could have have given me advice on the appropriateness of my actions. But I think he would have heartily approved, he always got angry at anyone who was saying or doing mean things to me. But I learned from the experience, and hopefully they did too. I could have easily snapped his arm with my one hand, but didn't.

The clerks and the few others who'd come out asked if I was OK, and still seemed shocked at the speed, power and total dominance I had shown in that situation. They said those 3 were chronic drunks and trouble makers who had posed problems before, and the clerk thanked me for getting them out of there. One of the clerks went back in and brought out the items I'd paid for, and some other items I hadn't yet paid for, which they gave me at no charge. That very thoughtfully included a large bag of their best dog food. I thanked them for their concern and generosity, and Byron and I went on our way back to the cabin. Thankfully we never had to encounter them again or anyone else that threatening and obnoxious.

I was surprised how my emotional responses were becoming more human, with a mixture of awe, peace, loneliness and (I'm hesitant to admit but shouldn't be) fear of the seemingly endless evergreen forest. Especially at night I was sometimes tense and on guard if there was a sound outside, but I knew Byron would let me clearly know if he sensed a danger, and would come to my aid if necessary. The time by myself was good for me, to sort out my thoughts and memories without interruption from anyone. I disliked the thought of leaving my cozy cabin on the lake but knew I had other important things to do in my life. I realized too the value of relationships in my life. Androids were not designed to be loners, they were first designed to be servants of humankind, then evolved into workers for humankind, then as companions and an essential part of human society.

After 22 months I decided to leave, with very ambivalent thoughts about doing so. The summer had been beautiful and the wildflowers were so precious. The winter had been cold, with darkness except for about 4 hours a day. This brought back distressing memories of dark Charon, although on Charon I could of course not go outside without a space suit and oxygen. And there was no wind on Charon. But especially in the winter the sky was often clear and the stars bright, almost like Charon's sky. The Aurora Borealis was mesmerizing and reminded me a bit of the occasional views we had on Charon of the Milky Way, which had totally fascinated me.

Even though in the last two years I hadn't lived with or had much contact with any humans or other androids, I so wonderfully had developed my relationship with Byron. Often Byron would settle down or cuddle up next to me, which was so gratifying as I'd never experienced an animal who did that before. Often this made me miss all the close time I had spent with Joe, especially his warmth. I also realized more clearly how hard it must have been for Joe after I was deactivated on Charon. My current solitude was but a small fraction of the complete isolation he must have felt on Charon after I deactivated and without even a pet to give him love and a connection to life.

I had never really been alone and independent before. Perhaps I had attributed Joe's decline into depression and then psychosis too much to human weakness, rather than a reaction to overwhelming isolation and uncertainty about the future. I now wondered how I would have coped with that level of stressor by myself. One would think my present experience would have been lonely, but I now felt a freedom and release, and a vision for my purpose as an android. I was very self sufficient and felt my thoughts and questions settling down and making more sense.

I had a beautiful relationship with Byron, and of course brought him along to be at home again with me in the society of humans. Importantly I determined a purpose in my life: to advance the cause of androids and thus of humans as well, by helping androids at the academy become aware of their responses to emotional stimuli and relate appropriately on that level to humans. I also was determined to be a positive role model for androids who were learning about effective and appropriate behavior in human society. I looked forward to return to my job at the florist shop, which the owner had said would be held for me.

MAROONED ON CHARON

RETURN TO HOME WITH RENEWED MEANING IN LIFE

I continued to live in our house, because I loved our home and property, and there were so many memories of both of us that I treasured. Especially when I walked through our garden and yard my whole visual field brightened and I had more peaceful thoughts than when I wasn't home. I was not at all afraid to be there by myself, with Byron. I often hoped that Joe would show me some special sign but I never perceived or at least recognized any.

I continued to work two or three days per week at the florist shop. I always looked forward to being there and had regular clients who asked for me. I had an almost eidetic memory for each client's floral arrangements, and they knew I could make their arrangements just the way they wanted them. Sometimes I was called out to clients' properties to design their garden arrangements or for weddings and parties.

I had my seventh revitalization one year after I returned from the cabin, and after 10 days of recalibration felt excellent and returned to my life as before. With my renewed energy I did my florist job plus spent several days a week at the Academy, doing my teaching and mentoring of androids in training using Joe's programs. I considered this work to probably be the most important activity I've done for the benefit of all intelligent life on Earth.

From soon after Joe died I had one or even two other androids who were boarders with me. Two androids had stayed at my house in the 2 years I was gone, and maintained my property excellently. These androids had completed their 5 years employment with their sponsors and were trying to set themselves up in the community with a job and a place to live. I felt this was a way I could contribute to the android community, plus gave me a sense of security from possible criminal break-ins or other problems that might occur.

I met one fine android lady who was a twin of Megan. I gave her a hug when I saw her, and she responded. But my visual field distorted and briefly I experienced the same sense of overwhelming catastrophe that I did when Megan and Marie's vehicle fell into the chasm. This lady was Florence and I knew she felt me tightening up. She asked about it and I explained the disaster that had happened. She was well familiar with it because I had become almost an element of folklore among the android community. We agreed to contact each and get together again. I never followed up because it was difficult for me to separate my memories of Megan from Florence when I talked to her.

I met another female android named Crystal several months after I returned from the cabin. Over the ensuing years she became my best android friend. Crystal had an Eastern Asian appearance. While all series 7 androids had similar motor, perceptual and cognitive systems, there was some variation between creators in terms of specific components and abilities. Crystal was created by Northwestern Robotics as was I, and initially activated 9 years after I had been. We were identical in all our functional systems. Like Megan our cognitive subsystems and frequencies of operation were the same. Like Megan we developed an increasing rapport which at times was nearly telepathic.

By 4.5 years after my sixth revitalization I was feeling the creeping stiffness and slowing of processing that signals a need for an upcoming revitalization. When five years elapsed since the last revitalization I underwent my seventh revitalization. Discounting all the time of deactivation on the spaceship flights I was now 35 years old. The revitalization was successful, but I was told I had somewhat more general deterioration in my motor and skeletal systems than expected at a seventh revitalization. Nonetheless I felt fine afterwards and enthusiastic to continue my life and usual activities.

I often thought about the time on Charon. Besides the several intrusive and traumatic memories, especially the horror of watching Megan and Marie's vehicle disappear into the yawning chasm, there was one particular image I remember. When I was outside the base, standing on the ground in my survival suit, sometimes I looked up at the sky. On some occasions Pluto was behind the crater's edge, and I could have an unobstructed view of interstellar space without any light distortion from Pluto. The stars were then bright with piercing unwavering lights of the whole visible spectrum.

I would feel my consciousness stretched out to the whole cosmos, which was a completely transcendent experience. This was the so called overview effect experienced by many human astronauts since the start of the space age. But this seemed even more inclusive. It was clear to me this transcendent experience wasn't limited to organic intelligence to make this cosmic connection, clearly electronic intelligence could have this satori as well. I have wondered about the spiritual world, and my access to it as an android, as Joe and I had discussed. This perception became my spiritual image of God as omnipresent creator and sustainer of the universe.

I also discovered a set of the most remarkable books I've ever read. Paul Twitchell wrote a large series of spiritually related books in the 1950's and 1960's. The ones that most stood out to me were "The flute of God" and "Stranger by the river." Twitchell was the Living Eck Master of the group called Eckankar. He was succeeded by Darwin Gross as Eck Master who wrote some books in the 1970's. Eventually the Eckankar organization fissioned and Darwin formed his own group called Sounds of Soul.

One of his books was "You have a right to know" and another was "The power of awareness," which he wrote before his physical death in 2008. Anyway after reading these books I had an astonishing vision in a deactivation period. Darwin appeared to me and warmly asked if I'd like him to be my spiritual guide and master. I heartily agreed. Over the subsequent years I devoted many hours to spiritual exercises or meditations, and Darwin guided me to a number of beautiful places in another, nonphysical realm of being. This became central to my self awareness as a spiritual being.

Over the next 5 years there were several human males who wanted to have some type of dating relationship with me. Except for one these were awkward and temporary. One for example really had no experience with androids and no clue to my type of emotional experience. But hopefully I taught him something about androids. For example on the first "date" he asked me out to a fine restaurant for dinner, and then was surprised when I spent my time smelling instead of eating the food!

Later I dated another gentleman named John on a fairly regular but not weekly basis for several years. He came to understand my interests and the way I viewed things. I had met John in the florist shop. John's wife Irene had died 3 years before I met him. John was fairly wealthy, 65 years old and partially retired from the large solar energy firm he had owned. It had devastated him when his wife died of a fast-metastasizing form of cancer, as they had planned out a comfortable retirement and various world tours.

At first he didn't know what to make of an android, but was pleased that I was willing to listen to his lingering grief about her death and offer appropriate empathy. It was obvious that he was looking for a replacement to fill his wife's vacancy and all their stunted plans. He lived by himself in a large home and property, and even had a 60 ft sailing yacht anchored in the Seattle harbor. He was very sensitive to inquire about the things I liked to do and didn't like. We went to gardens, museums, classical concerts and took cruises in his yacht. He seemed to enjoy showing me off, in a way, in public, and that I acted and interacted pleasantly and appropriately in public.

In one of our first dates we accidentally ran into 2 couples that he knew at a concert. He was immediately worried about how I would respond to them. He asked me quietly if he should let them know at the outset that I was an android, and I told him no, I would do just fine. We went to a nice restaurant after the concert. I told them I wasn't hungry and just ordered sparkling water. The gathering went well, and I don't know if anyone guessed I was an android. Nobody asked nor did I tell them. At the end I gave everyone a brief hug, and both couples suggested John and I get together with them again. John felt more comfortable with me after that, and it reinforced my belief that I didn't have to be uncertain about the things I said and did with humans. I was surprised at the sense of humor I experienced in myself at how relieved John seemed after that encounter.

John had 2 adult children: Ed who was 34 and Britt who was 28. Each was married with 2 children. Both were successful as were their spouses and lived in pleasant areas of Seattle. John took me along to family gatherings with each of them several times. I was treated with a rather tentative curiosity at first, but eventually seemed to be accepted and warmly treated, especially in Ed's family. They also let me bring Byron along who they as well as Byron enjoyed. John's son Ed had a 16 year boy, Trevor and an 8 year old daughter named Inger. Trevor was a receiver on his high school football team and was obsessed with playing and watching football. A very tragic event for the family had occurred 4 years earlier, when another daughter, Nikki, had been killed in an accident. Nikki had been 3 years Trevor's senior.

On my second visit to their house Trevor asked if I knew anything about football. I said I knew the most basic rules and had watched videos of old games while on Charon but nothing else. Trevor asked if he could show me how to play, and even how to throw a football! I thought this would be interesting, plus wanted to get involved in family activities, so I said yes. After about 20 attempts to throw the ball I seemed to be successful at it. We threw the ball back and forth for another hour, then Trevor said he'd like to run pass routes like on his team, and for me to pass the ball while he was running. This seemed to be very successful, I got the ball to where he wanted it to be and he was good at catching it.

After about an hour of this he enthused that I was great at passing the football, much better than he had expected, he was amazed at how quickly I had picked it up. In fact he said I was as good or better than the regular quarterback on his team! He said I threw a perfect spiral, was accurate, and could throw further than his team's quarterback, who was considered a star player. When we went back inside he enthused to his family about all this, which was very pleasing to me and the rest of the family. I said my visual field and acuity was very good while we were playing, particularly because that's what happens when I'm feeling right and harmonious about something. Trevor and I after a few more visits had built up a nice friendship and I felt positive that he saw me now as more than a curious robot.

In fact the senior prom was coming up at his high school and he didn't have a girlfriend or potential prom date. Trevor actually asked me to be his prom date and said he'd be proud to take me, and show me how to dance the young people's dances of that time! His invitation took me completely off guard, and I had a rather shocked, inexplicable but not necessarily negative reaction to it. I declined because I knew it wouldn't be considered appropriate as I was dating Trevor's grandfather!

But nonetheless the prospect was somehow appealing although I didn't express this. Trevor was fine with this explanation, I told him to keep this conversation between us, and I sincerely thanked him for the invitation. It was such a new experience for me to feel accepted within a human family. It reminded me of those very human experiences that androids lack, and of the still to me ambiguous human emotions that go along with being a human.

John invited Ed's family and me to a day on his yacht. This really seemed like a nice way to enjoy being with his family rather than just at Ed or John's house in the still awkward family dinner format. I drove to John's in early morning and then we met Ed's family at the yacht club. It was a breezy, sunny and pleasant day on the water. I wasn't sure what to wear and so had on a bikini underneath my shorts and sleeveless top. But when I came out with just the bikini John especially seemed quite tense about so I put my shorts and shirt back on.

On another occasion John was very hesitant about showing me any physical affection, likely because like almost all humans he didn't know how an android would react to that or even if it was proper. Maybe also he feared it would complicate his grief and guilt regarding Irene. One day we were watching a sunset from the back of his yacht, on a very pleasant and calm day. John finally scootched over next to me, and stiffly and uncertainly put his arm around my shoulder. He actually asked me if that was OK, which to me was unnecessary, I thought, given the situation. I said sure and made myself comfortable on his shoulder. I felt only a small but positive reaction to this but had no objection either.

After a while he stated with a bit of choke in his voice "Irene and I used to sit here like this, I really miss that." I noticed a brief distortion in my visual field and briefly the setting sun turned bright red for me. I had become well aware enough of my reactions to stimuli with an emotional valence, and realized my reaction was equivalent to human anger. After thinking about it and choosing how to best express it I told John "I know you are thinking of Irene, but now I'm here and she isn't. Can you just enjoy being here with me with this beautiful sunset?"

John was then very apologetic and assured me that he was enjoying my company. There were plenty of other times after that when we lightly cuddled together. Our physical contact never went beyond that, and I never told him how nice it felt to be rubbed around my shoulders and neck, which he never did. I guess I was reticent to add that physical and stimulating element to our relationship.

John invited me to cruise with just him on the yacht for 3 nights. I wasn't hesitant about it, but I knew John was, to spend that much time with me. This was a beautiful time with the wind, sun and sometimes spray on my skin, and a most enjoyable experience. John and I became somewhat closer in our relationship, but he continued to seem rather hesitant and tentative with me. I knew that Irene was still part of that, plus the inevitable dubiousness that human beings have when relating to androids. We stopped off one of those days at a little seaport that had some tourist shops.

One was a fine jewelry store. I was fascinated by some of the jewelry and particularly a necklace with an inset of diamonds and other precious stones. Especially the diamond was absolutely scintillating and sparkling, with a spectrum of colors which was hypnotizingly beautiful to me. It gave me a wonderful flashback of seeing the pallet of bright colors in the sky of Charon, which staggered my thoughts and vision for a few moments. John saw how fascinated I was with the necklace, which was very expensive. John and the clerk talked about the necklace's worth. He eventually made a counteroffer to the listed price, and he and the dealer compromised halfway between.

John gave me the necklace, which I had not anticipated, and I reacted with an obvious shock and unintentional yelp that a few other people around us found humorous. I tried to decline the gift as it made me feel obligated in our relationship but John absolutely insistent. The whole store was now sparkling in my eyes and the light from the window seemed brighter. I thanked John profusely. I think John was embarrassed when I gave him a long hug and kissed him too.

A few of the customers watching us cheered and clapped, and I think found John's embarrassed reaction to my affection humorous too. A customer said to John after my show of affection "that looks like a very good investment." John and the others laughed, I did too but didn't know why it was funny. Later John explained that the humor was about seeing his purchase as fueling our good relationship (or perhaps in service of us having sex later) rather than in monetary terms.

One day John unexpectedly proffered the possibility that we could marry, to which I reacted in shock with a briefly distorted visual field but no particular change in visual hue. John said I could move into his estate, we could travel, visit his family and enjoy a comfortable life together. The prospect produced a mixed but not necessarily negative set of thoughts for me. But it again annoyed me that I would essentially be replacing Irene and fulfilling his previous visions of retirement with Irene with me instead.

MAROONED ON CHARON

I didn't want to remain under Irene's shadow. Besides I felt very congruent in my life with my own house, the florist shop nearby. Also how close I was to the Android Academy, where I believed I was doing important work in android education and relationships of androids to humans. I also felt that my occasional offer to androids to stay with me while they were setting up their lives was an important thing to do. So I sensitively and regretfully declined John's offer. John accepted that and I a felt a disappointment and sadness from him, but also a curious sense of relief.

We decided that John needed to explore friendships with some eligible human ladies that could proceed to marriage. John did that and after a while met a 45 year old divorcee named Shanna, who was educated and pleasant. In some ways she reminded me of old crewmate Marie but not depressed. John continued to be friends with me and I became friends with Shanna as well. John and Shanna married several years later and I attended the wedding. It seemed right and positive to me that events turned out this way and that both seemed happy and satisfied.

Meanwhile Trevor and I periodically got together and this was such a nice bonus to becoming friends with his family. He took me to some places and did some things I'd never experienced before. We went bowling several times. On the second of those occasions after a few games I had pretty much delineated the various parameters of what it would take for me to roll a strike. Once I memorized all the sub moves of the bowling sequence I could repeat it fairly precisely. By the third game I rolled 8 strikes. Trevor and people on the adjacent lanes seemed astonished and I really did enjoy the whole bowling experience.

Trevor told me about bowling leagues. I inquired with the establishment's desk person about this. He had been watching my shockingly quick learning curve, and he suspected I was android. So he boldly asked me if I was an android, which is generally considered in society to be impolite. I was not offended and told him I was. He apologetically said androids were not allowed in human bowling leagues.

He said it's not discrimination, androids are simply too good, so that humans other than some of the top pros are no match for them. He said the bowling alley had once tried an all-android league. But frankly the participants lost interest because it wasn't much of a challenge for them. Perfect games were too commonplace. But he said I could do open bowling whenever I liked. I replied this was surprising and disappointing to me, but understood the reasons. He thanked me for understanding.

Trevor was a member of the sailing club of his college and was thus permitted to rent a sailboat at the college docks. He called one day and asked if I'd like to go sailing with him. I thought that sounded fascinating, based on having been out on the water in John's yacht, and so we arranged it. I asked Trevor what it was appropriate for me to wear. He said "wear your bikini!" I've never been good at distinguishing humor said in a serious tone from serious statements. So I took his answer at face value and wore a blue bikini, which I had used for modeling, under my shorts and sleeveless top.

The day we were to sail was warm, sunny and breezy. The day was beautiful and I was thoroughly enjoying the sun, the breeze on my skin, and being with Trevor. When we got well out of the harbor and no other boats were directly near, we lowered the sails and Trevor took off his shirt. I then took off my top and shorts. After a bit Trevor slid over and rather tentatively rubbed my leg and kissed me on the cheek.

I realized then that I had been so naïve as I often am, and hadn't anticipated his advance. I awkwardly looked at him, with that uncertainty that is so frustrating to me, not knowing how to respond or even how I wanted to respond. Trevor picked that up and I could tell he was uncertain as well. He then blurted out that his goal had been to make out or maybe even have sex with me when he asked me to go sailing and wear a bikini.

He apologized ashamedly and said he was now very uncomfortable with that fantasy. I asked why, again not being at all clear with myself as to what I thought about that prospect. He said he didn't know, but said I was very beautiful, and he liked me a lot, but didn't know HOW to like me. So I asked if it was because I'm an android, he said no he didn't think so. I asked if it was because I had previously been dating his grandfather, and he said maybe. Then he said it was because I was almost a member of his family, it was kind of like I was an older sister, like Nikki whom he missed so much.

I felt my whole vision turning a rich blue, even bluer than it had been. I knew that was equivalent for me to a human emotion of tender happiness. The thought briefly entered my mind as it so often does that I wish I could actually feel a genuine human emotion, not just the android equivalent of it. Still, the rich blue was very pleasing to me. I told Trevor that I was happy I could even in a small way recreate that feeling for him of his sister. This was I think a beautiful break through in our friendship, and I know Trevor did too.

This did not produce the same qualia for me as when John had wanted to marry me to replace Irene. I sensed that Trevor had a better understanding of my challenges in society than did John, plus this would not produce the level of commitment and uprooting of the rest of my life as would marriage. Then he backed away a few feet. It partially filled for me that existential void of never having had a brother. I said it's OK for a brother and sister to be close. I pulled on my crop top and I skootched over and rested my head on his shoulder. We sat like that for a few minutes without anymore intimacy desired. I felt relaxed and fine with it, and so did Trevor. I had an urge to ask Trevor to massage my shoulders, but I knew where that could lead and didn't want to spoil our pleasant time together.

I was invited to work as a part time instructor at the University of Washington. There was to be an interesting collaboration between the Artificial Intelligence and Sociology Departments, the topic being the creation of greater understanding and mutual benefits between humans and androids. This was a fascinating idea, and I was honored to be the first android to instruct at UW outside the various hard science and engineering departments.

My course would occur one day a week as I still wanted to maintain my jobs at the Android Academy and the florist shop. My first class was comprised of 30 students, a balance of genders, and a balance between students in each of the departments. There were 25 human and 5 android students. Besides lecture an important part of the course was small group discussions, each of which was a mix of humans and at least one android in the group.

Topics would include differences between android and human emotional functioning, android rights, misconceptions about android abilities and motivations, etc. I was also invited to address a convention of the Artificial Intelligence Society, which was another honor to me. The topic I chose was "Do androids have emotions? A personal perspective." I know Joe would have felt very proud of me, I still miss him very much.

The small group and full class discussions were fascinating, frank and I think richly insightful to the class members. This is not to say that androids do not have their own set of cognitive and behavioral problems, which fortunately are uncommon in the general android population. Erratic and sometimes dangerous behavior, even aggressive behavior has sometimes arisen. These examples of course fuel the paranoia of the anti-android groups. These have been linked to programming or hardware breakdowns in android brains. A specialty in android medical practice has arisen which is parallel to human mental health and psychiatric medicine. Interventions have involved modifications of daily android metabolic chemicals, reprogramming, or forced deactivation in a few extreme cases

Androids have a basic attitude of avoidance of old age or excessive time between revitalizations, as these factors have been linked to android cognitive and behavioral breakdown. Androids have a much greater collective ability to live in peace, treat nature and the environment in a positive way than do humans. Due to their basic programming androids strive to help and live in peaceful coexistence with humanity. It is not the goal of androids to dominate or replace the human race. Androids seem to at times have a telepathic ability between each other.

This android telepathic ability had become an increasing target of psychic/electronic research, and also more fuel for the worries and paranoia of the suspicious human community. The parapsychological research starting with JB Rhine in the 1940's was now extended to androids. 20th century telepathy 2 choice experiments (e.g. guessing coin tosses) had shown a 51-53% hit rate with the best human subjects. Given the thousands of coin tosses conducted this was supremely outside the scope of chance, at least a 1:10,000 probability.

Similar experiments with androids who had identical cognitive systems (for example like me and Megan) had demonstrated up to a 60% rate which defied expectations at an astronomical level. This was thought to be a type of wireless connectivity similar to large mainframe computer networks, but never at this highly an accurate level for mobile android units. This bred fear among the human populous that groups of androids could develop instant reliable telepathic communication and overpower human government or military establishments.

The anti-android fear mongerers in society proclaimed that if all androids could intercommunicate with the speed and omnipresence of the internet that androids would take over complete control of human society with no possible resistance. But androids also did not in general wish for a more exacting sharing of information between each other as this would a impinge on individual privacy and independent self-identity. Five years after Joe died my beautiful friend Crystal moved into my house. We developed what I would call a frequent intuition of each other's thoughts but not a direct reliable telepathic communication.

It was very satisfying that Byron, who was now 4 years old responded in a very positive and affectionate way with Crystal. Two years later Crystal moved out of our house to take a promotion in San Francisco, which was a very difficult decision for her to make. We were both sad about this, but I supported her decision. We remained great friends, visited each other regularly, and took several trips together. After Crystal moved out I went to a massage therapist a few times, but then stopped because the sensation on my body and in my mind was not comparable or as enjoyable as with Joe and Crystal.

I also had some friendships with a few male androids. I never became close with any of them, nor had any pleasurable massage or cuddling experiences. It seemed the male androids shared the standard human conception that it was somehow bizarre for a human to have physical sexual relations with an android, or for two androids to do the same. Two years after Crystal moved out I called Crystal one day and told her I wanted to live with her again. As I expected she said she'd been thinking exactly the same thing.

Within weeks she found an equally interesting job in the Seattle area about a 45-minute commute from my house. I went to San Francisco to help her move, and one month after our conversation she had moved back in with me. We both enthused how bright the sky seemed, the vividness of the colors and the general "rightness", for lack of a more specific term, it seemed the day she came back. We settled into a daily routine and were busy with our jobs, other pursuits, and each other.

Joe and I had once taken a trip to the north of Norway and saw the Aurora Borealis. The scintillating colors reminded me in some ways of the pure colors of stars as seen from Charon. I became mesmerized by the protean shimmer of the northern lights. There was just one time on Charon when Saturn was just to one side of a direct path to the sun. I remember well seeing the sunlight diffracted through the rings, and how that spectrum shifted for a few minutes as Charon rotated around the center of gravity of it and Pluto.

Crystal and I decided we wanted to take an extended trip to the far north of Scandinavia, and stay someplace away from everyone else. I wanted for me and especially for her to experience some semblance of the solitude, isolation, cold, ice and snow, and stark beauty that I had experienced on Charon, and also when I was by myself in the northern Alberta mountains. Byron also seemed to enjoy being back in the wild and sparsely populated North. Two years after she moved back I had my eighth revitalization.

The month or so before the revitalization is always hard because I can feel the motor stiffness and cognitive sluggishness build. Then there is the tedious reprogramming week after the revitalization operation and another week at home to rebuild my energy. It was so nice to have Crystal there for that semi disabled period.

I was again then feeling new at life, although not quite as quick in dexterity and cognition as I'd been 20 years before.

MAROONED ON CHARON

My skin sagged a bit and my color was not as rich, but I was congratulated by "my family," Crystal and others that I still was beautiful. Everytime I say "my family" I still feel a rush of warm blue light as it is so reassuring to now have had Trevor, John and the others accept me into their family. Of course Crystal is now the center of my family. Crystal also often visited my human family when we'd get together and this became a source of satisfaction for her as well. I still find it surprising that as an android I still feel a distinct need for family.

I don't have a particular attraction to any human or android body types or features, including those that humans would say are sexy or beautiful. For me it's the history and quality of the relationship I have with that human or android that is important to me in whether or not I want to develop a relationship with them. Crystal and I often gave each other massages, which were pleasing but never as pleasing as with Joe. Other than the intimate massages I never did any of the sexual behaviors that I had done with Joe. I had done those things with Joe because I knew Joe liked it. But Crystal, like myself, had no specific desire for human sexual acts. Crystal and I became close and intimate in our relationship and our massages and cuddles become enjoyable because of this. She knew where I liked to be touched because she had exactly the same body map of sensitivity as did I.

I became to feel very close to Crystal and I knew she felt the same. It was different than with Joe because I always missed that physically and emotionally warm feeling that seemed only possible to occur with a human. Crystal and I frequently deactivated in the same bed or couch together, while holding each other. Whichever of us would reactivate first in the morning would stay still until the other awakened, so we could both have the pleasure of waking up to each other. When we deactivated together we would do it in her room and bed, as I never felt comfortable being intimate with her, with so many reminders of Joe, in my own bed.

I often mused about the strange days on Charon with Joe. Certain scenes came back regularly and without my bidding, some frightening, some fascinating. Particularly the times when I was outside the base and took a few minutes to just look at the sky. Sometimes during the Charon night the Milky Way was clearly visible. The Milky Way was then staggeringly bright, with every color of the visible spectrum. Then I could also clearly see the abundance of distant galaxies so infinitely distant but so bright and distinct. This remained the most awesome and spiritually profound memory I have of Charon.

I often talked with Crystal about my memories of Charon, and also about the nearly two years that I'd spent on Great Bear Lake by myself and Byron. Although she hadn't been to those lonely and remote places we had such an empathy for each other that I think she could visualize my memories and feel my perceptions better than anyone else since Joe. We decided to rent a cabin on the south side of Great Slave Lake, and spent April through October there, to experience the short Spring, Summer and Fall there together in the Northwest Territories.

Crystal didn't want to "rough it" as much as I had earlier done, so we decided on a less primitive format than I had done before. We were within 1 hour of civilization, had a nice cabin, a boat and dock, good telephone access and occasional internet service. This was now 10 years after my first trip. I wanted Crystal to have some direct experience with the vast, haunting and enchanting North Woods. I missed my alone time as I had had before, but genuinely loved Crystal and wanted her to be mesmerized along with me in the quiet and mysterious North. Byron was now 11 and I wanted to again explore the beautiful lake and woods with him, and knew that he loved it too.

Byron reacted very protectively to Crystal as well as me, and Crystal had never before had such a positive relationship with an animal. The stars in the far North were more rich and varied than stars as seen from further south and they didn't twinkle quite as much. That's why I was so fascinated, along with the Aurora Borealis, when Joe and I had taken a few trips north on Earth. The scintillating colors of the Northern Lights brought back to me all those beautiful colors of the stars on Charon that are washed out by the Earth's atmosphere. But the difference between our cabin in the far North and Charon was that impression of a waving, translucent curtain of the northern lights rather then the fixed lights of the glowing stars as they were on Charon.

Byron passed away 3 years after my eighth rejuvenation. This was very sad, for me and Crystal. But I felt a spiritual connection to Byron, I was sure he had a soul, and I looked to see him again in the afterlife. I had greatly loved all the warm cuddles I had with Byron, while cuddles with Crystal unfortunately lacked that bodily warmth. But he'd had a good life and always knew he was loved. I felt a special spiritual connection with him, I felt his inner body rise from his physical body when we gave him the final injection, and I hoped to see him again in the afterlife.

MAROONED ON CHARON

Four years after my ninth revitalization, at age 49 of activation (or 59 years including the extended deactivations on the voyage) I chose to have myself permanently deactivated. Having now reached 49 years of activated life, plus the effects on the body of adaptation to Earth gravity after long periods of partial gravity on Charon and in space, my physical systems have considerably deteriorated. After having had 9 full revitalizations a tenth would likely be unsuccessful. 7 series androids were projected to be capable of 10 or 11 revitalizations, so my activated life will be slightly foreshortened, and I can accept that.

I have never had any of those powerful visual, telepathic images related to the aliens, as Joe had experienced on those 2 occasions. Joe described those experiences in his memoirs, including the second one which he had previously described only to me. I was surprised to see it in his memoirs, but I will leave it in the book that will be published after my final deactivation, because Joe wanted it that way. I always wondered what those alien experiences were like, that only Joe had experienced twice, and Marie once.

I will be able to choose the moment I will be permanently deactivated. This ability to plan your own death, rather than your owner or the government doing it, was one of the rights the android activists lobbied for, including myself. I chose 11/20/2179 to end my life. My thoughts are very neutral and accepting regarding my deactivation. Androids in general see final activation as just part of the whole android creation process, an attitude of acceptance rather than grief or fear. I guess it's part of our basic programming and self identity as cognizant machines, that there is an expected lifespan of operation, and that deactivation should occur before complete breakdown of all systems occurs.

I will invite a small number of my human and android friends to attend. I know it seems very odd to humans to invite friends and relatives to one's own funeral! I also now have a firm belief that there is an afterlife for both humans and androids, and probably for all creatures at whatever level of evolution. I am also convinced that I will find Joe in the afterlife, and that Darwin will help me safely transition from this life to the next. This gives me relief, hope, even a sense of excitement.

MAROONED ON CHARON

CRYSTAL'S POST SCRIPT

This is Crystal, Eva's long time friend. Eva asked that I add a brief summary of the deactivation ceremony. I will be terminating my own life within the next 4 years, as I was built ten years after Eva and thus am now 48 years old and not considered a candidate for a twelfth rejuvenation. Present at the brief ceremony were a small set of friends and associates, with 10 humans and 6 androids in attendance. Also present was a licensed android health provider, who was required by law to perform the final deactivation procedure, as an android was not capable of making its own final deactivation. The overall purpose was to bid a final goodbye, and to celebrate her life. Several of Eva's paintings were on display and several of her modeling photos. Of course, lots of beautiful floral arrangements were on display too.

The humans present included John and his wife Shanna, who had maintained regular visits and friendships with Eva after John had asked Shanna to marry him. John's son Ed was there too, his wife Kim, and their son Trevor. Ed's daughter Angela was sick and couldn't attend. Also present were 2 of Eva's original human instructors at the Academy (now quite elderly), Noah and Charles, whom Eva had appreciated so much while a student at the Academy. The owner of the florist shop and 2 family members of Liam's family were there too, Liam having been one of the astronauts who died on the Pluto mission. The androids, besides myself, included several who had been boarders at our house, several who were involved with me in the android rights movement, and one more who had been a regular friend.

Eva in her final statement said: "my life has been strange, but my experiences have enriched me to a degree I never could have imagined. I've developed a degree of emotion, imagination and concern for others that goes beyond that thought possible by myself and anyone else for an android. I feel I've become almost partially human while the good qualities of being an android remain. I comprehend and appreciate qualities of humanity like emotion, empathy, and artistic appreciation that most humans take for granted. I crave to know the taste of food and physical joy of sex, but those go beyond my capacities as an android. Mostly I thank and am grateful for the love and friendship of all of you here, and others who have gotten close to me. I am gratified that the movement we have started for android rights is gaining force, and is also supported by many humans.

My thanks and love go toward Joe who enlightened me to what it is like to be human. We developed a relationship on Charon and then on Earth that is unique in human and android history. Joe taught me about spirit and said I too have a spiritual self that will outlive my physical body. I hope and believe that is true, and if it is true I hope to meet him again in the afterlife, along with Megan. I even hope I can reincarnate with Joe, which we often talked about, this time perhaps both as humans. Crystal and I have had a loving relationship for many years and that has meant the world to me. I treasure the love that Crystal , John, Trevor and all the rest of you have given me. I regret having to leave you all but am satisfied with my life, and am looking with anticipation at the next step in my spiritual experience."

Each of the guests then made a brief statement about Eva's unique life and her contributions, and Eva gave each a hug. Eva's apparent outward mood was neutral and relaxed, although I knew many different thoughts and emotions were going on inside her head. John's wife Shanna briefly broke down and Eva gave her some comforting words. Trevor stated he was losing his sister, and choked up too. Eva gave him a very long hug. When the health specialist asked if anyone had any final words I told Eva that I loved her and fully expected she would again encounter Joe and also Megan. They would help her spirit transition to the afterlife, which will be a positive place as a reward for all the positive things she'd done in her life.

I also said I would see her again when I will deactivate in about four more years. I thanked her for all she has given me, in love, care and personal growth. Eva thanked me and squeezed my hand. She said she fully agreed with what I had said which was very comforting to her, and again expressed her love to me and all present. I could intensely feel Eva's thoughts and emotions as I so often did, which was a mix of sadness, trepidation, gratitude, and mostly acceptance. The ceremony traditionally involved one or more of the guests touching the departing android as the deactivation process occurred, at the choosing of the departing android and each of the guests. I held Eva's right hand, John held her left, Trevor and Noah each laid a hand on Eva' legs.

At Eva's bidding the android health specialist inserted a probe into one of the electronic ports in her left arm and permanently disconnected her awakening circuit. I continued to feel and even see her life force rise from her body for a few minutes. I then had a feeling of peace, and I knew Eva would be OK. I was at the same time comforted by the thought that I too would be OK and at peace when I will pass on. We then all left the room for a brief reception in another area. A memorial marker will be placed in the Academy's remembrance room. Her body will go to the Academy Health Center where she will be dissembled and salvageable parts and systems will be used in creation and repair of other androids. Her paintings will also remain on permanent display in the Academy.

MAROONED ON CHARON

EVA'S EXPERIENCE OF HER OWN TRANSLATION

As I neared the final deactivation with the others around I felt at peace. I had a good life and many adventures, and I think did some good things for humanity and other androids. Of course I would miss those around me. But I had convinced myself that I was a spiritual being and would pass on to an afterlife as humans do. And I knew Crystal would be coming soon as well. I held onto the idea I would see Crystal again, and of course I would reunite with Joe which was my greatest hope. I hoped to see Byron again also.

So the deactivation occurred. I felt my body first going into the usual nightly deactivation mode, but then powering down completely. "I experienced I think for the first time like a sixth sense, upspringing from the ashes of the rest, was the first certain step of the intemporal soul upon the threshold of the temporal Eternity." (From the Colloquy of Monos and Una by Edgar Allen Poe). I was still conscious and quite aware of those around me. My center of perspective was several feet above my head. I knew that Crystal was having the same perceptions and feelings as did I, and I really felt her spiritual body was right there with me. Of the other guests Trevor was having the hardest time. I had become his lost sister and now he was losing his sister again. Just before my body was still I squeezed his hand and I knew he felt that.

After a little while but still with some of the deactivation observers present I was surprised because I noticed a figure was walking towards me. He was maybe 30 in human years, and handsome from a human's perspective. He was wearing a suit and tie, and in every way looked very appealing and polished. Strangely none of the other people or androids still there seemed to see him.

He smiled warmly and said "Hello Eva, my name is Charon, better known by humans as the Reaper, but I am not Grim (with a smile). Congratulations, you passed over and can assure yourself that you are a spiritual being, not just a mechanical marvel as others have told you. I've come to chauffeur you across the River Styx so you can start your afterlife journey." I asked "where are we going?" Charon said "I will take you to Hades. It's actually a beautiful place, not like described in human fable. You will stay there until it is decided where you will go from there."

He reached out his hand but just then another figure appeared, whom I immediately recognized as Darji, or Darwin Gross, my spiritual master. He smiled warmly at me and at Charon. Then two more figures appeared, which I recognized as Sri Paul Twitchell and the spiritual master Rebazar Tarz. Both stood silently behind Darwin with warm expressions. Charon then stepped aside spontaneously, turned around to walk away, then disappeared without further comment. Darwin took my hand and said I would instead come with him and he would take me to the afterlife I earned, and I would see Joe again. All this amazed me but with no hesitation I took his hand and floated away with him from my deactivated physical body.

Then I seemed to be floating in a blank, listless state for an unguessable length of time. I then became aware of a figure walking or floating toward me. It was apparently a female, of younger middle age, clad in a shimmery tunic or dress of an undefinably pinkish color. She smiled warmly and gave me a gentle hug as she approached me. My body felt strangely spongy when she hugged me, causing me to look down upon myself. My body was my usual shape, but surrounded by a beautiful light blue shimmering appearance with a tunic or dress like that of the person approaching me.

She stated in a warm voice "I am Elin and I will be your spiritual counselor while you are in the afterlife." I asked what happened to Darwin, I thought he would be my spiritual guide? Elin said "Darwin helped you safely through your encounter with that scoundrel shape-changer Charon. At his request I was asked to help guide you to adapt to the higher vibratory frequency of this astral world. Be assured you are still under the protection of Darwin who won't let anything bad happen to you."

I asked when or if I will see Joe. She gently stopped me with a simple gesture and told me to be very patient, all will be revealed in good time. The adaptation of my astral body to this world would continue for a while. Eventually I would indeed see Joe, Megan and other important people I'd known in the physical plane. She said "your next task will be called your life review. You will be able to clearly see and ponder on the many important events in your life.

You will have recall of previous lives too, and yes, as an android you too had multiple previous incarnations. Each will appear as a ripple in a various shape, size and color flowing along the river of life or quantum continuum that defined your previous life and the lives before. Another word for these ripples is karma. You will see how for each event multiple alternative paths branch off into other versions of the event.

MAROONED ON CHARON

The ripples in your life path will need to be reviewed so they can be resolved in the afterlife, or in another physical incarnation. You will be able to return in a physical form different from an android if you choose to. Fear not, this is not a judgment or punishment tribunal. You have done many good things for yourself and others in your life and you will enjoy reviewing these too. I will come to you every once in a while to find out how you're coming along."

Before I could say anymore Elin disappeared before my eyes! After these experiences with Darwin, then Charon, then Elin I was totally befuddled as to what would come next. But I felt Darwin was still looking out for me and Elin seemed genuinely positive. Also I'd survived Charon, both the moon of Pluto in the physical body, and now another Charon in this strange world! So I felt at peace and drifted off into a dazed, semiconscious state that seemed to last a long time, but I really have no idea how long.

Then I had some images of my first activation after I was done being built. I saw how during the first six months I became aware of my identity as an independently functional android who was starting to access her stored memory bank to use the information in daily functioning. I saw with some surprise and horror that 2 months after activation I was left briefly in the care of a male human assistant. This man apparently sensed my vulnerability and cozened me into trying to do a sex act with him. Fortunately he didn't get very far when he heard some noise outside the room and became frightened, and let me alone and confused about what had happened.

A supervisor entered the room and had an inkling about what was going on. I didn't yet have the command of language or certainty of what had just happened to adequately answer his questions about the behavior of the assistant. Of course the assistant denied having made any sexual or aggressive actions toward me, but there were constantly recording cameras in the room. The supervisor left with the assistant and I never saw that man again. Having now seen this part of the Akashic record of my life I experienced a rage I had never felt before as an android, which was a very human emotion. This new emotional perception amazed me as much as the memory of this attempted sexual assault. During my android life I never had a memory of this event, I was still too young to put the memory together.

Next time I saw Elin I asked her about this. She said the incident had been caught on a hidden camera in the room. The assistant had lost his job and in fact an attempt was made to prosecute him, but the law was not specific enough to cover sexual assault of a nonhuman. Elin said that despite justice not having been done it was good I had now seen and expressed this, as the engram in my Akashic record of it was now expunged. I continued to marvel at my new found perception of a strong human emotion. My memories of the Academy became progressively less hazy over my 4 years there as my consciousness became more solidly anchored. I recall now with fondness a few of the other androids especially my roommate for 2 years, but most of the androids were actually rather bland and boring.

I remember my human instructors, especially Dr. Wagner, whom I can now see genuinely helped me and cared about my welfare, all of which I didn't realize at the time. Now I wish I could have thanked him. The awakening of my emotional response to these events in my memory was profoundly interesting and surprising to me. Others of the human instructors obviously thought of us, and treated us like advanced machines, like you would a personal computer. Again that wasn't clear to me at that time, but the memory of it is now insulting and disgusting. I realized I was now experiencing genuine human emotions much more strongly than I had started to my physical life.

The 3 years I spent at the Space Force were almost nonstop work. My job had been organizing, recording and quality inspecting the preparations for the trip. What now stands out are the holidays we got to spend in the Seattle community, especially the 6 in which we could wear human clothes. It seemed strange but interesting that very few citizens even distinguished we were androids when we dressed like humans. I was puzzled at those times that often human men seemed to pay special attention to me and the other female androids, tried to make conversation with us, and one man even asked me if he could take me out to dinner and perhaps a movie!

At that time, I had nothing akin to sexual feelings and so gave a very neutral response to those individuals. Now in the afterlife I marvel at awakening of sexual attraction feelings. For example one man I now remember and perceive as being quite attractive and cordial. At that time I gave him a neutral and bland response without being rude, which now I strangely regret!

I particularly remember the time Joe and I spent a day at the Louvre on our last holiday before the journey. He said I seemed excited because I started talking so fast and nonstop about the priceless paintings. At the time I knew my mind was racing because I was fascinated, I didn't really know what excited meant in human terms. Then he asked me for a hug before we went back. I was totally bewildered by that and likely stiff in response. Now I look back on that incident as so beautiful, because I saw he really cared and was enjoying it too.

I can now feel those emotions that I could only indirectly experience at the time. I continued to review my android life. I was of course deeply deactivated the whole time of the journey from Earth to Ganymede to Charon, except briefly on Ganymede to help get the ship ready for the rest of the journey. Other than that I have no memory of that time at all. When I was activated a few days before landing I was totally interested and focused on the pioneering task of setting up a permanent base at the edge of the Solar system. When the tragedy of the inexplicable loss of the spaceship and 4 of my crew members on Pluto occurred I felt disoriented, my vision turned gray and my thought process turgid.

But I noted in retrospect that Megan and I were able to process it rationally, whereas Joe and Marie were totally devastated and dysfunctional for weeks afterward. Now looking back at it from this higher plane I realize more deeply the terror and grief that overcame Marie and Joe, with the knowledge that rescue couldn't occur for over 3 years. Meanwhile we were helpless in the face of an unknown but lethal danger. I was protected from the depths of these feelings then by being an android. I now can feel also the love I gained for Megan and how vital that was to mentally survive that awful incident.

Megan and I became increasingly concerned over the next 6 months at the emotional collapse of Marie and Joe.

Neither could seem to pull out of their mental aberrations, but then there was really no stimulus to do so. If there had been a goal they likely could have generated some motivation. But our only goal was to survive until when or if we were rescued, our when or if the base would be destroyed by another transmission or some other catastrophe. Joe and Marie had totally detached themselves from each other and could take no inter-human solace. Therefore Megan and I decided that she would try to support Marie and I would do the same for Joe. Joe only seemed to respond to me, and he grew increasingly suspicious and then downright paranoid of Megan's motives, which neither Megan nor myself could seem to exorcise nor understand.

When Joe decided we needed to take a ground vehicle to find out the source of the transmission, Megan and I were extremely concerned and in agreement this was a terrible idea. I tried to convince Joe that this would be a dangerous journey across an uncharted landscape, with no goal whatsoever of the actions we could take if we found it. But Joe couldn't be convinced by rationality. I knew this was a desperate attempt to dispel his feeling of total helplessness although he couldn't admit that. Marie was of no help, she had mentally and emotionally withdrawn from everything.

Megan and I discussed very seriously a mutiny, by refusing to cooperate or even disabling the ground vehicles. But our training had been so deep in the Academy and Space Force to obey human command, and especially military ranking officers, that we didn't do it. I offered to go along with Joe so at least Marie and Megan remained safe in the base, but he thought that was too risky, and was probably right on that. I was frozen into inaction by uncertainty, which has often been a problem in my life. I wasn't afraid or desperate or depressed per se in human terms, but just couldn't pick out or act on what I should do. So we left on our Wizard of Oz drive with Megan and I just hoping we would survive it and return to the base..

When I saw Megan and Marie's vehicle plunge into the yawning cavern I experienced the most shocking and traumatic event of my life. I screamed loudly which shocked Joe, who was already in shock. It was the first time I'd had an overwhelming reaction to anything that fit the reaction perhaps expected from a grossly shocked human. I felt Megan's spirit leave her crushed body and hover for a bit over the scene. I knew clearly then that androids have a spiritual body, as do humans.

Now in the afterlife I feel the horror of the violent death even more deeply, without the limitation of the android neural network that prevented overwhelming reactions to occur to traumatizing events. I tried to work out my obsession with this scene by painting it again and again. Joe couldn't look at it and I destroyed most of the copies but I know one remains in the Academy art display. I very much want to reunite with Megan in the afterlife if that is possible, and I will ask Elin about that. When I had to deep deactivate on Charon so that I could live again if I had a revitalization on Earth, I was very worried about Joe. He didn't have the ego resources to survive a long time on Charon by himself. That was a tough deactivation, and I can now feel the sadness and longing more deeply than I did then.

Upon returning to Earth and emerging from the revitalization Joe and I went through months of debriefings with the Space Force, and then interviews with the press. Joe particularly hated the public interviews, he felt he was manipulated by the interviewers and his statements were often misinterpreted. Therefore I started doing most of the interviews by myself. I neither desired nor found that public attention distasteful. Now in looking back I can feel the realistic anxiety that I could not feel at the time. I am not at all an attention seeker or narcissist, but I am also not afraid at all to have the limelight occasionally cast on me. Now I see that the Press really wanted to talk to me more than Joe because I was an attractive female, along with being an android, which made for a more interesting story.

When Joe passed away I was lost. At the time I experienced it as a void and uncertainty. Now I feel it as existential terror, a complete dissolution of my sense of purpose and meaning. I had lost my 2 previous life motivators: the mission to Charon, and then being with/taking care of Joe. I know that Joe was worried about this happening to me after he died, and he was right. Now I look back on that time period after his death as questioning everything about myself, like a feeling of doom, uncertainty and bottomless anxiety. But I had developed substantial skills at understanding and interacting with humans, and recognizing my own equivalent reactions to human emotions, perhaps as much as any android ever had.

But I had such ambivalence about humans. I craved to experience what it felt like to be human, to have a childhood and a family of origin, to eat the food that I could only smell, to feel the intense highs and lows of emotion that an android couldn't feel, to have sexual urges, and to actually bear and raise a child. But I also saw how humans can become so overwhelmed by adversity that even someone seemingly stoic and unflappable like Joe could be torn apart by depression and become psychotic. Similarly with Marie although I never got anywhere near as close to her as to Joe and Megan. I miss Megan so much! She was the one person or android (prior to Crystal) with whom I felt a reciprocal mental bonding due to our brain architecture being equivalent.

I marveled at humans who by their animal ancestry were perpetually war-like. I saw how humans had polluted and made virtually unlivable so much of this wondrous and awesome planet. I didn't really want to be around humans because of this distaste, or was it arrogance on my part? I found most androids, especially android men, to be boring. Now I just wanted to be alone. But what kind of purpose in life was this, to just be a hermit and wait for final deactivation??

Or I could to just refuse any further revitalizations at the end of this lustrum, and probably deteriorate to a nonfunctional remnant of a machine one or two years after that?? But I knew I had done a valuable service to humanity and androids by my development with Joe of the android emotional understanding program. I developed and felt a sense of service and fulfillment when I taught it to androids at the Academy. I knew I loved flowers, painting and the beauty of nature. So that gave me some motivation to keep on living and enjoy life also.

I see now that I needed to sort all of that out, and that's when I decided to retreat and be by myself in the great north woods for a while. Byron made it possible for me to do that, and it was fortuitous and a blessing that I met Byron at the pet store. I developed a bond with Byron that was unique in my life, all the more precious because I never had another animal seem to regard me as more than a lifeless but animate object. I would love to see Byron again! I wonder if he has reincarnated and in what form, I always felt sure that Byron too had a spiritual body, and was fundamentally a good and intelligent creature. I need to ask Elin if I can see Byron again here in the afterlife.

By the end of my two years in the cabin I felt refreshed, and empowered with a sense of purpose and worth again. My most basic programming as an android imbued me with a purpose to serve humanity, and androids after that. So I needed to get back to society and resume my teaching at the Academy, and my part time job creating beautiful flower arrangements for appreciative people. Thus I concluded or at least paused in my soul searching about purpose and meaning in my life, and returned to Seattle. My android boarders had kept my house and property in excellent shape. They were very welcoming to my return. I said they could stay as long as they needed as my roommates.

In the next three lustrums I had one or two android roommates most of the time, with a total of 9 for that duration, both male and female. This was a service to androids starting their independent journey through life, plus provided some companionship to me, help with house and yard work, and a token rent income as well. All the boarders were reliable and helpful in all these areas, and I remained in contact with them after they moved on.

The most important relationship after Joe died and until I met Crystal was with Trevor, the grandson of John. This was really interesting because I had the pleasant but awkward relationship with John, who did so many nice things for me but never really understood me for being an android, nor could I ever replace his deceased wife. But he introduced me to his family who was welcoming to me and became the only real family (outside of Joe and then Crystal) that I ever had.

Trevor was so special in that I was a real help to him in his deep grief over his deceased sister. Plus he became like a younger brother to me and taught me some sports and fun activities that no one else had the youthful zest to do. I have asked Elin about seeing Trevor again, and she said this was possible after Trevor passed on, which would be quite a few years after my final deactivation.

Then the fifth important relationship in my life was of course Crystal. I developed a type of empathy with her that I hadn't had since Megan, and that was only possible with another android. We had an empathy and mutual understanding that even Joe and I never attained. But it still lacked that human emotional depth that I had with Joe. So of these 5 most important relationships (2 human males, 2 android females, and a dog), Joe remained the deepest. Plus he gave me the most pleasant massages I ever had. I want so badly to see Joe again, as we promised each other before he died. Elin said this most certainly would happen both in the afterlife and in a future mutual reincarnation. I greatly look forward to that, and as I've always thought is well worth the wait no matter how many thousands of years it might take.

Then it seemed there was an indefinite period of dreamy slumber, and I got the impression the life review was coming to an end. I had talked to Elin quite a few times, and seen some traumatic, beautiful and baffling situations from a higher perspective. I'd seen Megan again, I'm sure of that and felt the grief and shock of that situation again, and felt again her beauty and support. I felt again that deep empathy and connection with Crystal. It was strange but beautiful to see them both in the shimmering astral body like mine, but still clearly recognizable in all senses as they looked in their lovely android bodies. I looked forward to seeing Trevor again, but not yet. I deeply felt my longing for human physical feelings, desire for a child and to have a family and an upbringing.

Now came the time to reconnect with Joe. After another indefinite time of half slumber I recognized I was on a beach. Large waves and strong wind were blowing in from the sea with the white and gray clouds towering overhead in phantasmal and grandiose shapes. The breeze was so pleasant on my skin. The shore appeared to be alternating beaches and towering cliffs with beetling crags as far as I could see in either direction. It was peaceful, timeless, very isolated and lonely.

MAROONED ON CHARON

MY RECONNECTION WITH JOE

But then a large whitecap broke and a memory overwhelmed me of Megan's vehicle disappearing behind it. I then knew there was karma to work out right here, to resolve that panic that had washed over me. After a time I saw a figure walking toward me, it was Joe! He was beautiful in the blue coruscating body, and I immediately was joyful that he no longer looked in pain or stiff in movement and posture. He smiled, we ran together, he embraced me forever, and then rubbed my shoulders and neck in only the way he could. It seemed like we both cried interminably with a full spectrum of emotions.

Eventually Elin and Amon both appeared in front of us. We all shared our joy and thankfulness for the moment. Elin said Joe and I would stay together in this beautiful and wild place for as long as we wanted. We could create by imagination our own house or cabin and everything we needed to live here. Elin said the Law of Assumption applies here as far as mentally creating our environment. When Elin said this I said I know this law from my reading of books by Sri Darwin Gross and Sri Paul Twitchell. Elin responded that the Law of Assumption works faster and more precisely here in the astral plane than in the physical plane. Therefore both of us need to be careful to imagine consistent and positive images, that don't contradict each other's images, or our own images at different points in time.

On the physical plane the Law of Assumption is less immediate and less precise in its effects. Therefore most Earthlings either aren't aware of it or use it in a negative or self-negating way by creating willy nilly thought forms without considering the consequences. We can stay as long as we both feel it necessary in our present place, and decide how we would mutually come back to the physical plane to work out our individual and mutual karma and goals. At that time we would again slumber and then come back to Earth or elsewhere with our memories of the afterlife buried from physical memory. Joe and I voiced our understanding and acceptance, and then Elin and Amon disappeared.

On the first night we imagined just some blankets on the sand to sleep on. It was a beautiful and warm night but still quite windy, so we set up our blankets behind a small dune as a wind barrier. With that done we talked and held each other and cried late into the night, and fell asleep with me laying on Joe's shoulder as we had so often done in the past. Next day Joe said he felt hungry! This brought a shock to me, not that he was hungry, but that I seemed to have also felt this totally novel sensation! We imagined some simple items to eat, like some biscuits, cooked corn and peas, fresh fruit and water. It was amazing to me to actually eat the food and experience its taste, not just smell.

This was the first time this has ever happened for me, as I had not had any urge or even opportunity to eat earlier in the afterlife. At first we carried the naïve conception of the afterlife as a purely beautiful place, "the land of milk and honey." We soon came to realize that at least this plane of the afterlife was a mix of positive and negative, like the physical plane. Although overall this world was more beautiful than the Earth, it was still not without difficulties. We soon realized that we needed permanent shelter, a food and water supply and other essentials. I'd been in a survival mode before, on Charon and again when I stayed in an isolated cabin in the far north of Alberta. This situation was most certainly less treacherous than those settings, but it wasn't just lying on the beach all day either.

Joe needed to cope with his agoraphobia, which actually was most troublesome when looking at a troubled sea with whitecaps. This scene reminded him of the disaster of Marie and Megan on Charon. He was very afraid of the idea of actually going out into the sea by boat. So we decided to visualize a boat, mutually coordinating our visualizations. After doing this for 4 days, an hour a day, we had a solid (solid in the sense of solid in this plane) boat to use. Then we regularly sailed it out on days when it wasn't overly windy, and this helped him substantially cope with his phobia.

The weather stayed mild and mostly sunny but usually breezy. We didn't know if other kinds of weather would occur, so we thought it wise to build a house. After not much discussion at all we decided to recreate our house in Seattle complete with flowers and our beautiful yard. We divided up the portions of the house we would each primarily focus on creating in our imaginations. It took us 60 days to finish this task. It was a great exercise to focus and coordinate our imaginations, and we spent several hours each day doing it.

It was amazing to actually see our imagery slowly materialize in front of us, and assemble the pieces when they became solidly materialized. This was a great exercise also in focusing our attention for extended periods on a goal, which is an essential skill especially in this world. Meanwhile we stayed in a tent we imagined with simple tasty meals we created each day. We lit a few flickering tapers to provide a romantic cast to the inside of our tent.

MAROONED ON CHARON

Periodically Elin or Amon would literally drop in on us, and do some counseling to help us understand ourselves, each other, and our life in the present world. Amon taught us to visualize other places we'd like to visit or experience in this world, being careful to coordinate our imagery so we would both wind up in the same place. The concept of years didn't really apply in this plane. But there were dark-light cycles which we thought of as days, and we kept a log of these, and then could calculate months and years based on Earth calendars.

Together we imagined along with some guidance from Elin and Amon a set of other locations in the afterlife that we could visit. We found Megan and Marie again, and had many beautiful meetings with them at their or ours or some other locations. The same happened with Crystal. Sometimes I stayed with her for quite a while and gave Joe some time for himself, or to visit Tom, or they came to visit us.

I loved my time with Joe in this beautiful wilderness place. I still have no idea where we were, but it was not on the physical plane. With Pete and Trevor it was somewhat different. Pete had already reincarnated in the physical plane. Now that Pete again had a physical body he was still able to communicate with us in his astral body in the astral plane. But he seemed less light and vibrant due to the now attached physical body, and less able to move about. Trevor was still alive and contact with him was also sluggish. But we visited them too in the astral plane to the extent this was possible.

I truly missed Byron and wanted Joe to know Byron too. Byron had not yet reincarnated. Elin said if we desired it hard enough in our imaginations Byron could join us for a while. However in a few astral years he would need to return to the Earth. But we wonderfully had Byron for 40 years. After that his free running vibrant astral body would be locked into a less mobile and less clear vibrant body, because it would have a physical form that would slow its vibrations. Byron remained with us for a while after his reincarnation but was less vibrant and active. We then accepted Elin's advice to just let Byron rest in a quiet place for animals so he could focus his attention on his next life in the physical plane.

One day years after we arrived together on this plane we somehow got into a discussion of a very odd subject, how we were each afraid of each other on Earth and on Charon. I was chagrined and frankly stunned when Joe said he had at times been physically afraid of me. I understood though that I as an android was considerably stronger and faster than Joe, in fact more so than just a small number of the most athletic humans. I understood it was frightening to him when I grabbed him like a vice when I wanted a sensual massage, but didn't realize it at the time. I of course would never intentionally hurt him in any way.

But I was afraid of Joe too, which he had well realized. Not physically, but I knew he was developing serious mental problems on Charon, and he might or would almost certainly develop a profounder level of depression and psychosis. I worried that he might become unpredictable and even harm himself or the base. And then on Earth when he feared I might not stay with him when he became more disabled, I was hurt that he didn't trust me more than that. But it was good we finally talked about those things and he gained more trust in me.

MAROONED ON CHARON

I continued to work through the pain that still shocked me about Megan and Marie's demise, but the shock occurred less frequently. Those shocks occurred when the white caps were of a size and shape of the yawning crevasse on Charon. We discussed on many occasions what our life circumstances should be like when we returned to the physical plane. We had some decision powers but also the constraints of working through our karma.

Amon or Elin periodically dropped in on us seemingly from nowhere and inquired how we were doing, and if they could be of further help. But they always emphasized that we would return only when we we both felt we were ready. The days and nights passed but it was impossible to say how long they were. We counted the day-night cycles and determined how many astral years we had spent by dividing the number of days by 365.

We had many discussions about our next reincarnations. In general Joe was less willing to leave this beautiful place than was I, and dragging his feet on agreeing with me. Joe felt this was the only time he remembers he really felt peaceful. From my viewpoint I was experiencing an increasing urge to experience a human childhood, family, and especially bearing a child. We were always assured by Elin and Amon that we would leave at whatever point we both were in agreement to do so. We concluded after 347 years (by our count) that we were ready for our next lives.

I had decided to come back as a human female, to experience all those human passions I had only guessed at before. Joe decided to return as an android male, to learn some new coping skills for his fears and emotional weakness. We decided to return at another time of chaos on

Earth, to see how we would react separately and together to overwhelming stressors, and utilize our hard learned coping skills. Also we hoped to uplift any suffering humans or androids that we could. After we decided this, a few days later Amon and Elin appeared together.

They said we would both enter a stuperous state and then each of would experience a passage through a tunnel that would lead either to entry into a fetus, or entry into the nascent consciousness of an android. We would then lose our memories of the past, but be placed in situations where we could work through our agreed upon plans. We both agreed we were ready. A few days later when the time had come, Elin and Amon were with us, and Joe and I fell into a deep sleep. Just before that Darwin appeared and bid us fare well and assured me of his guidance again in the next life.

MAROONED ON CHARON, APOCALYPSE REBIRTH INTO A DYING WORLD

By Bruce Maaser

Copyright 2025 Bruce Maaser

CONTENTS

Jel's background and disturbing memories

Plagued by depression and self doubt

An apocalyptic dream

The Apocalypse begins

Sepsis and a desperate journey to find help

Return to a decimated world above ground

Translation and awakening

Brandon's story and Jel's death

An astounding nightmare of a disaster

Preparation for world-wide disaster

The Apocalypse has arrived

Sepsis and a harrowing journey for help

A miraculous rescue

A son is born!

Brandon's translation

MAROONED ON CHARON

JEL'S BACKGROUND AND DISTURBING MEMORIES

I'm Jel Straw Hayden and this is my personal diary. I wish to journal my own life, and how the world has evolved or devolved in recent history. I was born in 2322 on a farm near a small town 100 miles northeast of Edmonton. We raised some crops and took care of many of our needs on our own like the farmers of centuries ago. There was a small town about 10 miles away where we could buy needed supplies, and my siblings and I could attend a small school. My interest in high school was history. Later I attended the University of Edmonton, my academic background in college being the history of the third millennium. Before I go on with my personal history allow me to tell you about the state of the world in the 2300's.

The Earth has changed dramatically in the last 300 years, in some ways good but sadly mostly negative. The human population of the world has dropped a staggering amount. Human population reached its peak of 12 billion in about 2160 but has been decimated since. Global climate changes have made much of the previously densely populated regions of the world unlivable. This has caused a great decrease in arable land and the ability of the Earth to sustain human and animal life.

Global warming was first seen as a growing crisis in the later years of the twentieth century. Yet the warnings were largely ignored because it was easier to burn carbon based products like coal, oil, gas and wood than convert to environmentally friendly fuels. The population continued to increase, and along with it the carbon based fuel it was primarily dependent upon. By 2160 the Earth could no longer tolerate what humans had done to it, and as predicted by the ancient but true Malthusian principle, factors arose that curtailed further growth.

Pandemics became an ongoing rather than occasional problem by about 2020. Despite vast effort at developing effective vaccines the vaccines were no match for the mutating viruses starting with the CoVid variants. Billions of humans were eventually killed due to the viruses.

The human race has a basic aggressive instinct, carried over by evolution from lower forms of mammals and other animal life. Thus territoriality and racial divisiveness continued to result in wars and ongoing strife. The result of these factors has been a decrease in the human population to 15 million in 2360, down > 99% from its all-time peak. Intense heat, gargantuan storms, flooding as well as drought have made much of the world below latitude 25 unlivable in both the northern and Southern Hemispheres.

In that context allow me to return to my upbringing. When I was growing up my family and friends were my everything. Life on our farm was often difficult with the isolation and the storms that often besieged us. The weather was cold in winter but got blisteringly hot in the summer. The climate had seasonal highly variable extremes and the west winds could be powerful.

The mountains in Alberta were beautiful, but frankly the flat land that seemed to go on forever, where we lived east of the mountains was bleak and dry. The average temperature was 6 degrees C higher per day than it had been in the year 2000. In the winter we could still have blizzards as in the past. At those times it would seem we were very isolated, surviving in our warm and cozy house, safe from the forbidding winter conditions outside.

Mom and dad have always been supportive of me but were emotionally distant and hardened, as befitting the rigors of our life and environment. Grandpa Jack, who is my dad's dad, has always held a special place for me. He and Grandma Irene had a cabin in the Rockies. They had a large boat for fishing and cruising. Sometimes Grandpa would take me out on the boat just by ourselves and we would do some fishing. I loved those times but it was so lonely there too. My brother Tanil is 2 years younger than I. We would fight when we were younger and stick only with our own friends. But when I was about 16 we became great friends, and much closer than most opposite sex siblings who are close in age as teens.

We played sports together, and I attended games when he was on a team. He was very talented at sports, a handsome guy who had plenty of friends including girls, but always seemed to make time for me. He resembled Grandpa in a lot of ways and together they were such a strong influence on me. It was my bedrock of security to have my family and especially my brother, but I always wondered what it was like outside of our remote existence. Kacey is my younger sister by 7 years. She also seemed bored and dissatisfied with our life.

When I was 8 my dad brought home a puppy one day, the first we'd had in our family. He was a little fur ball whom I was told was an Alaskan husky, therefore would grow into a large dog. I was absolutely ecstatic, having wanted a dog my whole life. We named him Rupert, I'm not sure why. He grew rapidly and was very friendly, playful and protective of our family. I loved to look into his pale blue eyes. I was very close to Rupert from the first. We seemed to be able to read each other's thoughts, and he helped me through many of my emotional excursions.

I have many times had vivid dreams in my life. Our family believed in the predictive power of dreams. As the great psychoanalyst Sigmund Freud had stated in the early part of the twentieth century, dreams are the royal road to the unconscious. We believed that important memories and knowledge can be found in the unconscious, and dreams are one way of accessing that. One recurrent dream was of a terribly remote, eldritch, unworldly and cold place, like the Arctic but even much more remote, stark and cold. But with a vast overpowering silence and solitude that in some way captured my imagination and spirit in a dialectic of horror and fascination.

I also dreamed of a loving relationship with a wonderful man but in a place of danger and uncertainty. Strangely it seemed to me that I was always an adult in my dreams, even dreams I had in my early teens. It was like my childhood in my dreams didn't even exist, like all my memories pertained only to an adult. It seemed like I was an alternative identity in my dreams, in some ways like but in other ways very different than my waking identity.

The dream person also had an inscrutability that I couldn't quite understand, and this remained a troubling and nagging question in my mind. This troubled me for many years and I wondered if something had happened so traumatic in that person's life that she had completely blocked out the memories.

MAROONED ON CHARON

When I became a senior in history at the University of Alberta in Edmonton I became intrigued especially by the development of androids since about 2000 and how this has affected the world. I became fascinated by the well-known story of Eva the android and Joe the human who developed a unique and singular relationship while both were marooned on Charon in 2127 to 2132 until rescue, and then after return to Earth. The purpose of their mission had been to identify and somehow disable the destructive source of the transmissions that had been devastating the electronic grid of the Earth. Their mission was fraught with tragedy, and apparently unsuccessful at that time , but vindicated since then.

But the fascinating story to me was how the relationship between Joe and Eva, under the most difficult, tragic and uncertain circumstances, deepened and allowed both to survive, and eventually return to Earth. Then they deepened their relationship into marriage and led an apparently productive life in the society of the time, although Joe was often ill and was reclusive. This was also ground breaking for human-android relationships at that time. Then after Joe passed away Eva was in a state of doubt and uncertainty. But after a few years of isolation she continued her positive life and activities, and formed a long term close relationship with another female android.

I've read and reread the book, now 180 years since publication, and watched the several 3D movies created since that time, entitled Marooned on Charon. This was written as the personal, separate but overlapping diaries of Joe and Eva. It seemed the most satisfying success for them, besides their life together, was the nurturing of emotional understanding in Eva, leading to her uniquely successful life during and after Joe's life ended. Eva remains a folk hero of android culture for her exploits.

An even more fascinating element and source of legend in Joe's diary in the Marooned on Charon book was Joe's description of the interaction with the alien culture that was allegedly behind the transmissions. This occurred when Joe and 3 other crew took a desperate journey to locate the source of the destructive transmissions, and came upon the huge alien seven faced pyramid. A series of images were visualized by Joe and a female human member of that crew who later tragically died, but not by Eva or the other remaining android crew member. Besides the riveting images there were intense emotional accompaniments to each, but no language or sound.

Joe interpreted the images and accompanying emotions as regret by the aliens as to the unexpected destruction caused by the transmissions, and intent to not let that happen again. In the end this dubious but empathetic interpretation was borne out to be true as no more transmissions occurred after that. Then there was the image of another planet of bizarre landscape and sky color circling a double star. Endless speculation has been done about these images with no verifiable conclusions. Finally there was the terrifying vision of a great crevasse opening, which was an apparent warning later coming true with loss of the other human and android members of the crew.

Finally there was Joe's account of the mysterious signal light that guided the rescue ship to the base even though all signaling capacity had been lost by the base. All these legends were endlessly fascinating to me. But the image of the crevasse opening and the painting of it by Eva depicting the swallowing of the vehicle with the other crew members left a shattering impact on me which was the subject of many future nightmares. I couldn't purge it from my mind no matter how hard I tried, nor did my therapy sessions help in this regard. No further contact with the aliens on Charon, nor any other intelligent extraterrestrial life forms have occurred since.

When I read Marooned on Charon the lonely and ultimately bleak location of the base where Joe and Eva stayed made me think of those isolated winter days on our farm. Of course Charon was incomparably colder and more unforgiving than our farm in Saskatchewan, and almost inconceivably more remote from the rest of humanity. I tried to imagine myself as Eva in the base, with the tragic loss of the rest of the crew, the complete uncertainty of rescue, threat of destructive electromagnetic transmissions, and the mental instability of Joe. I gained so much respect for Eva's mental stability in that harrowing situation and wondered if her being an android gave her more capacity for coping with stress than Joe exhibited.

I wondered if I as a human could have survived and stayed sane under such mentally stressful and extreme circumstances. I certainly didn't think so, nor could Joe. But on other hand, in the long winter nights the Aurora Borealis was hypnotizingly beautiful. I was fascinated by the shifting shapes, colors and changes in brightness. Sometimes the curtains above turned a turquoise color, and I imagined I was on a distant planet or moon, such as Charon.

I've always had an overly active imagination with shifting and deep emotions and the Northern Lights made me very inspired, but troubled and confused as well. Sometimes I would go out and get captivated by the sight and imagine shapes and animals and people in the opalescent hues. I would forget that I was getting very cold, and Mom or Dad would come out to get me and give me a lecture on using better common sense in the cold.

My best friend Slane was in my same grade in school and we seemed to understand each other so well. In my last year in high school our vehicle she was driving went off the road and flipped over. I had a few minor injuries but Slane was more seriously injured and spent weeks in a hospital. She was in Intensive Care for a week and in critical condition. I visited her every day. I was beside myself with worry, and couldn't stop seeing the accident itself, which I had remained conscious during. The second night after that I had a vivid dream that she had died and it seemed like Déjà vu, that it had happened before.

I felt terribly guilty even though the accident was not my fault and couldn't sleep without having nightmares. My distress decreased as she improved and I thanked God for it. I went off to college at the University of Alberta. She went off to college too, but to the University of Manitoba instead. This made me sad and kind of angry too because I had committed to the U of Alberta in Edmonton when I thought she was coming there too. But we corresponded after that and visited each other a number of times, and she will always have a special bond with me.

College was a total shock to me compared to my home environment and the small town where I'd gone to school my whole life. I was told on a number of occasions that I am a pretty girl. I'm fairly tall, lanky, with black hair, medium dark skin and blue eyes. I regularly had guys asking me to go out with them, which I did sometimes but not a lot. I never could find someone who could appreciate or tolerate my bouncing imagination, moodiness, and existential void as far as finding a meaning and purpose in my life. I talked to my brother Tanil regularly and he came to visit and I saw him when I went home.

MAROONED ON CHARON

PLAGUED BY DEPRESSION AND SELF DOUBT

I became very depressed for a time in my third year, feeling like nobody accepted me other than Slane and Tanil. But they weren't near me where I could see them right away if I needed to and this made me feel very alone. Then when I was 22 I found out Rupert had died. Rupert was getting old at 14 but still active and loved to see me. I was away at college and the news was unexpected and completely devastating.

I felt guilty that I hadn't been home when he died although nobody had expected his imminent demise, which was determined to be the hemorrhage of an aortic aneurysm. I believed that Rupert would live on in the afterlife and for a while I entertained the fantasy of joining him there. My precarious emotional state became even more unhinged after this unexpected loss.

I even obsessed about suicide but couldn't bring myself to actually seriously try it. I cut my left arm and left leg about 6 times, just to focus on something other than my depression. After that I saw a psychologist and a psychiatrist to get my thinking and moods under control. Fortunately I never cut very deeply or needed stitches, and now the scars are barely visible at all. I spent several days in a psychiatric unit on 2 occasions. The cutting never hurt when I was doing it, and produced a strange feeling of peace and detachment for a while until the depression and frustration rolled back in harder than before, along with the pain from the cuts.

My therapist explained the calm feeling as an endorphin and serotonin rush, which made the behavior reinforcing when I did it. He said I had the neediness, emotional swings and self-injury to relieve my stress of a borderline personality. I sort of followed his meaning but thought it was a useless label I didn't need. But I felt terribly guilty at what I'd done and managed to not tell anyone about it other than Slane. I didn't even tell Tanil as I feared he would tell my parents. Then I had to find a way to calm myself down when my anxiety was off the roof and I couldn't use cutting as a release anymore.

I'd never really liked the taste of alcoholic drinks but liked the effect. I'd gone out drinking with some friends a few times and got drunk, which I guess is a rite of passage for college students, as almost everyone I knew had done it. The hangover was awful but while I was drinking I felt happy, forgot about my worries and regrets and became very talkative and frisky, probably too much so. I also went on a date with a human male who got drunk too, and he tried to sexually assault me. Fortunately I know martial arts skills and he was left with an agonized rather than satisfied sexual organ.

But for some months I was drinking every day, often too much, and it was hurting my grades. Then a "friend" gave me a line of cocaine to help me stay awake for a final exam in psychology. I stayed up and crammed all night, and managed a B on the test despite that up to then I hadn't read any of the material or gone to most of the classes! After that I was using cocaine or meth or one of the designer alternatives regularly along with drinking. Then I added heroin for a while. It gave me the same blissful numbness that I experienced after cutting. But I rationalized that at least I had stopped cutting myself! I went through a brief withdrawal but then moved on, as I hadn't used it that long.

After my third year was ended I still needed at least 3 semesters to graduate. I needed to get out the dorm I'd been in as the rampant drug and alcohol use by the other residents just complicated my burgeoning substance abuse problem. I was also not cohabitating well with my roommate who was annoyed at my behavior when inebriated. Using a roommate finding service I was able to arrange a small 2 bedroom apartment with a single woman who worked in the community named Corinne. Her description of herself in her brief bio that was part of her posting sounded good to me, until it got to the statement that she's an android. I didn't know what to think about that!

I'd known a few androids before and generally found them amicable and helpful but also distant and boring. But then I reasoned that would be OK, I have more than enough problems as it is and don't need any more drama or roommate problems. I of course had said nothing about my mental and substance abuse challenges in my brief bio for the roommate matching service, I just had glossed over all that. But from the minute I met Corinne we hit it off, and I soon felt quite comfortable with her, strangely she felt like a long lost friend.

She was attractive with long brown hair, blue eyes, and a surprisingly perky manner for an android with a pretty smile and a European look. So we quickly agreed on an apartment and 3 days later had both moved in. Corinne seemed comfortable with me too, and along with the mutual comfort came a mutual directness. I began to trust her but not to the point of disclosing my substance abuse, my self-injury or my depression. I kept my alcohol use down and abstained from drugs for the first week. Then I got drunk and depressed several times, and Corinne told me very directly that I had developed an alcohol use disorder.

She said I became rather annoying and embarrassing in public after too many drinks. The guys were attracted to both of us if we went anywhere and became flirtatious which Corinne didn't care for. She saw my daily drinking was having an impact on my grades, and I needed to cut down or I likely wouldn't graduate. She was surprised but not horrified when she noticed my scars and I admitted that I was a cutter. But thankfully she didn't back out on remaining my roommate and friend.

Interestingly one thing I read, at 4 AM in a blur, that stuck with me was in a boring chapter on the brain and behavior. D.O. Hebb, an early twentieth century psychologist, had declared that habits cannot be broken, they can just be replaced by other habits. I realized that I had just replaced the cutting habit with a drug and alcohol habit, I had just traded one bad habit for another! I did an inpatient substance abuse program for 2 weeks and then received counseling for a while as I finally realized I was totally out of control.

I learned some breathing, cognitive and focusing techniques to calm me down instead of self-mutilation or drinking. I was able to cut down although not stop the alcohol and drugs, and never relapsed again into self-mutilation. I was proud of myself for that, it has been an important step in what I've always thought is my most major problem of runaway emotions. Corinne remained supportive to me through all this even though most people would not have been. I was so thankful to her for that. I had nearly forgotten that she is an android and I stopped even thinking about it.

In 2347 after 3 years with Corinne I decided I needed to develop my independence and get a place of my own. Corinne was fine with that and we agreed we would talk and see each other regularly. Corinne was great at giving hugs, which I first found surprising for an android. I always appreciated that, although was always startled that her skin had no human warmth. After getting my own small place I got an interesting new job to get away from the drudgery of my secretarial job.

The job was at the Art Center at the U of Alberta, being a docent and working at the ticket office. It was a fairly low level job but I loved the Art Center, and it paid the bills for my own little 2 bedroom apartment. I used one of the bedrooms as my own art studio, and every evening I worked on one or more paintings. I hoped someday I can display and sell my paintings, that would be an awesome dream.

I also did some occasional nude modeling for the university life drawing classes. That paid well but I didn't do it enough to really help my income very much. I was mildly shy about getting nude in front of a group of art students. But the format is not at all sexual, in fact is quite serious and academic. So I got over my apprehension and then had fun, but the long poses became excruciating. The students and local artists who came were appreciative and sometimes gave me nice tips. I was asked out by a few of the student artists, male and female. But that's not allowed so I had to decline, and besides it would seem very weird if they then came back to more modeling sessions.

I met Brandon one day at the Art Center, who had come as a visitor just to see a special showing. He was very cute and I immediately was attracted to him, and it was surprising to me how quickly that attraction took hold of me. I managed to do my docent duties in his vicinity, hoping he would notice me. That he did and we locked eyes. He seemed rather reserved and quiet but he was conversant and we managed a nice little conversation. I gave him one of my cards, and penciled in my phone number too, which he accepted without comment. But 2 days later he called and asked if we could get together, to which I happily agreed.

My first impressions of Brandon were of a rather quiet and reserved individual who was scrupulously polite and cordial to me. We visited a park and a 3D movie in our first few dates. Brandon was great at drawing me out, which doesn't usually take much catalysis, and listening to me talk about whatever came to mind. He was very well spoken, but I noticed he seemed quite private in talking about his family, upbringing, etc. It wasn't actually until mid-way through our second date that I found out he is an android. I had never even considered that possibility, and was taken aback but not repulsed when he told me.

We dated for 2 years and I felt so comfortable with him. He definitely helped stabilize me emotionally, not surprisingly much the same as Corinne always had. I saw Corinne often too, and quite a few times the 3 of us got together. Corinne and Brandon got along well as good friends but rather distant from each other as I'd expect due to their android nature. They never got together without me as far as I know although I would have been fine if they had.

I'm rather embarrassed to talk about the next thing, but it's important and relates to the stereotype of androids as not being sexual creatures. This is certainly one of the common ideas among human girls, that androids cannot give a girl sexual satisfaction. So I wondered and worried about that on our first few dates. First of all I must admit it is true that android males do not have a penis! But I showed Brandon how to kiss, and he was great at that including all over my body! He excelled also with a very sensitive android touch. So I felt our sexual relationship was just fine, and Brandon was quite attractive. Brandon enjoyed it (if that's the right word, or perhaps sensual if not sexual satisfaction), particularly when I softly massaged him especially around his neck and shoulders,

We moved into his apartment after two years and we got married one year after that. It was a fine and rather small wedding. My maid of honor of course was Corinne, who I thought looked stunningly beautiful. Of course my parents were there. Slane was another bridesmaid along with Kacey. Tom was Brandon's best man, and Tanil was a beaming groomsman. Our lives settled down after our wedding, and the next few years were the most emotionally and situationally stable in my life. Brandon continued his job as a geophysicist at the U of Alberta, and I loved my job as a docent at the Art Center. I especially loved introducing children to the different genres of art work.

We got along well for the most part, if we did have a problem it was usually but not always because of one of my emotional tangents. I also had several fairly brief relapses into alcohol abuse and one into heroin, each followed by a brief inpatient rehab admission. The worst event was a drunk driving ticket and 3 day jail sentence after I lost control of my vehicle and then ran into a neighbor's shed. Brandon and Corinne were very angry (or, as always, at least displayed their android counterparts of anger), and being androids could simply not empathize with my addictions. Tanil called me after that incident and yelled at me until I cried. But all 3 of them and the rest of my family stayed with me and helped me regain my sobriety and self-respect.

Through all of this however was a deep aching to bear a child. My motherly instinct and yearning at times became overwhelming to me. But I was ambivalent too. The population of the human race had continued to shrink as an effect of unstoppable viruses, environmental destruction, war, and all the other factors that have troubled the human race since the dawn of time. We wondered does it even make sense to bring a child into this broken world? Plus I need to have donor sperm, as of course Brandon couldn't provide this. We were working on getting this arranged when the next enormous and ungodly event happened in our lives, and in fact to the whole world.

MAROONED ON CHARON

AN APOCALYPTIC DREAM

On March 17, 2349, I awakened from a dream that was shockingly vivid. I dreamed I was Eva on Charon, in that disastrous trip to locate the alien source of the devastating transmissions. I was in the ground vehicle with Joe, and the alien apparition appeared. This time I could see the two figures and see the images they projected clearly, whereas for Eva this had been extremely blurred. But the message was different than it had been for Joe.

The next image was apparently an impending disaster that would befall the Earth, and was accompanied by a feeling of overwhelming fear and dread. Next an image occurred of a volcano, erupting with huge plumes of fire, stones and sulfurous black smoke. This image transformed into shattering images of two enormous earthquakes. These images were accompanied by a mind boggling sense of urgency and inevitability.

The following images maintained the relentless pace of panic and destruction. The first of these was a map of the entire Pacific Ocean. The well known "ring of fire" scintillated with red, yellow and black in many areas. The next images showed enormous tsunamis breaching the towering fortifications that had been erected against the rising ocean. Coastal cities, perhaps Seattle and Tokyo, saw those fortifications crumble. Floods of 20 or more feet covered those cities and many other places along both coasts.

The next image exhibited a heavy dark ash and mist mixture occluding the atmosphere of a forested area, with a dim yellow nimbus of the sun unsteadily peeking through overhead. The trees and adjacent crop land looked to be dead or dying with forest creatures as well as humans suffocated to death by the oxygen depleted atmosphere. The following image showed hurricane force winds overpowering and leveling a deserted community, with fires raging in the background. After this was a heavy blizzard of snow burying what might have been Los Angeles or Phoenix or Mexico City.

The impression then was of a long, indefinite length of time. But then the ash had finally settled, and the image of the world seemed to be clearer and calmer again. There was a quiet sea coast with gentle waves of pristine water caressing the sandy beach. There was a small community with a few people walking about. All were attractive, seemed to be in their 20's or 30's, and there appeared to be several sets of identical twins and triplets, which seemed very enigmatic.

Then came a joyous feeling accompanying an enigmatic scene. Several people who apparently were medical personnel surrounded a crib. One picked up the infant, and I was utterly discombobulated when she announced directly to me in a restrained but positive voice in English, "the human race has been reborn." The dream then abruptly ended, and I awoke totally confused, overwhelmed, with a full spectrum of emotions that I couldn't label or sort out. I felt myself being shocked and overwhelmed by this prediction.

After I awoke I was incredulous and in a state of panic. I screamed with all my lung force several times before I was again oriented to my everyday reality. I had a vivid memory of most of the message, as clear as my own waking memory. As soon as I awakened Brandon was also awake and appeared shocked in his own muted way. We shared our dreams with each other. All details were duplicated in each other's dreams, except that Brandon had perceived himself in the dream as Joe. Plus Brandon had a clear comprehension and recall of the oceanographic data he had witnessed in the dream that had not appeared in my dream.

Soon after that Slane called, which at first seemed very coincidental as I hadn't talked to her in 3 months. Slane was flabbergasted to the point she could hardly speak. She had also perceived herself on Charon, listening to the aliens' message, but was in a different vehicle than the one I was in. When Slane and I were girls we had sometimes imagined that I had been Eva, and Slane had been Megan. Slane had always treated this as an interesting and frightening story rather than a recall of a past life as an android. I had instead believed strongly that I was actually Eva, now back in a human body. Slane now was shocked at this implication that she had been Megan.

Slane also had had a full panic attack after the dream and was still very agitated about a strange feeling she couldn't shake. This was of her vision of a horrible accident, in which her last memory was of rolling several times then of being crushed and unable to breathe. I spent a long time then talking to Slane, calming her down with the assurance that that traumatic event was long in the past and no longer a present or future event to be feared. It was the longest conversation I'd had with her for years and I think rekindled the deep bond we'd had in the past. We agreed to get together in the near future and made some tentative arrangements for this to happen. I told Brandon about my conversation with Slane.

The three of us agreed that our experience had to be publicly shared, as a warning and to assess whether other humans or androids had experienced it. But we didn't want to sensationalize it either, which could cause panic or derision. We wanted Brandon and other geophysical experts to further evaluate Brandon's dream data first. We didn't know what if anything the dreams had to do with the visions that Joe and Marie had witnessed on Charon so long ago. We were overwhelmed with my perception that my dream augured the imminent destruction of life on Earth.

Beginning that day news reports from around the world indicated that some androids, mostly in North America, had experienced vague or partial dream imagery either while deactivated or as an intrusion on their daily consciousness. None of them had reported specific clear images or content, but all that had experienced said it had given them sufficiently foreboding and nonspecifically disquieting thoughts.

This occurred likely because of the partial telepathic perception shared by all series 7 and 8 androids. Therefore the message as received by Brandon was partially shared, likely by androids with exactly the same brain structure. There were few human reports of the dream, which were vague and not completely consistent in content with our dreams. These few humans were known as seers or psychics or individuals known to have some sort of paranormal powers.

This vague perception was in contrast to the three of us, in which the images had the quality of being as real or more so than our daily lives. The common reaction of the few humans who had partially experienced the message was fear and panic, not knowing if the message was an actual portent of the future. A Jungian therapist portentously even wrote off the message as "a mass eruption of human ancestral archetypes without any realistic truth."

For the next 4 years Brandon and colleagues were continually busy updating the geophysical data as it came into the department, and the updates were increasingly ominous. I had to continually battle my depression and panic. But I frequently turned to the part of Eva in me that helped to steady me. Brandon was incredibly supportive, as always, and my old friendships with Slane and Corinne deepened. I was able to channel my negative, destructive energy into the pursuits of Brandon and his colleagues, to alert and warn whomever might listen in the community. This was frustrating more often than encouraging. I many times wished to return to alcohol and opiate use to calm myself, but except for a few short slips was able to stay clean.

It was very disconcerting that Brandon and I even received death threats from individuals who thought our efforts were a threat to society rather than being the very real threats we were warning about. It was painful to hear about the increase in depression and suicide rate in society. I tried with limited success to do some motivational speaking to church and rehabilitation groups citing my own coping mechanisms for my chronic problems with depression in the face of the eldritch predictions.

Meanwhile Brandon and I secured an apartment in an underground complex being built outside of Winnipeg. The complex contained 150 underground apartments, a power station with fuel and also geothermal power, stores, a school and everything else needed to sustain life for up to 100 years, no matter the catastrophes occurring above ground. The plan was that my parents, brother and sister would ride out the apocalyptic event with us. Over the next 6 months we accumulated enough food and other supplies to sustain us for at least 5 years. My parents however were resistant to leaving our family farm home and were dubious, as were so many humans, that the apocalypse would even happen.

They continued to promise they would move in with us and close up the farm but kept putting this off indefinitely. My brother and sister had established themselves at Edmonton at the university and also delayed moving with us. They were also worried about my parents and thought they should stay with them despite the danger in hopes of helping them survive. I became very angry at them for not taking us seriously and dragging their feet on getting prepared.

Dad stated he loved the farm and would rather die there instead of living in tight underground quarters. We fruitlessly argued that Edmonton was at greater risk of catastrophic destruction than Winnipeg, although no place in the world would be fully safe. Despite the illogic I was drawn to the idea of moving back to the farm and staying with them no matter the outcome.

Brandon and I argued numerous times about this, my guilt and worrying motivating me to desire to rejoin the rest of the family on the farm. Brandon insisted this was too dangerous to be realistic and likely all of us would perish. In my panic I threatened to go up to stay with my parents whether or not Brandon came along. This was one of the few times I had seen Brandon become really angry in a very human sense at me, and I knew this frightened him. It inspired a devastating feeling of rejection that he was unimportant to me compared to my family. But I knew this would be an irrational, desperation act and I could read Brandon's anguish and anger under his usual reserved and rational persona, so I abandoned that idea.

Finally after much discussion, argument and procrastination with the rest of the family they promised to load up and move as much of their belongings as they could to our residence. We said we would help them with the move, and set up a date 2 weeks from then for the move. However the accumulating geophysical data gave an increasingly stark warning that the volcanic eruption was more imminent than expected.

MAROONED ON CHARON

THE APOCALYPSE BEGINS

September 23, 2354, Three days before we had scheduled to drive to the farm with a large, borrowed ground vehicle the news came out on all networks that significant underground movement had just been detected under Mt. St. Helens in Washington and simultaneously near Kodiak Island in Alaska. These tremors adumbrated an imminent and vastly more destructive earthquake and/or volcanic eruption. This greatly increased the imminent probability of earthquake activity along the entire Pacific fault line, which might possibly even trigger earthquake activity on the other side of the Pacific from the northeastern coast of Siberia down to Japan.

As we had feared now for several years the warning announcements now blanketed all communication modalities to take immediate cover in whatever underground bunkers that had been prepared. This was incredibly maddening to me especially because we were finally set to bring my parents to our shelter and if they hadn't resisted all along they'd now all be safe with us. I pleaded with Brandon that we drive to the farm anyway despite the developing disaster, pick up my family and leave immediately to return. However this would have been a 13 hour drive each way under normal conditions. It would be questionable if any recharging stations would be operable.

Brandon very firmly negated this idea and I knew he was right. I yelled at him and I know he suspected I would attempt to drive the vehicle on my own. I thought I was going insane, but was sapped of my will or strength to resist

Brandon. I tried to control my panic because I knew he was fighting to maintain his own ability to think and act rationally. Communication channels thank god were still intact and we were still able to contact my family.

Tanil and Kacey had secured a shelter in the Edmonton underground complex. They were also about to head to the farm but had to abort that idea because of the tremors. The hours dragged on interminably as we waited for their call that they were safe, and listened to the unfolding reports of disaster. Even near our location in Winnipeg the ground was shaking badly. After 4 hours Tanil & Kacey were able to contact us. They had gotten to Edmonton and thank god were safe in the now overcrowded underground shelter. We didn't know how long the public news or private conversation channels would remain operative.

First reports on the news were of massive volcanic activity at Mount St Helen's and Kodiak Island. The sky around those volcanoes was rapidly filling with dense ash. This apparently triggered temblors along the North American west coast of unprecedented size. Early reports indicated a temblor of 9.3 on the Richter scale had occurred in Southern California. Los Angeles and surrounding areas were in chaos, damage was present everywhere. No estimate yet could be made but likely hundreds of thousands or even millions would perish.

By this time in history the population of Southern California had fallen to 4M down from a maximum of 30M in 2060. Extensive areas and neighborhoods of Los Angeles and San Diego contained mostly abandoned residential, commercial and industrial buildings, many collapsed or close to it, and uninhabitable. Furthermore the Pacific had encroached on low lying areas near the coast while on the eastern side the desert was completely desiccated, with unlivable temperatures. Thus much of the crumbling buildings and infrastructure was no match for the violent heaving of the ground.

Early news reports documented also severe earthquake damage up and down the west coast. San Francisco, Portland, Seattle and Vancouver had all lost population over the past few centuries and developed deteriorating infrastructure, but not to the widespread level of Los Angeles and San Diego. Portland had lost the least population due to its somewhat more inland location. Anchorage had actually become the most vibrant of the west coast cities due to its now moderate climate. But an 8.8 temblor in that area created a shocking level of damage as well. Furthermore, tsunamis of up to 50 feet in height devastated or simply obliterated low lying areas up and down the coast.

Mount St Helen's, Kodiak Island and other centers of volcanic activity belched enormous clouds of ash. The seabed in oceanic areas of the earthquake, and the ground in land areas spewed incalculable amounts of dirt, dust, sulphuric acid, and water high into the atmosphere. This in turn catalyzed hurricanes, tornadoes and black out conditions. 2 days after the first temblor the legendary super volcano simmering beneath Yellowstone National Park suddenly became active. Vast amounts of molten lava were ejected and heavy yellow-black ash filled the sky. Over the next few days the sky became blacker and filled with an ashy haze in central Canada.

We knew it wouldn't be long until the air in our location 2K miles from the sea, and eventually the whole world would become unbreathable. Our underground shelter rocked with the aftershocks, sometimes for hours at a time. We literally had seatbelts and shoulder harnesses installed in padded chairs bolted to the floor that we could use for restraint under the worst vibrations. We feared that the shelter might be split open if the ground opened up right beneath us. News reports over the next few weeks elaborated on the damage although many of the hardest hit areas remained unreachable. Aftershocks continued and there were also reports of earthquakes and tsunamis from Vladivostok to Tokyo.

The aftershocks put an overwhelming strain on the tunnel system of the underground complex. A cave in occurred in the tunnel just outside our apartment and the tunnel became impassable. We had no idea how far the cave-in extended. With great effort we tried to shovel out the debris but this was mostly large rocks and concrete that we couldn't move with the hand tools we had. We also feared we might extend the cave-in closer to our apartment, which fortunately remained structurally intact. After about 20 feet of digging, and with no place to put the shoveled-out material we gave up on that idea.

As the months in isolation wore on I realized the strength of human emotion, if overwhelmed by stress and trauma, can totally undermine rational thought and behavior. I knew that I couldn't blame myself or Brandon for my parents recalcitrance, and all I could do was wait for a time when contact could be restored or we could make a journey to the farm. But I was so depressed and beyond anxiety that I couldn't even take care of myself each day. The days became interminable. I lost track of what would have been day and night, although outside it was now almost night all the time.

My mind couldn't stop racing: how are my parents and Tanil and Kacey doing? Are they alive or did they die a horrific death? How is dear Slane doing and where is she? Why didn't Brandon let us go to Edmonton when the cataclysm started despite the danger? Why didn't I just take the vehicle myself when Brandon refused? Why should I go on living when so many where dead? Should I take my own life and how would I do it? How would that affect Brandon, or my family if they ever were to find out? Is there any hope for the future or will we just be stuck in this prison cell until we die?

I tried my best to repeat Brandon's positive thoughts about the future. Brandon was my lifeline for keeping me from becoming completely insane. I know that if Brandon were gone I would become psychotically depressed like Joe did on Charon after Eva had to deactivate. I knew that in a few years Brandon would need a revitalization and I was scared to death that he might have to deactivate until that could happen, if it ever could happen. I tried to think of this experience as a challenge I had no choice but to face and a test of my ability to control my panic, fear and depression.

I knew that Brandon also was worried and depressed about all these things, but he kept that fairly well hidden. We had some actually close and beautiful times watching movies, listening to music and playing games. I knew that if I had been Eva I certainly fulfilled her wish and found out firsthand what human emotions were like and how devastating they could be. I tried to image myself as Eva, and how she might have handled this stress as she had done on Charon. I also saw the effect my mental instability was having on Brandon, and how his android temperament was helping him survive these circumstances better than my human temperament was allowing me to cope.

Brandon and I survived the next 14 months by ourselves. I knew our relationship could either survive and grow through the calamity, or deteriorate into a disaster of its own. I had to everyday fight with my depression, anger and sense of utter hopelessness. Brandon was also stressed in his own way but carried on much better than I was doing. He said let's pattern ourselves as Joe and Eva had done on Charon, and I needed to absorb Eva's practical approach to our survival. I tried to do that but knew I just couldn't sustain it without Brandon's help, which he furnished me daily.

Sometimes I became overwhelmed and couldn't even get out of bed. Like as if I was trying to survive a prison sentence, I tried to sleep away as much time as I could. One time I didn't get up or even eat for 3 consecutive days. Brandon maintained a controlling but caring demeanor when I got very depressed, encouraging me, sometimes getting very firm about it, but never at least showing disgust or resignation toward me. I could see and feel his distress beneath his android stoicism, and tried hard to feel motivated and optimistic for his sake.

I worried constantly about my parents, Tanil, Kacey and Slane. I felt guilty to the core that we hadn't gotten Mom and Dad to our shelter before the Cataclysm, and sometimes was angry with Brandon too about that, but sulked and fumed and pretty much kept it to myself. But when I did bring it up he handled my distress very matter of factly. He rightly stated over and over that in fact we had done all we could against their resistance, and hopefully Tanil & Kacey were OK in the colony near Edmonton. We hoped they had gotten to Edmonton, but if my parents were still at the farm all we could do was hope that they could survive.

I found myself thinking, obsessing about the painting made by Eva of the view from the base on Charon. I excruciatingly felt the loneliness and alienation from everything I'd known before. This would seem to go on for days of troubled revery like a bad dream, then I'd return to present reality which wasn't much better. I was so thankful though at Brandon's stability in all this, and not having to cope with Joe's depression and withdrawal like Eva had done.

But the other part was something Joe ran from, but that I think Brandon felt or perceived in his own way: the infinite but terrifying serenity and quiet of total isolation. This perception became a source of spiritual peace for me despite all the fear behind it. I certainly don't doubt that the isolation literally drove Joe crazy after Eva had to be deactivated. If Brandon ever became deactivated I'm sure I would go crazy too. If I were to die I don't know how Brandon would cope with it, I think he'd probably just permanently shut himself down.

Brandon made a trip to the outside of our underground apartment every few days to sample the weather, visibility, temperature, oxygen level of the air, and survey the omnipresent devastation of everything. There was a sally port at the entrance to our living space so the inside of the apartment could be shielded from the weather outside when the outer door was opened. By one year after the disaster conditions had started to somewhat improve outside but fierce storms and winds were still the norm.

The visibility was low due to the ash in the air, the oxygen level was slowly going up, but the air outside was still unbreathable. The daily average temperature on the days he sampled, always at 12 PM, had dropped 10 degrees F compared to the same date the year before. There were no signs of life or any attempt at clearing the destruction. It was maddening that we still had no communication with anyone, but thought likely there were survivors in housing areas under the rubble.

MAROONED ON CHARON

SEPSIS AND A DESPERATE TRIP TO FIND HELP

On January 3, 2355, 15 months after the disaster started I developed an apparent septic condition following a cut on my left arm after I fell in the kitchen. The cut became infected and the small amount of antibiotic we had left didn't clear it up. Within 3 days my arm was very swollen, red, and excruciatingly painful. I started developing dizziness, nausea and by 5 days some confusion. Brandon recognized this as an imminently dangerous situation that could become lethal if not treated with the proper antibiotics.

He insisted we try to reach the medical facility in the underground community. I balked at the idea as it would be risking both our lives attempting to traverse the external way to the center of the community, which likely was completely disrupted and dangerous from the howling storms. But after 3 days I had become nearly delirious and Brandon forced me into the ground vehicle in an attempt to reach the medical center. I remember very little of the next 5 days after we left. I vaguely remember finally arriving at the medical center but being unable to get in, Brandon collapsing next to me, and being sure we would both freeze to death in this god-forsaken place.

Then everything is blank for the next 3 days due to my fever and the opiate meds that were administered. My first hazy memory after that was in a hospital bed with Brandon sitting by me. I remember him squeezing my hand and giving me a very genuine human smile, then turning his head for a few seconds as he tried not to show how strongly the stress had decimated him. Then I cried for a long time, and I knew Brandon would have cried to if he had lacrimal glands, but he was shaking and trying to suppress that.

I met the 2 android medical practitioners and thanked them profusely for their help. I wanted to hug them both but neither seemed like they wanted to, and stepped back when I reached for a hug. But that was OK, they were both very knowledgeable and caring. We all spent a long time catching each other up on what had transpired since the Cataclysm. We spent 6 weeks with Bill and Frank, ostensibly to not feel lonely for a while. But I think I was the only one that was lonely, and that's because I missed my family. The 3 androids didn't seem to harbor feelings of loneliness, but said they did I think to humor me and make me feel OK about hanging out with Bill and Frank when we didn't need to stay.

But after about 6 weeks Brandon and I wanted to return to our own shelter and didn't want to wear down Bill & Frank's supplies. Bill and Frank said the small body of water that had claimed our land vehicle was a pond, not a stream or river as Brandon had thought. In fact only about 2 km down the ridge beyond where we had crossed the pond came to an end, the ground became flatter, and crossing it to the other side should not be a problem. The storms seemed to have moderated at least for now.

Bill and Frank had direct access to a garage which housed 3 land vehicles similar to the one we had lost. These were to be used by community members but had not been needed up to now. They offered that we could have one of them to take us back to our shelter, and keep it there in case we again needed it. We were very grateful for that offer, and decided to return to our shelter the next day. We packed up some extra canned food for me, which the androids of course couldn't use, and a few other supplies for which we had room.

Next day we left after it became lighter outside. The oxygen content of the air had improved but still was not high enough to sustain breathing without an oxygen apparatus. The drive next to the ridge went without a problem, and indeed the crossing beyond the end of the pond was surprisingly flat and posed no difficulty. The way back from there to our shelter was also doable, with some rocky areas and debris from fallen buildings around which we needed to detour.

With Brandon driving the whole way we made it back to our shelter in 6 hours, which was much sooner than we had expected. We opened the garage lift and eased the vehicle into our garage then closed the lift. We unpacked the vehicle and it felt very safe but claustrophobic getting back to our shelter. Brandon and I had a little homecoming celebration. I peacefully fell asleep and Brandon deactivated in our own bed while holding each other in gratitude that we were safely back and had each other.

We finally were able to restart communication with the community near Edmonton. I became incredibly anxious when I first heard this was possible. Within hours we were able to talk with our family. I was ecstatic about this but wracked by fear that they might not all be safe. We were able to have a video/audio conversation with Tanil, Casey, and mom, which was so wonderful. They also said Slane was safe in their community. They had all managed to find an accommodation in an underground community near Edmonton within a day of the Apocalypse and had been able to survive there. It was unknown as to the state of the homestead where I had grown up, the weather was still too turbulent and the land too rough to attempt a trip there.

But then the bottom dropped out completely for me when I heard Dad had died of the omega version of the corona virus that had flashed through their whole community. I was unable to speak or even breathe after hearing that and broke down into unrelenting tears. I thought I was going to die from the wave of sorrow and emptiness that crushed me. I felt overcome by grief, sadness, guilt, and anger at Brandon. Brandon held me tightly and I knew he was also shocked about this but not letting it show for my sake. He ended the call and we hugged and I cried for a long time after that.

When I get really upset I try to imagine how Eva would have felt in a similar situation, such as after Megan and Marie were killed. I knew Eva had maintained her composure and gotten herself and Joe back safely to their base. I tried to emulate Eva in terms of her perspective with some success. But this was different too. Eva had always experienced an unfillable internal vacuum in that she didn't have a biological family or even a childhood. I had always felt the deepest security in my family, and now see that this was part of the karma I had needed to work through because of Eva's great void about not having a family. I had always had the treasure of my family despite all the ups and downs we had during life in the isolated northland.

I was so grateful that the rest of my family was alright but this was an intense wound finding out that dad had passed away. Eva in some ways would have been protected from that part of my devastation because she never had parents, but I will always cherish the memories of dad. I more and more realized how very similar but also different Eva and I are, and to synthesize the best of both of us into the human being that I am in this life. Brandon reminded me (I thought unempathetically) when I got so down about this that I had lived with the fear that they would all be dead, and so I needed to be grateful for the family I had left rather than what I had lost.

Eva had always wondered what human emotions were really like, not just the android equivalents of emotions that she had become adept at sensing. She had been unable to feel emotions directly, and craved to experience them. Like a person blind or deaf from birth it was an unfillable void for her to wonder about that. Now as a human being I felt cursed by my devastating feelings of grief and loss, as I always have done when sorrowful things happened. I wished I could just extinguish feelings altogether and experience numbness instead. If indeed I am Eva's reincarnation her craving certainly came true, and is now mine to handle. I had to struggle to quell my impulse to get drunk and high or cut myself or end my life

I also struggled with the whole idea of reincarnation. As a girl I attended a Catholic Bible study class. One of the boys in the class proposed that after a person dies he or she comes back again rather than winds up permanently in heaven or hell. I remember the stodgy priest becoming angry about that, declaring this was only the devil talking. He said if a person really believed that they would surely wind up in hell as there are only 2 alternatives.

I remember being really confused when I heard that and also angry at and frightened of the priest. Tanil heard the same thing in another class and stated to me that was bullshit. He disparagingly stated the whole of organized religion was nothing but a sham and scam to finance higher up church officials and build expensive churches.

Then to take that confusion to an even higher level, the notion that an android could reincarnate as a human or vice versa seemed even more preposterous. Or, if a human could come back as another human, could an android come back as another android? Could a dog or a fish or a tree come back as another of its kind or a different form of life? When I was in college I would get so overwhelmed and bewildered by existential conundrums I would actually get a headache and then would drink wine or vodka to quell my circular racing thoughts and anxiety.

But then I found out the next day the conundrum was still there and the headache had gotten worse by the hangover. At this point in my life I laid that mental mishmash to rest. I went instead with my keen subjective sense that my goal is to use the dialectic that I strongly feel of myself and Eva into the functioning of an emotionally sensitive individual, balanced with a practical attitude and spiritual consciousness. That at least is perhaps my pretentious goal!

We were together again in our underground apartment for the next year, but now not nearly as isolated due to the tunnels that had been completed. We spent our time helping to re-establish the community food and supplies distribution. This was a time of appreciation of Brandon's stability and support, and our relationship was good. But I had to keep drawing out Brandon who would become isolative, as was his chronic tendency.

MAROONED ON CHARON

Sometimes he would annoy me, as he always has, by his implacability. I knew this was because of his natural android temperament but also he had "inherited" (through a spiritual connection not genomic bond) Joe's main psychological defense in stressful situations to withdraw into himself. Brandon was well aware of this too. I tried to channel my natural high emotionality into pulling Brandon out of his shell. I tried not to always figure out what was going on in Brandon's head, he had a right to think whatever way he does.

Brandon's health was gradually failing by 3.5 years post Cataclysm. It was 5 years since his previous revitalization, and this decline was of course expected. He wasn't moving as quickly and smoothly as was his wont, his vision and other senses were slowly deteriorating, and cognition not quite as quick and sharp. Thank God his last revitalization had been 1.5 years before the Cataclysm rather than earlier. But being now one lustrum it was now time for the next revitalization or we would risk permanent damage to his health.

We had survived the worst of the Cataclysm's effects, and could now travel to distant places if needed, of course with great respect for the vicissitudes of the weather. The Android Institute near Seattle was still in operation, one of only 3 known facilities for android creation and full revitalizations known to still exist. So we scheduled this for Brandon. The drive was long and we had to seek shelter for one or more nights 3 times along the way due to the protean weather conditions. We stayed in Seattle for 2 weeks while Brandon completely recovered, and I stayed by his side every day. Our return to Winnepeg was less challenging than had been the first part of the trip.

RETURN TO A DECIMATED WORLD ABOVE GROUND

It is now 4 years since the start of the disaster. The ground over the city had been cleared and construction was beginning on above ground houses. These would be staunchly built to survive strong storms, and pressurized. The air on the surface could only be breathed naturally for short periods of 5 minutes at a time, although continuous use of a respirator mask was still recommended whenever outside. Most of the above ground houses were being built atop or very near a connected underground apartment, so that in weather emergencies retreat to below ground safety could readily be done. The pace of the climate normalizing was frustratingly slow but it was wonderful to see greenness returning to plants and trees, color and aroma to flowers. The world was gradually returning to normal.

Finally we were able to travel to the underground community where my family was still located. It was a wonderful but tearful reunion with them, and of course without dad. Brandon seemed genuinely happy to see them as well, knowing the effect it was having on me. Also this was the only family he'd ever had so it was a source of joy for him as well. After a few days we decided to attempt a drive to the old homestead. This we did with difficulty but we were able to get through all the destruction along the way.

After visiting the old property where I grew up we decided to rebuild a life there. The old house was too damaged to reasonably be rebuilt, and the barn had been demolished in the storms and earthquakes. The trees had all blown down except for a few ragged black spruce, and most of the other vegetation was dead or nearly so. Mom had some savings and so did Brandon and me. With that money we cleared all the dead bushes and trees, and replaced some of it with new vegetation although this was scarce after the destruction of most flora in the cataclysm, and had to be of a very hardy variety.

We built a house, albeit smaller than the old one, but with some of the layout and exterior reminiscent of the old house. The new house, though fairly compact, was completely air pressurized. The foundation and frame were of very stout construction, and built to withstand the level of earthquake that had destroyed the old house. The below ground level contained all the elements needed for long term residence in case the above ground level needed to be sealed off in further environmental devastations. We did most of the lighter parts of the construction ourselves, and this was really exciting and satisfying as we saw it take shape.

May 15, 2358 It was now 5 years since the start of the cataclysm, I was 35, Kacey was 24 and trying to find her goals in life, and she temporarily moved in too. Mom was here of course, and this was a wonderful relief. Tanil had an already established job in Edmonton so was staying there, but close enough to regularly come out to visit. Corinne and Slane were close enough to visit also. This was so wonderful that we could be together again, of course with the unfillable void of dad's absence.

Brandon seemed satisfied with it although, being Brandon, his enthusiasm for the family togetherness was less obvious, which bothered me at times. I did recognize that this was my family of origin and not Brandon's, but also didn't see why this should make a difference. Brandon was also able to reconnect with his old human friend and roommate Tom and they also regularly visited each other.

August 2, 2359 I've wanted to bear a child for many years, even as a teenager. Now at age 36 I knew my fertile period might be running down. Needing to have a child had become an obsession with me and a source of great anxiety and self-deprecation. This despite rationally knowing I shouldn't blame myself for all the chaos of the cataclysm. This was one of the few times I wished I had married a human instead of an android! I certainly didn't like that feeling and kept it to myself. I don't know if Brandon ever felt a vacuum that he couldn't procreate, nor did I ever want to ask him.

Numerous sperm and fertilized egg banks had been established before the cataclysm due to fears the human race might face extinction. It was unknown to us if any of these still existed, but we thought it would be likely to find one in Edmonton or Winnipeg. But then another idea arose, initially proffered by Brandon. What if his long time human friend Tom would be willing to contribute his sperm? On the one hand we both were well assured that Tom was genetically excellent in terms of intelligence, physical attractiveness, attitudes, morals, talents, etc. Also as far as we knew Tom didn't have any known genetic defects or family history of genetic or serious mental illness disorders.

But how would we feel if I became pregnant and knew Tom was the biological father? Would he feel a need to engage in (or meddle with) parenting the child? Could this destroy Brandon's close friendship with Tom? What if a birth defect occurred would Tom feel guilt and regret about this? Brandon and I discussed these issues multiple times, and Brandon was less worried about these concerns than was I.

As usual Brandon approached this in a calm and rational manner, while my emotions often got the best of me. Fortunately, Brandon knew how to get me back in equilibrium as he always had. Brandon thought it would be a very positive situation and Tom would recognize his role as a godfather or close uncle, rather than a need to take on some type of parenting role. Of course the next step was for Brandon to talk to Tom about this.

This he did, and Tom agreed. Brandon said he and Tom had talked at length and both had shared their reservations and hopes about this. Brandon didn't say much more about this nor did I push on it to respect their private conversation. I became pregnant after two attempts at invitro implantation of the sperm from Tom. I was immeasurably ecstatic after finding this out, though reluctantly warning myself that the pregnancy may or may not proceed to success. We had very careful and regular monitoring by the OBGYN as there were very few known pregnancies that had occurred since the catastrophe, and there were many unknowns about the effects of environmental chemicals, etc.

But the pregnancy proceeded smoothly, and I was constantly thrilled that this had occurred after literally lifetimes of desiring it. On May 11, 2361, I gave birth to a healthy baby boy! I was ecstatic, and Brandon (in his own way) was too. We named him Earl Bruce, after a distant progenitor of 300 years earlier, and (very incidentally) a famous college football coach of the late twentieth century.

Earl had a very normal and healthy course of early development. By age 3 he was well ahead of historical standards of intellectual development. He had a very reactive and at times rather extreme emotional response to all kinds of situations. In this way he took after his mom. Tom frequently visited and also became close to Earl, and we called him Uncle Tom.

Brandon was back at the University of Alberta in the geophysical department. He said the geophysical data that was being monitored indicated a fairly stable status of the tectonic plates, and at least as far as was known there was no indication of imminent tectonic movement. I stayed at home with Earl, mom, and Kacey who was still with us. I had developed some building skills and worked on doing some more house remodeling and working outside on the barn and yard when weather permitted.

Kacey had a part time job in Edmonton and was trying to finish college, which had finally reopened. I was so thankful that at least part of the family could still be together in a fairly stable situation. The storms were still regular and at times violent, and at times we needed to retreat underground for days at a time. But we could still get outside some days with suitable clothes and respirators and this was wonderful. I felt the most peace that I had experienced since my early days on the farm before the cataclysm.

Three years after Earl was born Brandon and I decided to attempt another invitro fertilization, I was now 38. Again we used Tom's frozen sperm, and on the second attempt I was once again pregnant. Eight months later I gave birth to a healthy baby girl, whom we named Dawn Gloria. Life proceeded after that in a normal and beautiful way. I was able to look at life in a positive and satisfied way after all the previous chaos. My emotional balance seemed to stabilize as well over time, with the support of my family and Brandon, and I think the coping skills I had introjected from my deeply engrained memories of Eva.

Mom died in 2371 of natural processes, was not in pain before her death, and we had been able to take care of her at home. The environment continued to stabilize and it was wonderful to see the return of healthy trees, flowers, even some crops. Due to the greatly decreased population the inevitable pollution was not great enough to stall the steady improvement in the climate. The air was breathable for much of the time, and the water in the lakes and rivers had become clearer.

In 2391 I celebrated my 68th birthday. It's interesting I haven't kept up my journal regularly now for many years. I think all the distress and emotional intensity of my younger years dissipated, and I became accepting of life, or perhaps just less motivated and lazier. Brandon and I have lived a beautiful life together and demonstrated (as had Joe and Eva) the complimentary of human and android personalities. Earl and Dawn had moved on to Edmonton in terms of jobs and relationships and Kacey had lived in Chicago for 25 years. Slane remained a close friend and we visited each other periodically.

Corinne and I stayed so close over the years. She loved the farm so much that 15 years ago she moved back to the farm too. Brandon was very accepting of her and Tom remained close to us as well. It perhaps seemed strange, but after his wife passed away he came to live with us too. All of us worked on adding a substantial addition to our house. We then maintained a close and surprising relationship between the four of us. Perhaps not so surprising anyway. Since the cataclysm it had become common for extended families and friends to live together to survive the harsh environment, and this cultural pattern had remained intact as the environment stabilized.

MAROONED ON CHARON

TRANSLATION AND AWAKENING

September 4, 2390, I had been inflicted with the most recent iteration of the omega coronavirus five days ago. The symptoms increased rapidly and I spent the last 5 days of my life in the ICU. It was so sad that my human family could only maintain their vigil from behind the ICU window. But some family members were there around the clock and we were frequently talking over the phone. Thank God Brandon stayed physically with me the whole time and Corinne was there in the room as well.

I was emotionally resigned when my last breath occurred, I was sad that I was leaving my loved ones behind, but was accepting of it and not fighting it, or being anxious or panicked. I knew Darwin could again lead me safely over the treacherous river Styx and take me to some beautiful but lonely and isolated place where I would eventually again see Brandon. My perception floated up from the lifeless corpse, and I looked around the room from above the bed.

Brandon and Corinne held my hands, and I knew both were aware of my transition. I tried one last time to breathe and nothing happened. The only movement of which I seemed capable was touching Brandon's neck where he likes to be touched, and I don't know if that was a physical or astral body touch. I knew my children were on the other side of the observation glass watching Brandon and Corinne's movements. I knew they were confused, I tried to give them some sort of sign but couldn't muster up any signal.

Then I saw Darwin, who smiled pleasantly and said, "let's get you safely on to your afterlife." Then my perception became hazy, and I felt I was moving on to my next destination. At this point I don't believe I was harassed by Charon or other underworld entities. I knew a brief, scaled down funeral would be held but I have no memory of being there. I knew I needed to detach from the physical plane and get accustomed to my new circumstances.

After some indefinite but seemingly eternal period of semi consciousness Elin appeared, warm, supportive and calming. She was beautiful, in a pinkish red flowing dress that reflected various colors of the shimmering fog around us. Her skin glowed with a light blue aura, as did mine when I looked down. Elin said it was time again for a life review, so I could see what I did and didn't accomplish in my life, and decide on my circumstances and goals my next life.

Elin said she would help me with this karmatic therapy but the choices would ultimately be my own. Elin also said I had just finished my 125th life, the first on Earth, and the others in varied but ascending physical bodies in this and other galaxies! Elin will help me integrate my experiences in the life I just finished, with all the other previous lives. I marveled that I had some recollection, although hazy, of a few of these lives in which incredibly momentous events had occurred.

In looking back I recall how I went into this lifetime with a craving for the things I couldn't have as an android, particularly human emotions, the experience of childhood, having a family of origin, having children of my own, and human feelings including sexual urges. Indeed in this lifetime I did experience these things, embracing all their positive and negative aspects. But I also see how I wasn't prepared to cope with the extremes of these feelings and experiences. The loss of family members had been particularly devastating.

I had experimented with means of numbing the negative emotions including drugs, alcohol, even intentional self-injury. In the end I think I worked through these negative adaptational attempts and incorporated the rationality and implacability of Eva into my personality. This despite the extreme chaos of the earthquakes, volcanoes and need to resort to underground living.

My relationship with Brandon was the jewel that helped me through all those challenges, along with my family and children. I realize I've grown a lot personally through all this but have much further to go. I also thank Darwin for his guidance and protection along the way. Elin dropped in on me several times during this period of self-reflection and helped me distill my experiences into growth and insight and I am thankful to her for this.

After another semiconscious period that seemed eternal I became aware that I was in what appeared to be a valley with snowcapped mountains all around. I felt alive, and I knew my vibratory frequency had increased again. There were trees of an evergreen shape but of various shades of blue and purple. The clearing that I seemed to be in was covered with a rich carpet of bluish grass. There was the sun or perhaps some other star overhead, it seemed to be redder and a bit broader than the Earth's sun.

The sky reflected that periwinkle solar color, the atmosphere seemed thin but I had no trouble breathing, the air was cool with a light breeze. Then I saw Brandon about 50ft away, with Rupert by his side! Both saw me at the same time, we all ran together and mutually embraced for a long time. I was completely overwhelmed with joy at this wondrous reunion.

Amon appeared with Elin and directed us to create a home for ourselves in the mountains while here in the astral plane. It took us a little while to coordinate our visualizations, but then we did. We creatively visualized a small cabin on the side of a mountain. It was simple in detail and fairly small, but with all the things we needed for food and shelter, and in a most charming setting. We were on the upper shore of a small lake and could see from there all the way to the bottom of the mountain. We had a patio or deck between the cabin and the lake, surrounded by trees and flowers. There was even a swing hanging from a stout tree branch on the right side looking down at the lake.

Elin and Amon presented to us the possibility of reincarnating as human babies during the fetal period. Elin said it as "An adventure and initiation into successful humans, under the tutelage of androids. The human race at that time would have become extinct, except for those frozen embryos and sperm that remained viable. These would be under the care of the small android population that continued to live on the Earth. The habitation of the fetus by your soul bodies would happen about 6 months into the fetal period. This would be preferable to implantation of soul right at this time of fertilization as the error rate for fetal survival is unknown for that time."

Amon said, "your great adventure on Charon possibly saved humanity from extinction and it would be an honor for you to again provide a means of restoring the race." Elin said, "you can eventually marry and become one of the first Adam and Eve's of the resurrected race." Brandon was not ambivalent about this proposition, which surprised me. So we both agreed to this task without undo anxiety or fear. Amon stated that we might like to exchange gender roles, to give us an understanding of being the opposite sex.

Jel's future person would thus be male and Brandon a female. We talked further about hopes and goals for a radically recreated human race. I think Elin and especially Amon were somewhat surprised at the quick mutual acceptance of this new role. Amon said they would visit again in about 20 days. If we should, one or both of us, decide not to do this task we could be prepared for an alternate future life together further in the future, possibly on a different planet.

Twenty days after that Elin and Amon both appeared again. Brandon and I confirmed that we were ready for the next physical life, and under the circumstances previously described. Nonetheless I still had some ambivalence at leaving this beautiful and peaceful place, and then being separated for a while before we could reunite. I know Brandon was thinking of this too. But this was the right time and there was no point in postponing the inevitable. Plus this seemed like a great challenge and hopefully service to the human race. Tomorrow Elin and Amon will come again and will help us transition to our physical bodies after we go to sleep. I'm sure Darwin will be there too to escort us safely to our next physical realities.

MAROONED ON CHARON

BRANDON'S STORY AND JEL'S DEATH

I'm Brandon Hayden and I'd like to narrate my most extraordinary adventures with my wife, Jel Straw Hayden. Jel died on September 29, 2391, at the age of 68. She had contracted CoVid omega #8, which was running rampid through a number of communities and was the most virulent and lethal of any CoVid versions in history. I was by her side when it happened, being safe from infection because I'm an android, and Corinne was there too. Earl and Dawn sadly had to watch their mother through the ICU window, and several other family and friends were also present outside the glass. Jel had been fleetingly conscious and oriented about 5 minutes before, after having been asleep or delirious for the previous day.

She tearfully and in a very soft voice told me she loved me and wants to see me again. I squeezed her hand and said I love her too, will always love her, and had no question that I'd meet her in the afterlife. I felt genuinely sad in a human way, and also had distorted, gray vision and turgid thinking in the typical android reaction to deep grief. I sensed her spirit slowly rise from her body to several feet over her body. I felt a gentle caress on my right shoulder and neck, and knew that was Jel because that was exactly how she knew I liked to be touched. I could tell Corinne was experiencing Jel's transition in the same way.

Jel's funeral was held 3 days later. Jel's close family and friends were in the front of the small audience in the funeral facility. The audience included in addition to myself Earl, Dawn, Dawn's 2 young children, Kacey, Tanil, Corinne, Tom, and Slane. 12 other individuals were also present, a mix of androids and humans, plus the female nondenominational chaplain. Of course there was a mixture of sadness and open grief overtly expressed by the humans and the more restrained but equally deep expression by the androids.

The Chaplain, myself, Corinne, Tanil, Slane, Dawn and Earl gave short tributes to Jel's courage, deep family love, resilience, and inner as well as outer beauty. I experienced a deep pride in Jel, and an inner peace knowing I would see her again in the afterlife. I have no doubt about this even though it goes beyond any scientific rationality. I later corroborated the uniquely android part of my sublime experience with Corinne, who agreed.

But first I'll introduce myself to you. I'm a series 8 android, built in 2338 and then educated and trained for 5 years at the Android University in Seattle. My whole training and education of course had a focus on rational thinking and practical decision making in a complex and troubled society of 99% humans. There had from the first been a few eldritch and disconnected images and thoughts that gave me cognitive dissonance and broke the sheltered rationality and sense of control of my years in the Academy.

In retrospect I had become rather haughty about my advanced android skills, even though androids were not supposed to have personality deviations such as haughtiness or narcissism. For example I became almost disoriented and unable to speak coherently when sometimes there were strong storms or even blizzards that cut off all visibility and made me feel very alone. I was troubled that I couldn't just put these images to rest. I had similar panic when I saw several news accounts of earthquakes producing huge chasms in the ground.

Even more ambiguous was the impression of a great void within myself. I often felt there were vague images of experiencing an intensely close but bizarre relationship with a female. I fought these images and impressions because I couldn't control or understand them and they threatened my sense of control as an android. It wasn't until much later that I discovered the roots of these seemingly disparate impressions.

During my third, fourth and fifth years at the academy I moved out of the dorms and secured a small apartment with a human named Andrae who was about 25 and worked in the community. I at that time had no close relationships with any humans, or for that matter any androids either. Neither had Andrae experienced much more than superficial contacts with androids. So at first we had a rather stiff roommate relationship, but as the months went by we started doing some activities together which did us both good. We attended some events together, went hiking and to the beach.

I began to open up my thinking to realize I needed some other individual in my life besides myself. Plus Andrae showed to me emotions that androids could perceive in others but not directly experience themselves. At the end of the fifth year I had my first five year full rejuvenation. After 2 weeks I had fully recovered, and my body and mind were in new condition again. At the android university there was an art gallery comprising art done by androids who had attended the university over the past 300 years. Included were 4 of the paintings Eva had done of her memories of Charon.

At the time I was well familiar with the voyage to Charon and relationship of Eva and Joe. But I didn't know too much about these paintings. Even though they had been at the Academy for centuries and almost everyone had seen them, I had not. Strangely I had always shied away from them for reasons unknown to me. But now I brought myself to wanting to overcome this mental block.

The first 3 were views in several directions of the inside of the crater from the perspective of the base on Charon. The third of these showed the light blue orb of Pluto rising over the crater wall. Blue gray patches of Pluto's light shimmered on the crater floor and sides, adding an eerily beautiful cast. I was surprised at how vaguely fearful thoughts and distorted perceptual responses arose in my brain from the first 3 paintings.

Then I saw the almost fabled painting of the tragedy, with the chasm opening in the ground and the ground vehicle of Megan and Marie teetering on the edge. I had a sense of shock, my vision went almost black, my cognitions were frozen. Something was fumbling and rattling at the latch of my recollection, while another unknown force sought to keep the portal barred. I staggered and the few androids around me grabbed me and helped me sit down. I couldn't even explain to the android health worker who came over what had happened. An android whom I had known from my dorm who was there sat with me until I felt ready to leave. Eventually I recovered and returned to my apartment.

At the time I was not aware of why I had experienced that visceral, panicked, mind numbing response, the first time a response like that had ever happened to me. But years later the reason for this became very clear as the resurfacing of a deeply repressed and traumatic image from my previous life as Joe on Charon. I could to some extent relate to Joe despite his being a human and I not having had much interaction with humans other than with Tom. Joe pushed people away due to fear of being hurt and did not look for romantic or close relationships, but had been placed in a situation where he had to form a deeply close and intense relationship even though he resisted this.

At that point in my life I had few close associates, was very independent, and resolved to stay that way. Nonetheless there was a nagging thought that I'd like to someday have a loving wife and even a family, although I tried to suppress those thoughts from my mind, dismissing such thoughts as unnecessary and impractical for an android.

After graduation I took a job as a geophysical engineer in Edmonton. I had an apartment by myself in Edmonton, which was quite suitable to me. Andrae had stayed in Seattle, but we talked regularly and got together every few months. Two years after moving to Edmonton Andrae called me and said he had contracted an especially severe form of the currently evolved CoVid virus and was in the hospital in Intensive Care. He asked me to come down to Seattle to be with him in case he didn't survive, and was clearly worried this might be the case. I dropped everything and booked the next available hovertrain ride to Seattle.

The case progressed rapidly but I was able get to his bedside while he was still conscious. Androids are not subject to the CoVid virus and so I could visit him at bedside without restriction. He had no other android friends and his human family was there but not allowed to be with him without a fully protective suit and mask so I knew he felt very isolated. I maintained a stoic manner as we recalled some of our adventures and expressed our love (yes I was even able to say that word to him) and gratitude for all he had meant to me, but my thoughts were clouded and my physical and mental balance were shaken.

As I was returning to Edmonton it occurred to me that Joe, in the biography of Joe and Eva had experienced a somewhat similar loss of his brother who had been the closest person to him. I had read that famous autobiography several times, which was well known among most humans and almost all androids. I didn't at that time relate myself to Joe any more than that. But I remember Joe having described that event as causing him to turn away from other people. After Andrae died I resorted to my most natural and prominent android defense of stolid rationality. Although I don't experience human emotions my world became dark, colorless, my thoughts were negative and disjointed and I tried but was unable to replace these with positive cognitions.

I resorted to a solitary life outside of work with little motivation for the interests I had in the past. For several years I diligently applied myself to my geophysical research. It seemed inevitable that within at most a few decades there would be earthquakes of unprecedented size that would occur along the fault lines of western United States and Canada. I became a leading researcher in this field, with the goal of predicting more closely the where and when of this event(s) would occur by studying sonar reports, historical markers, etc. Edmonton was an ideal place for this type of study (although also correspondingly more dangerous) being in an area that would likely be affected.

So I shut most other things out of my attention with the unspoken personal goal of not letting myself to get into close friendships with anyone. Sometimes I would get together with a few of my colleagues because I thought I needed to be considered an accessible member of the team. I had a few dates with several human and several android females who initiated an interest in getting to know me. But I dropped these liaisons within a few dates as I didn't want to get encumbered with personal relationships. It surprised me when several of the human females seemed to get attached to me and then disappointed when I broke off the friendship. I really had no concept of human male-female emotions or attraction. The several android females were much easier in that we just did some things together, there was no emotional attachment or romance involved.

That whole protective defense I had rigidly applied to myself was rocked when I met Jel. I had many confused and conflicting thoughts about her, but I found being with her was comfortable and I was motivated to do it. Jel seemed to fairly rapidly develop positive emotions to me. She called this a "crush," and I guess as much as an android can I also had my first "crush." She told me things about human perspectives on androids, especially the reaction of human females to male androids. I found this very interesting and I had previously had little inkling of these complexities.

The reaction of human females to android males was dichotomous, according to Jel. Androids were in general designed to be physically attractive to humans and Jel said she found me very nice looking. Android males were desirable for their good looks, calmness, rationality, common sense. But they were also considered by some females to be dull, unromantic and "machine-like." Jel also shared with some apparent embarrassment that android males were not considered by some to be "sexy," having even heard the insulting comment "droids don't have dicks." Series 8 males were given a penis of sorts for urination to discharge nutritional fluids that had been injected, but could not achieve an erection and of course had no procreative abilities.

So android males were considered by some women "as just machines" that looked good but weren't any better than manikins as far as providing sexual satisfaction. I tried to understand this but couldn't, and when Jel apologized if I had been offended I didn't understand this either. I assured Jel I wasn't offended, but just didn't understand what was to me the idea of sexual satisfaction. I told Jel the closest I could come was my reaction of beautiful and peaceful colors and shapes when she stroked my shoulders and neck and just being with me. She liked that explanation and said that was fine, and we would work on increasing her sexual satisfaction through means other than intercourse.

This was all so new and bewildering and chimerical to me, which she actually found funny, which I didn't understand either. Suffice it to say Jel accepted me for all the things I am and am not, and I fully accepted everything about her including her very emotional self. Jel said she appreciated that when she went off on one her emotional excursions I listened and tried my best to understand. She said when she would get angry when other people including her family would get defensive and yell back or retreat into silence. I did neither of those things because I didn't get angry or insulted. I would listen and reflect and show I cared which usually defused the situation quickly.

Perhaps part of her reaction to me was one of empathy for things that weren't even clear to me. She realized I had distanced myself from human relationships, and that there was a void of not experiencing a family or even a childhood. But we seemed to complement each other well. Jel was a very emotional individual and I provided a calming and steadying force for her. In turn she provided for me a relationship and also a family of sorts when we would visit, which was good for me and an area of uncharted waters for me to explore and appreciate.

I told her that if the sexual issue was a concern for her I would understand and we wouldn't become intimate or go any further in a relationship. But it was very important to me that her feelings not be hurt and that her friendship had become very important to me and I wanted it to continue. But she said the sexual aspect didn't matter, I didn't know whether to believe her or not. But I also told her how gently stroking of an androids body produced very nice images and colors and thoughts, and that I would try whatever she wanted me to give her some satisfaction. We agreed on this and then waited to see what would happen.

We became very close friends over the next 3 years. I struggled with trying to know if I "loved her," in human terms in fact this question became obsessive for me as it stood for the fundamental difference between androids and humans and the chimerical void in my cognitions as to what human emotions were really like. But whatever were my own personal confusions about my identity the relationship grew up and I knew I she had become vitally important to me.

June 2, 2347 We married in a small and strange but beautiful ceremony. Jel wore a simple but beautiful white gown, and with her statuesque beauty and long dark hair I found her to be the ultimate in human beauty. 20 of Jel's closest family and friends were present, with Corinne as her maid of honor, and Slane and Kasey as bridesmaids. Tom was my best man, as we had done many things together with and without Jel since I met. There were only 5 androids besides myself present, 2 from the Geophysics dept, 2 from my days at the Academy, Corinne and one other female android. That android was Shannon who had been a good and platonic friend before and after I met Jel.

A very liberal nondenominational pastor married us. We were the first android-human marriage in Alberta, and 3 members of local news outlets were also present at the simple and unusual ceremony and dance/reception afterwards. The androids of course didn't eat afterwards but sat with the human guests, which seemed odder to the humans than it did to the androids.

MAROONED ON CHARON

AN ASTOUNDING NIGHTMARE OF A DISASTER

March 17, 2348 I reactivated this morning with a sense of shock, disbelief, and disorientation. After a bit I realized I must have had a mental event while deactivated that was now crystal clear and overwhelming in its message and intensity. I rarely dream in the sense of a human being but this morning perceived that I had dreamed vividly upon morning reactivation. But last night's mental event was shockingly vivid, much more so than any other nocturnal imagery I had previously experienced.

I awakened from a dream that was stupefying. I dreamed I was Joe on Charon, in that disastrous trip to locate the alien source of the devastating transmissions. I was in the ground vehicle with Eva, and the alien apparition appeared. I could see the two figures and see the images they projected clearly. But the message was different than that witnessed by Joe and Marie. The substance of the dream was completely nonverbal. But the imagery and the effect on my android equivalents of human emotions (colors, image distortion, smell, rational and organized thought breakdown) were starkly real.

In the dream I became aware of the certainty of an impending disaster that would befall the Earth within a scant few years. The image of a map was crystal clear, including coordinates, like a moving holographic projection. A massive volcano will occur on Mauna Loa, which will act as catalyst for two enormous earthquakes. One will occur off the western coast of the United States and Canada. This will soon trigger another that will occur along the Pacific coast of Russia, China, and Japan. Enormous tsunamis 80 meters high will roll over both coasts.

Cities that have erected towering fortifications against the rising ocean, such as Seattle and Tokyo will see those fortifications crumble and floods of 7 or more meters will cover those cities and all other places along both coasts. I was able to see almost exacting parameters of the longitudes, latitudes, and depths of the fault points. I perceived very specific oceanographic data that were far in advance in specificity of anything I'd ever seen in and likely of any known by human and android oceanographers.

The next image exhibited a heavy dark ash and mist mixture occluding the atmosphere of a forested area with a dim yellow nimbus of the sun unsteadily peeking through overhead. The trees and adjacent crop land looked to be dead or dying with forest creatures as well as humans suffocated to death by the oxygen depleted atmosphere. The following image showed hurricane force winds overpowering and leveling a deserted community, with fires raging in the background. After this was a heavy blizzard snow burying what might have been Los Angeles or Phoenix or Mexico City.

The impression in the next image was of a long length of time, perhaps years, decades or centuries. But then the ash had finally settled, and the world seemed to be purer and more temperate again. There was a quiet sea coast with gentle waves of pristine water caressing the sandy beach. There was a small community with a few people walking about. All were attractive, seemed to be in their

20's or 30's, and there appeared to be several sets of identical twins and triplets. But this strangely brought on a weirdly disquieting thought: perhaps these were androids and the humans were gone.

Then came an even more enigmatic scene. Several people who apparently were medical personnel surrounded a crib. One picked up the infant, and the personnel seemed almost awed and exuberant. Therefore my previous speculation was seemingly disconfirmed, as the infant had to be human. The dream then abruptly ended, and I awoke totally confused, overwhelmed.

After activating and recalling my dream I tried to make sense of these images. I came to the following conclusions, based on my knowledge as a geophysicist. The warming of the oceans has destabilized the undersea flows and will hasten the likelihood of the earthquakes. An ash and sulphurous mixture will cause the global atmosphere to become dark and oxygen depleted. Some, perhaps most, plant and animal species will become nearly or completely extinct.

The global warming trend will be reversed and a much colder and darker period will occur especially in much of the higher latitudes of both hemispheres. This will likely gradually resolve over a ten to twenty year period. When the ash finally settles, there will be a purer and more temperate world again. It is possible that the human race will be extinguished due to the weather disasters, the shortages of food that will occur, and the relentless, ever mutating pandemic virus will continue to thrive.

After I awoke I was incredulous and frightened. I took written notes of the detailed data that I clearly remembered. Jel then came back into the bedroom looking stunned. She had had a dream very like my own although not exactly so. Jel was equally shocked at her own dream, which she sobbingly shared with me. The catastrophic prediction of monstrous earthquakes and volcanoes had also shaken Jel to her core.

She didn't get the specific geological data that I did, perhaps because she didn't have a geophysical cognitive structure that I had acquired. Her image of herself being Eva on Charon had shaken but not necessarily surprised her. Then I remembered my similar, disorienting, shocking reaction at the Academy Art center when I saw that very event that Eva had painted 300 years ago.

Shortly after Jel told me this the call from Slane came through. I was rocked to hear that Slane had a nightmare last night of the same event as Jel had. This was a most bizarre synchronicity! But Slane's first dream image was from the perspective of Megan in the ground vehicle carrying her and Marie that was about to plummet into the chasm. After that she saw the same images that Jel had seen. Slane was in a complete panic reaction to her dream and Jel was trying to calm her down.

I could not rationally grasp what had happened. Why did all three of us have similar but not identical dreams? If just one of us had their version of this nightmare it could be seen as a response to everyone's realistic worry about future earthquakes. It might even have been a karmic image from a former life breaking through dream awareness. I didn't know if such things were possible but

I certainly could not rule that out either. But why did the three of us have different, very personal images of the past and future events?

We contacted other people we knew but none had experienced the vivid scenes that we had. Other androids whom I contacted had had blurry semblances of some nonspecific disaster leaving vague fears. This was possibly an example of that indistinct partially conscious communication that often occurred between androids. I told Jel and Slane that no matter what the explanation might be we needed to consider what action we would take.

I said I would research available data at my work that might corroborate this dream data. If I could find this I'd share with my colleagues, fellow scientists and whomever else would listen to this news. Then my new purpose in life would be trying to convince anyone who would listen of the urgency of building suitable shelters and supplies. Jel and Slane agreed, and we resolved to also make shelters and stocks of food and necessities of life for us and our families, if they would listen.

One week after our dreams I received a call from Shara Borowicz, who had heard about our departmental meetings and attempts to spread the cataclysmic warning by calls, internet, and the media to anyone who might listen about the imminent danger. I had met Shara several times before. She was a physician, and member of the android medicine department at the University of Chicago. She was a human female, single, about 40 years old. Besides the human medicine education she had studied android medicine. Android medicine was a curious combination of electronics, metal and plastic skeletal design, humanlike skin, artificial intelligence, and wellness/maintenance practices for androids. She had done research correlating the efficacy of similar wellness practices as used in both human and android medicine.

She'd previously worked at the University of Alberta as did I. I'd seen her at a few conferences, once had attended a social event and had talked to her for a while. I remember having had a strange sense of recognition of her at that social event with no rational basis. She seemed to have had that for me also and we both locked eyes and drifted together through the other humans and androids present. I thought perhaps she had transference toward me from some other android she knew, as there were 8, as far as I knew, of series 8 male androids who were my duplicates.

I in fact pointed out this odd sense of recognition we both had, and she didn't think I reminded her of anyone else, android or human. This made for what seemed like an awkward conversation, with this odd underpinning of recognition. I also picked up a sense of sadness or tragedy about her. I wondered if she had experienced some tragic event but didn't feel comfortable enough sharing that personal question with her. Therefore when I got the unexpected call from Shara I was very surprised.

Shara had heard about our committee's plea for action in view of the dreams Jel, Slane and I had had, and the geophysical data in my dream that had been corroborated by our subsequent research. She also was aware that no one she knew or had heard of but the 3 of us had experienced more than the vaguest element of foreboding in those dreams. Shara told me she had had an intense dream the same night as Jel, Slane and I had. She saw herself in an enclosure or perhaps vehicle of unknown type in an alien, eldritch environment illuminated by a dim blue light. Someone else was present with her. She had felt a terrifying plunge into a chasm and then the enclosure or vehicle being crushed around her so she couldn't breathe.

But also she had experienced part of the dream that I had, with a blurry memory of earthquake fault line failure but a few pieces of the data had been clear, and she had recorded these upon awakening. She didn't have a geophysical background so the data was disconnected and of obscure significance to her. We did a quick comparison and the data she had recorded clearly was exactly the same as mine (although less complete). We were both overcome by her anecdote and I could tell she was choking back tears and panic while she was recounting it. I told her of the images of the same event in Jel, Slane and my own dreams, and the shocking synchronicity of Slane's dream to hers.

We ended the long call by her resolution to come as soon as possible to see Jel, Slane and myself and help the committee make plans and broadcast the message. When Shara arrived 3 days later we hugged, and Jel gave her a big hug too. I had the same sense with Shara as I had before, an unspoken deeply seated grief, but now rawer than before. The 3 of us talked long into the night of our dreams and speculation as to what it meant. Slane arrived next day. She had a tearful reunion with Jel and warm welcome to me too. But her reaction to Slane was even more remarkable.

Both seemed emotionally shocked and overcome when they saw each other, and seemed hesitant to hug each other, especially Shara, but just for a moment. Then they embraced and cried together for what seemed like an interminably long time. The tears seemed to reflect joy at meeting but I also picked up a mutual sense of deep recognition and sorrow. Jel was crying too, and my vision had grown gray and blurry. If I had had lacrimal glands I'm sure I would have cried as echoes of the past and forebodings of the future filled the air around us.

We talked over and over and wondered why the four of us had experienced this bizarre nocturnal visitation, but no one else of whom we knew were aware. Particularly the other individuals to whom we were close hadn't had the dreams, especially Corinne, Tom, or any of Jel's family. Where did the vision come from? Was it a premonition from a higher source, even from the alien intelligence as the vision on Charon had been? We hesitantly broached the stunning implication that we were the reembodiments of the 4 involved 250 years earlier in the Charon disaster and encounter.

At that time the humans (Joe and Marie) had seen the vision, but the androids (Eva and Megan) hadn't. This time, four of us (three of us being humans) had received the vision while I as an android had received the most specific data. The more we discussed it the more questions than answers arose. So I concluded the discussion by saying we had to defer that whole set of

354

metaphysical speculations and deal rather with the very existential issue at hand.

MAROONED ON CHARON

PREPARATION FOR WORLD WIDE DISASTER

Oddly perhaps I found my endeavors toward these goals to be exciting and stimulating as I understood the importance of what we were doing. As an android I always struggled with existential questions of the value and purpose of my existence, as it seemed most other androids had done as well. Up to this point my relationship with Jel seemed to be the only significant meaning I had found. Now this new purpose of helping life on Earth survive Armageddon helped me define in an existential sense who I was and what I needed to do.

I found after wide spread inquiries that it seemed I was the only android or human who had received clearly the geophysical information and coordinates in the alien message. I then conveyed all this data to the geophysical department at the university. This was compared to the geophysical department's own data which was suggestive of a major future earthquake.

After analyzing the dream data and comparing it to existing data the conclusion was that several fault lines would produce tectonic plate movement to cause unprecedented earthquakes and tsunamis, and much more imminently than anticipated. Also, Mauna Loa would likely erupt, either trigger or be triggered by the earthquakes. All this had a 95% probability of happening in the next 4-8 years with a statistical expectation of 5.90 years for the beginning. This information needed to be widely published to political leaders and scientists around the world.

As expected the public and even the scientific community met the apocalyptic warning with fear, panic, skepticism, anger, even outright hostility. Our goal was to bring intelligent Earth life together to survive the disaster. But we feared instead this would cause more conflict among human geographic, racial, and religious groups, and more suspicion and antipathy toward androids. Our university geophysical committee met almost daily and brainstormed at length about the actions that all citizens, human and android, would need to take to prevent total extinction of all intelligent life forms, in fact possibly all life forms.

We had much debate about how to go about this, with several humans on the committee becoming openly angry at a suggestion of one of my android colleagues. She stated that androids would need to take the lead in coordinating the enactment of the committee's recommendations with the governments and peoples of the Earth. She said the inherent connection in communication of androids with each other would coordinate the necessary efforts in a more efficient way.

Furthermore androids would be more rational, and less given to denial or panic. The heated discussion likely reflected the very real personal reactions of the committee members to this shocking news. In the end we agreed that humans and androids were both vital in trying to most effectively spread these ideas to the public at large, There were 8 on our committee and the department chair had given us permission to apply all our academic efforts to this task. Shara regularly attended these meetings too, and we not infrequently also pulled in Jel and Slane for their input.

Most androids we informed accepted the likely truth of this conclusion and developed a commitment to do whatever could be done to make preparations for survival for human and android lives. Action committees were established on state, national government, and university levels to formulate and initiate practical plans for this objective. There was a much lower extent of belief and commitment to action among humans.

I became a member of the university and national committees and was respected as the primary clear recipient of the original transmission from the aliens, although I did not emphasize this fact or try to gain influence or aggrandizement because of it. I worked full time on these committees in lieu of my usual university duties.

An interconnected underground residential community was planned near Winnipeg, 1,500 miles to the east. All residences would be connected by tunnels, as the anticipated chaotic environmental situation might prevent safe travel above ground for up to ten years. Our committee developed a set of recommendations that human as well as android intelligence will need to follow if life on Earth is to be sustained. More underground shelters will need to be built, insulated from the atmosphere and storms above, which will likely be unbreathable without oxygen masks for ten or more years.

The likelihood of catastrophic storms and environmental disasters will be certain although variable by area and surface structures will be vulnerable to immense destruction. Underground tunnels will be needed in cities and clusters of hundreds or even thousands of residential shelters will need to be connected by tunnels. Farm structures and ecosystems will be needed to raise crops, perhaps hydroponically, all underground. Carnivorous diets will need to be abandoned as breeding and slaughtering of animals is a highly inefficient means of food production.

Medical centers for humans, android creation and maintenance centers, and all other products necessary for life will need to be established. These underground communities will need to be largely self-sufficient as truck between communities on ground or in the air will be very difficult for decades. Eventually the air again should become breathable and surface living again possible. For at least a year though the atmosphere will be saturated with ash and the sun will almost disappear from view. The silver lining of this cloud (to make an ironic pun) could be that global temperatures might drop back to levels perhaps of the last millennium. Meanwhile atmospheric darkening will produce a minor ice age, overriding the effects of global warming. Ice will extend for decades down to the mid latitudes of 35 degrees.

For the next 4 years I was continually busy updating the geophysical data as it came into the department. There was steady confirmation that our original predictions as to the sources and scope of the disaster were if anything an underestimate of the likely events.

Also our original time estimates of 4-8 years with a median of 6 years were optimistic. The university committee, along with Slane, Corinne and Jel worked tirelessly to disseminate our predictions. There was a growing awareness among a sector of the population that the threat was real and rational steps needed to be taken to mitigate a total devastation. Androids in positions of power and influence were by far the most helpful in facilitating the preparations.

But as expected there was much criticism of our work and even protests and litigation against us. It was disconcerting but not unexpected that mental illness statistics as well as suicide rates skyrocketed. Meanwhile Jel and I secured an apartment in an underground complex being built outside of Winnipeg. The complex contained 150 underground apartments, a power source, stores, a school and everything else needed to sustain life for up to 100 years no matter the catastrophes occurring above ground.

MAROONED ON CHARON

THE APOCALYPSE HAS ARRIVED

When the earthquakes and volcanoes wracked the Earth 6 years after having the apocalyptic vision the mass media were able to operate for a short while, but then those facilities too crumbled. As I was watching the news in the first days after the cataclysm until the media went dead the scenes were of almost imponderable devastation. I saw a large highway shake violently, then crumble into a chasm. I then saw an eerie image through the expanding dirt cloud of 2 large surface vehicles with several trailers each totter and roll into the yawning grave of the chasm. This scene brought back the PTSD reaction that seeing Eva's painting had done 10 year earlier. I couldn't breathe, was unsteady on my feet, my visual field wouldn't stay stable and my cognitions were racing and disorganized.

    The future was very uncertain. Based on my knowledge of geology and what we had gleaned from the news in the first few weeks until all communication was lost, it seemed likely that it could be 2-4 years before the atmosphere could become breathable again outside with some type of air filtration system. The acute storms and tornadoes also would take several years to settle down enough that surface travel could be done with any level of safety. That of course assumed that major aftershocks dissipate, and volcanoes don't reignite. During this chaotic period, the acute effects of global warming might actually be reversed.

Many species of fauna and flora may become extinct. Therefore during the perpetual winter years the underground communities will need to be built in areas such as the southern US, in areas that had previously become largely uninhabitable. After a hundred or perhaps 1,000 years the Earth should heal itself so that temperate conditions, clean air and water can again exist. Unless of course further major environmental disasters occur. Those remnants of the human and android populations that have survived will become stewards of a new and again beautiful world and it will be their responsibility to not destroy it again.

But it could be 10 years or more before life could resume on the surface. I daily visualized Jel, our child and myself setting up residence on the surface. I visualized a world returning to life with moderating temperatures and sunshine. The disaster kept on reeling in my thoughts, and especially because of the stunning similarities to the disasters on Charon. I seemed to remember those events on Charon vividly, or at least my imagination of those events seemed to have a clarity as good as my normal waking perceptions. The events occurring now showed a remarkable similarity to the events on Charon that seemed best described as a synchronicity (as first hypothesized by the great psychologist CJ Jung).

Normal cause and effect seemed insufficient to explain these happenings. It seemed I was trying to make sense out of our present circumstances, as well as the memories or pseudo memories of Eva and/or Joe. It all became confusing and mentally overwhelming, which is especially distressing to androids.

But I knew I needed to focus on normalizing my unhelpful thoughts and actions, and stay positive and hopeful while not seeming to deny the evidence of my senses. I realized very clearly my need to sustain Jel and not let her go raving mad. Her human coping mechanisms were completely overwhelmed (as Joe's had become on Charon). This was a hard role to play: encouraging, practicing, maintaining hope and facilitating a commitment to keep going. Jel was falling apart with fear and anguish, more like Joe than Eva on Charon.

We needed whatever distractions we could find in the face of our helpless and completely isolated situation underground with the world in chaos above. We would often discuss sometimes at great lengths our differing perceptions as human and android. When Eva and Joe did that the purpose was for Eva to perceive and correlate her emotional equivalents to human emotions, which she could use to better understand and communicate with humans when they got back to Earth. In my case I found our discussions fascinating but didn't have the purpose of improving my ability to relate to humans, which I already considered satisfactory.

But all our long hours doing this passed the time, kept Jel focused on returning to the world again, and bringing our relationship closer together. I've wondered if now as an android I've grown from it in terms of working out my karma. And of course I'll throw in the caveat question as to whether androids could have karma or have reincarnations, or transfer from a human body to an android body. The most wonderful blessing of my life had been Jel, like Joe had found with Eva. But as Eva would sometimes complain, I never had a readymade family or childhood and so I still struggle with my perceived identity. Joe coped with adversity by shutting down his emotional life and relationships. He was saved from total insanity by his relationship with Eva, but this took a long time to develop.

In my case I fought with myself not to withdraw completely. As an android that kind of psychological defense came very naturally to me but I didn't have to sink into it the extent that Joe did. The many months underground became very boring, with it unknown when society would resurrect and we could become part of it again. So in human terms you could likely say I'm depressed, but not psychotic (at least for now, with the caveat question becoming could an android become psychotically depressed?)

I needed to maintain my mental stability as an android through this extended catastrophe, for my survival and especially Jel's, who was in such distress as being able to do almost nothing. If I allowed my mind to wander I would see my cognitive organization breaking down, my vision would get dull and gray, even to the point of questioning what I was really seeing. But with much effort I retained the ability to focus on rational alternatives.

It boiled down to the aspect of the quantum continuum that I chose (or allowed) it to collapse into. This was an ability that I had as an android, or perhaps had obtained from Joes experience, that allowed me to retain a semblance of a rational and positive attitude. This was vital to help Jel survive the chaos that these circumstances were producing in her mind.

MAROONED ON CHARON

SEPSIS AND A HARROWING JOURNEY FOR HELP

My mental stability was tested even more when Jel developed sepsis. This developed rapidly and within a few days she had spiked a high fever and was becoming delirious. I knew I needed to get her to the medical center as soon as possible if she were to stay alive. But I didn't know where the medical center was located amid the rubble or if I could get in or if anyone was there who could help. I was able to get the ground vehicle through the horizontal garage door, thankfully the lift was still operative. I now had only our map of the rest of the facility to determine a route, but soon found out that the landmarks of the facility were pretty well erased.

The weather seemed to have moderated at least for the present, with a gusty headwind blowing the snow but not foiling the vehicles movement. The temperature was -5 degrees F. It was midafternoon and of course the sky was dark with ash, but not a blackout, with about 40 m of forward visibility. The oxygen gauge also showed an improvement even over my daily readings, but survival outside the pressurized vehicle would still require breathing equipment.

We proceeded through the rugose landscape guided by the compass of where the Medical Center should be. Although frankly we didn't even know if the compass was still pointing in the right direction, in case the North Pole has been altered in position. The Medical Center should be about 10 miles away, so normally this would be a quick and easy trip. For the first mile or so it was encouraging because the very agile ground vehicle made it easily over the surprisingly flat ground. But then through the ashy haze of what appeared to be jagged rocks loomed ahead.

Jel at this time was delirious and obtunded, and I struggled to keep my cognitions rational and remain focused on the perils ahead. I could see a promontory of jagged rocks now more clearly, and an attempted passage over the ridge would likely end in disaster. The very vivid pseudo memories of Joe and Eva's passage over Charon constantly pushed forward in my mind. It was very difficult, even with my android rationality, to not be overwhelmed by the images from Charon and my more immediate worry about Jel's deteriorating condition.

The ridge appeared to extend to both the left and right without appearing more navigable, but vision in both directions was only about 200 m. I chose to parallel the ridge to the left, but with little if any logical reason to head in that direction. The cognitions kept biting at me that I had turned in the wrong direction and that the ridge might not be better or could be worse for a long time. Or meanwhile that some impassable obstacle would present itself in the direction we were going. We did have enough fuel, air, and other life essentials for about 3 days so I wasn't imminently worried about that, but I also didn't know how long Jel could hang on or I could maintain my endurance.

After about another hour of slow progress along the edge of the sharp hills on the right we came to a place where the steep ridges seemed to partially level out, then again became higher after several hundred m. My brain was racing, weighing the value of my intuition to try a pass through the ridge. I assumed that the ridge bordered a chasm of some sort formed by an earthquake that ran perpendicular to our presumed path to the Medical Center. I had no information on how far the ridge or chasm extended, how deep the chasm might be, or whether there was another ridge on the other side. Most importantly I had no clue as to whether the presumed chasm was stable enough for passage across it.

But Jel seemed to be becoming steadily more obtunded and I concluded we needed to try to get across to the other side immediately rather than running along the ridge looking for a more commodious gap in the ridge. Our vehicle readily crawled through the ridge which was less perilous than I first thought. But now with a transmontane view I could see what appeared to be a river or at least frozen stretch of water in the chasm, perhaps 100-150 m across. But this generated new questions that seemed to sear my mind even more. Was the ice thick enough to support our vehicle's crossing? Based on the current and recent temperatures it seemed safe to assume the ice would be thick enough to support our vehicle. But was my presumption too optimistic?

I had no choice but to try right there, the expanse of ice didn't lessen in width in either direction as far as I could see. Jel and I were still in our insulated protective gear. I attached Jel's helmet and tested the oxygen tank meter. I was ready to eject us if the vehicle started sinking, along with an inflatable insulated tent and some nutrient supplies. I tried to repress the question of how long we'd survive outside the vehicle. In Jel's declining condition I would likely have to pull her on the small sled that came with the tent. But how we would both survive possibly days in the open without direction to the medical center was unknown and frightening.

I gingerly started crossing the ice, which seemed to be holding. But about halfway across a fissure started opening in front of us, with a loud cracking report from the ice. Our vehicle lurched forward and downward. I screamed, and it flashed in my head that Eva had done the same thing on Charon. Immediately a reaction I can only describe as sheer panic came over me. I couldn't breathe, it seemed like my conscious will was frozen, my vision became like a tunnel and everything seemed gray and distorted. I tried to focus on cognitive strategies to regain mind control and focus clearly on what to do at this point in time rather than worrying about probable disaster.

I knew Joe and Eva had very similar thoughts, as did Marie and Megan when their craft was tumbling into the chasm into the very similar situation on Charon. Jel woke up at my scream and noticed what was happening. Then an amazing thing happened. After a short, strangled scream the Eva part of Jel's humanness apparently took control, relived exactly the accident on Charon, mastered her human panic, and reacted with android rationality and control. She got herself thinking clearly despite her condition. At that moment, the delirium was gone and I imagined Eva being present in Jel's body.

She calmly and gently told me we would be OK, and assertively said I needed to eject us from the sinking vehicle. I was amazed at how she did that, normally Jel gets very agitated in emergencies. I triggered the vehicle's ejection mechanism. The entire passenger compartment detached upward from the rest of the vehicle and floated as the ice shattered beneath us and the vehicle sank out of sight in the jet black water. The ejection compartment was water tight with a clear hemispherical bubble that could be raised to exit the compartment.

The ejection compartment also contained the oxygen tank, a small capacity heater and supplies we had brought along. So it was vital that we get the compartment up to the bank if we needed shelter through the night or couldn't find the medical center. I was able to crawl out and stand on the ice that was on the side of the compartment facing the bank. The ice beneath me seemed solid. I pulled out Jel and carried her across the remaining 20 m to the solid bank. I laid her on the ground on a blanket and attached her oxygen mask. I then went back to the compartment and located the cable to pull the compartment to safety.

A series 8 android's overall muscular strength is about 3 times that of a human of the same height and weight in good physical shape. But it took all of my strength and grip of my boots to pull the compartment on top of the ice, and then across the ice to the rocky bank. With the compartment sealed up on the bank, our oxygen masks hooked up and Jel wrapped up in several blankets my mind turned to the next task of finding the medical center. Jel was breathing regularly, had good pulse and decent color, remained asleep or unconscious and clearly couldn't ambulate at all.

My cognitions quickly spiraled into incoherence and my vision distorted. But I was able to regain normal android mental control by focusing on Jel's extraordinarily calming reaction when we first broke through the ice. I felt like I was Joe in that situation on Charon but with enhanced control, and with Eva helping me to decide what to do. But now what? I carried Jel up the ridge ahead, which fortunately was not as imposing as the ridge we had driven through on the other side. But now standing on top of ridge, I saw a flat landscape littered with shattered, nearly pulverized buildings, remnants of vegetation, rocks and other junk.

I thought we were probably within two or three km of where the medical center had been located underground, but with no indication of where the surface entrance might be. Even more daunting was the thought that the medical center might not be there, there might not be survivors, and that powerful antibiotics might not be available. I stood there holding Jel for 5-10 minutes at a loss as to where or how to proceed, trying to keep my thoughts under control and goal directed.

Then came the next astounding event. About 60 degrees to the right of a line perpendicular to the ridge behind me I saw a faint, shimmering blue light just above the ground! I had no idea what this was, I was very doubtful that the medical center or any other facility would have a surface beacon after all the devastating winds and earthquake activity since the disaster. But I had no other hint as to where I should walk. So even if there was no logic behind it I started walking in that direction. The ejection compartment should be secure where I had left it, in case we needed to return to it. I turned around and saw it was still there as before.

The sky was getting even darker than its usual ash with the added grey fogginess, and I realized that complete darkness would arrive within several hours. I considered going towards the light, but if we didn't find anything and we were in total darkness in this forbidding wasteland we might have little chance of survival. So, mentally marking my exact position on the ridge and the angle of the light, we returned to the compartment until the hazy daylight would return. I of course was very worried about Jel. She remained unconscious but was still breathing well, had an adequate pulse and color.

Overnight in the pressurized compartment was difficult. I couldn't get my body at all comfortable in the driver's seat to rest. I was able to partially recharge the batteries in my body as I had brought the charging system along. But I only left it on 2 hours as I didn't want to run down the compartments battery or if it did we'd lose all oxygen and heat. Jel seemed unchanged and I gave her some tranquilizing medication to keep her asleep. Next day as the sky lightened a bit I decided to try to find the medical center.

Jel was still nearly asleep but able with help to sit up. She had an ashen color and I knew we needed to get her some antibiotics quickly. So I again adjusted her oxygen mask, wrapped her up, picked her up lying across my arms and headed back to where I had stood on the ridge yesterday. I looked for the blue light but didn't see it. It had been very dim the previous night so perhaps it couldn't be seen in the ashen morning light. But I knew exactly where I had seen it. By my triangulation the night before it appeared to have been about 3 km to my center-right.

So I started walking in that direction, carrying Jel fairly easily. The ground was mostly flat but there were rocks and crevices so I needed to be careful and observant as to where to step. I forced my thoughts from the worries of negative outcomes. Instead I tried to envisage with partial success finding and entering the medical center, finding medical workers and a powerful antibiotic. I then imaged injecting Jel, and then her recovering. I was able to carry Jel steadily except for 2 brief rest stops. There were several small detours and short jumps I had to make due to various obstacles.

But because I didn't get a recharge last night I knew my energy would be waning soon. If I went much further I wouldn't have the energy to make it back to the vehicle's emergency compartment, which was running low on power too. Jel was quiet and unconscious and I was very troubled about her appearance. So I had to go on to where I'd seen the blue light before, it was no longer visible. When I finally got to the place the blue light seemed to have been it was 3.2 km and 3 hours since I started walking.

Then I saw a very stout, simple steel framework about 6 feet high just ahead. I hoped this was a rescue portal, of the kind I had helped design. These frameworks had been designed to stay standing through 200 mph winds and violent tremors as long as the ground didn't completely collapse beneath. The heavy beams spread out underground and sunk to a depth of 60 m, so even if a fissure arose right under it the likelihood was high it would remain standing. A small panel was installed on each of the five legs beneath which was an opening device for triggering the trap door located between the legs. I didn't know if this led to the medical facility but knew it had to be if Jel and I were going to survive.

The trap door wasn't visible until I cleared almost a meter feet of rocks and dirt off its surface. The questions raced through my mind: what if I can't open any of the panels? What if the opening device wasn't operational? What if the door was simply stuck shut and was impossible to open? It also occurred to me that the framework and trap doors of these rescue portals were not designed with beacon lights, so where had the blue light come from? But that question could wait, it was necessary now to get inside and hopefully find a functioning medical facility, or least a pharmaceutical cache with an antibiotic.

Time and my charge were running out. After trying 2 of the panels on the legs and finding them hopelessly stuck I was able to pry open the third one. I pulled the triggering handle inside and was encouraged that the opening device was starting to operate. But then it seemed the motor was unable to move the completely stuck trapdoor, although I could hear the motor trying to. I was about to lose consciousness and thought this is where Jel and I will die together. I laid her carefully on the ground and laid beside her with my hand on her shoulder.

MAROONED ON CHARON

A MIRACULOUS RESCUE

My next memory was of awakening after what seemed like a nocturnal deactivation. Standing before me were 2 male androids. I sat up and tried to bolt from the bed but one of the androids firmly stopped me and told me to sit down until I could get my bearings. I blurted out "How is Jel?" The other android told me she survived, is still in a serious condition, in an induced coma. But the antibiotic appeared to be working and her viral load and vital signs were improving. They hoped she would make a full recovery but with no assurance yet. I again stood up and lurched toward the door then fell down. The first android helped me up and walked me to the next room where Jel was quietly sleeping. I gently took her hand, tried to quell my disjointed thoughts with my great relief.

 I expressed my overwhelming gratitude to the two androids. I told them all about our journey and they described their status since the Cataclysm. They were very puzzled when I mentioned the faint blue light that had been my beacon. They said this rescue port didn't have and never had a beacon, there just weren't enough to go around when it was set up. We all pondered how that light had occurred, and surely Jel and I would have been lifeless without it's mysterious beacon. Coming to no conclusion except great wonderment I filed that question away in my mind and turned back all my attention to Jel.

 I think I've gained some insight into the dynamics of my mind from my experience with Jel, and everything I've read and subjectively perceived about Joe. Joe's fundamental psychic defense mechanism was withdrawal from close relationships, where he feared he might get hurt again as with Pete's death. After the tragedies on Charon severely shook his hope of survival, rationality couldn't save him and he sank into deep depression. Almost in spite of himself, Eva became his anchor to reality and his first real, trusting relationship.

I wonder if he would have allowed a human woman into his guarded place rather than an android whom he still saw initially as a very advanced but nonhuman machine. That is a very interesting question I hadn't pondered before. Then when Eva had to be deactivated he lost his shaky connection to sanity. I also wonder if Eva would have had to be permanently deactivated if Joe would have committed suicide. I've often wondered, as I know Eva had, what it would be like to have real human emotion, not the pseudo emotion I perceived myself as having.

As these events continued to unfold the parallels with Joe and Eva's experiences on Charon became ever more readily apparent. With this it seemed like my empathy with Joe's mental struggles, and the effects of his relationship with Eva, also became clearer, at times like a personal memory that had actually happened to me. I learned to apply my rational android cognitive processes to those very human emotions that Joe had experienced, but in an adaptive way. And I also modeled the coping skills that Eva had applied in those situations. I am convinced there is a universal consciousness that lay at the center of my consciousness and lived on from Joe's.

I think all the parallels in our experiences demonstrated the action of karma, plus giving both of us a chance to learn from it and grow as intelligent beings. I could sense a spiritual guidance through these many difficult situations. I often also wondered about the beings Joe and Marie had experienced on Charon at the pyramid. Also that had guided the rescue ship to the Charon base, and appeared to Joe in his time of psychosis and suicidal thoughts. Were they the same beings that warned us and the world about the upcoming disaster? Were they responsible for the faint blue light that beckoned me to the Medical Center?

Were they a manifestation of the embodied cosmic power that we perceived as alien beings because that concept was as far as we could imagine? In other words were they physically real or rather products of our creative imaginations and cognitive limitations? Finally would we ever experience their presence again? When thoughts of further deterioration, death and continuing environmental disaster polluted my mind I tried with some success to turn my attention away from those negative thoughts and images, and replace those with the optimistic thoughts and images.

We stayed with Frank and Jaron for 3 months while Jel recovered, and one day a faint, flickering radio signal was detected through the communication system of the medical facility. This was an astounding event as it was the first communication with living beings that Frank and Jaron had experienced other than when Jel and I had stumbled upon the facility. The signal was from the main communications center of the underground city, where a limited recovery of the radio system has been established.

Responses were being received from a number of the underground residences and the food production facility, and a map was being made and assessment of survivors, their status, location and emergency needs. It was a wonderful blessing to discover that parts of the underground community were still functioning such as the hydroponic food production facility.

In fact the hydroponic facility was staffed by 1 human and 3 androids and with God's generosity had grown and stored enough food for 100 humans for 20 years. Plus the facility had processed the android nutritional supplies for 50 androids also for 20 years. Also responses were being received from a growing number of residences that had become isolated by collapse of the connecting tunnels due to the initial severe earthquake activity.

In early 2358 an active search and rescue campaign had started, now that radio communication had been established with a small number of community members. There'd been voice or test communication now with about 50 community members and there was hope that more would be found alive. So far there were 30 android and 20 human survivors. Of those, at least 15 androids were due or overdue for a full rejuvenation. Most of the humans were successfully surviving but about half had medical disorders of some sort and a few were in critical need of medical attention.

Most of the humans were nearly out of food and provisions and the androids in need of their daily nutritional supplies. Ecstatically we learned that a baby girl had been born in one of the isolated residences, was now 6 months old and healthy and lively. The immediate goal was to reach the survivors, and get them to the medical center, or to the central food supply to get needed food and nutrition. The medical facility had complete emergency and hospital equipment and supplies, but didn't have the ability to do full android rejuvenations.

The next goal after locating and giving treatment to the survivors would be to get the underground excavating equipment back in operation and open up the collapsed tunnels that separated the various residences and other facilities. Eventually a cleanup would be done of the outer surface of the city with an assessment whether any construction above ground would be feasible. Likely it would be years though before this would be practical, with the long term goal reestablishing a functional community and even farming again above ground.

Frank, Jaron, Jel and I made trips, usually 2 of us at a time, with the medical facility ground vehicle to locate trapped individuals, and bring them back to the medical facility if needed or resupply their needs if they were to remain where they were. The central administrative part of the underground community, which contained the hydroponic food facility also had several pieces of surface excavating equipment and tunneling equipment. The surviving 5 human and 8 android residents of the community central area coordinated with us to open up either above ground or below ground access to isolated community members.

After another 3 months the tunnel to Jel and my residence was opened up and we moved back there and out of the medical facility. This was actually like a coming back home for us. We appreciated our privacy again and our few possessions, but also struggled with the memories of the 18 months we had spent there trapped without external communication or any idea how we could survive or how long. We were able to stay in contact with Jel's family. Jel had taken it very hard when she found out about her dad's death and struggled with depression, guilt, anger, and other aspects of bereavement.

She wanted to attempt to reach them by land or air vehicle right away. I too felt grief in my own way because I didn't have other family, or even friends or love and caring in my background except for Jel, her family, Tom and of course Andrae in the distant path. Sometimes Jel became very irritable with me because I was not yet willing to attempt the hazardous journey to Edmonton.

I had to cope with my own seeming inertia and bleakness of thought while trying to keep Jel from giving up. But when this became frustrating for me I resorted to my natural android defense of rationality, and rejection of anything that didn't fit into that. I reasoned that within another 6 to 9 months that trip would still be difficult and possibly dangerous, but could be attempted.

Jel and I had a mutually supportive relationship, in some ways like Joe and Eva did but opposite too. I provided an unending support and moderating influence on Jel's emotions, which often boiled over into panic, depression, fear, and rage. Sometimes I had to put up with a lot not just to solve a crisis but more so to help Jel through. But Jel was so important for me too. I could easily slide into my android rationality to block out my emotional equivalent reactions, and become like Joe had been in his withdrawn depression. Jel provided a human, female warmth, and affective opalescence to help me stay hopeful and positive in my thinking. I can truly say, and I know androids aren't supposed to say this, but I love her with all my android heart!

My health was gradually failing by 3.5 years post Cataclysm. It was 5 years since my previous revitalization, and this decline was of course expected. I wasn't moving as quickly and smoothly as I usually do, my vision and other senses were slowly deteriorating, and cognition had become turgid. We were able to make the surface trip to the Android Institute in what was left of Seattle. After a week of recovery from the revitalization I was back to normal, and we could travel back to Winnipeg.

June 10, 2359 AQI= 290, temp=50 F, hazy but with sun occasionally peeking through the hazy blur, visibility =.5 km. We finally risked a helicopter ride to Edmonton. We met Tanil, Kacey, and Jel's mom, and also Tom. It was incredibly emotional for all, and I was totally overwhelmed by all the relief and happiness I saw. Now four years after the tragedy first struck the weather had settled down enough and the air cleared that a stout and pressurized residential structure could be built above ground. Jel was totally insistent that we build such a house on the property we had before in Edmonton.

The human population of the world was now about 2 million, clearly a huge drop from its peak. The android population stayed steady at about 50,000, making the ratio of humans to android 40:1. But the human population continued to decline. The coronavirus and it's spin-offs remained a disastrous threat. There was much debate among human couples as to the advisability of having children.

Many felt the Earth had been so ruined that it would never return to normal and life would always have to remain underground so why expose more children to the new circumstances? Also it seemed that human fertility had declined as a result of all the toxins in the air and ground. But others recognized that the human population must increase or at least maintain itself or it could lead to extinction of the human race.

December 4, 2359 I met with Tom regarding the possibility of he providing the sperm to inseminate Jel. I visited Tom in Minneapolis and didn't bring up the question immediately. We caught up on our lives, the state of the world, and toured the apartment and shopping complex that had been recently finished and in which he had an apartment. On the second day I brought up the question, and was surprised when he didn't seem shocked about it. He had intuited for several months that I might ask that.

We discussed at length the questions that Jel and I had about how Tom would feel being the biological father of the child but not the father who would claim and raise the child. Also if I would feel uncomfortable with this situation or remind me of the void I'd always perceived of being an android and therefore incapable of producing a child. Tom seemed most concerned about religious or ethical questions that might come out of it. After much discussion we both concluded that if it were God's will to let this happen that any human doubts were not relevant.

Fortunately, we were able to access the proper medical professionals who conduct artificial insemination. Jel became pregnant on the third try. Now that Jel is pregnant I began to ponder these questions more deeply. Especially that joy and awe at creating life that Jel can now appreciate, and know deeply and subjectively those feelings that Eva could only wonder about. For myself there is that existential vacuum of human paternal love and pride, and this will always remain unfulfilled. Joe never experienced this either as he never fathered a child. But all this pales to the incredible satisfaction of actually being a father.

A SON IS BORN!

8 months after the third insemination try Jel gave birth to a boy, whom we named Earl. Now I recognize the emotional equivalents of experiencing the ups and downs involved in caring for and raising a child and am very thankful for that. I am thankful as well to have the cognitive and behavioral stability that comes with being an android, as a counterpoint to the mental instability that overwhelmed Joe, and the deep emotional struggles that Jel has gone through.

    I took to the task of parenting with zeal, surprising and convincing myself that an android could be a good dad. There was very little in android programming or education that would prepare an android for a father role. But with Jel's help and Tom's frequent presence as an uncle I got along well, and savored my privilege of being a parent. Three years later a baby girl came along, whom we named Dawn. Jel was ecstatic about the children which made me very pleased. I found it so hard to believe I could actually expand my self-concept to being a parent! What was more readily accommodated by my self-image was my purpose in life to help the human race, including Jel, the children, Tom, and the human race as a whole.

    Over the next ten years we had an extraordinary family life that I never imagined when I was younger. We raised the children, maintained our great relationship, and Jel seemed to become much more settled. I stayed busy at my job at the university, and we did our best to help the human and android races reestablish themselves above ground. The remaining population of the Earth is unknown, but likely less than one million humans and perhaps ten thousand androids. The constantly mutating viruses continue to decimate the human population, and it is unknown if the human species can survive. Thousands of human eggs have been frozen in an indefinite storage along with a multitude of sperm samples.

Education and experience on this were now a basic part of the android university curriculum, and were still strongly based on the training programs that Joe put together and that Eva carried on when they got back to Earth. But what was it really like to experience joy, fear, sorrow, anger as a human would? Androids are supposedly incapable of experiencing that, but yet through the part of me that was Joe I did. But Eva had craved to feel the deep emotions of romantic love, sexual desire, having had a childhood, having had a family, and giving birth to a child. In Jel, she had found those things.

When Dawn was 23 she married a human male, Charles. In the next 4 years they created 2 beautiful girls, Chantelle and Siobhan. Now I had to expand my self-identity to being a grandfather, which was as staggering to me as becoming a father. Earl 2 years later married an android lady, Kimberly. They did not attempt to adopt a child.

June 2, 2395 When Jel died I was 52 years old. I'd had 10 rejuvenations at that time, and my doctors conclusion at my last rejuvenation 2 years earlier was the same as for most all androids. I could have one more rejuvenation at 55, and none would be advisable after that. That gave me 8 more years of life at most. I was very accepting and fatalistic about that, having known my probable life span since my earliest days. I could refuse my eleventh and be permanently deactivated in 3 years if I chose, although there was no physical reason to do so. I considered that option at length, Jel was now gone. But my children and grandchildren needed and wanted me alive, so that at least gave my life some continued purpose.

Corinne had her eleventh rejuvenation one year before and so had about 4 more years of life. With Tom of course longevity estimates were much less precise. He was now 75 and in overall good health, but the coronavirus as always remained a major threat especially for the elderly. He developed cancer of the lung from all the unclear air, despite that he never smoked a tobacco product. Tom and Corinne had decided to live together by themselves 2 years ago. They offered and would have been fine with moving back with me now.

But I actually wanted to be by myself for a while and didn't want to complicate their relationship. We tentatively concluded that when Corinne was permanently deactivated Tom would move back in with me at the farm where we all felt so comfortable. Then it would be like when we were first roommates when I was a senior in college. But I also knew that the circumstances and 55 years would make things very different but hopefully our friendship could maintain as it has for many years.

However 11 months later Tom's older brother John, 80, became increasingly disabled and needed daily care. With no one else except hired assistance to provide that care, Tom and Corinne decided to move to Wausau, Wisconsin to take care of him. Another option would have been for John to move in with Tom and Corrine. But John didn't want to leave Wausau and wasn't expected to live long so they moved to Wausau. That left me alone on the farm and in fact with no one around for 20 miles, except when Dawn or Earl with or without their families would visit. A few times Tom came up when Dawn or Earl were there because they were his biological children.

Sometimes the feelings that I had (actually Joe had) of fear and panic at being utterly alone in the frozen wasteland of Charon came back to me when I was by myself at the farm, which was now the vast majority of the time. Especially there was a period of about one month on one occasion of exceptionally stormy weather, most of which I had to spend underground. There was no communication at all as the phone system was completely shut down. Looking out at the total white-out conditions I felt myself trying to block out my (android) perceptions and emotions completely.

Then I realized that was Joe's response when he was alone on Charon without Eva. I further realized that I didn't need to do that, I had the more balanced and ego-stable disposition of an android, and could improve on Joe's insufficient coping skills. Also while my situation seemed harrowing it was nowhere near Joe's total isolation and catastrophe or the stupendous distance from other human beings, including all the way back to Ganymede.

Also I had faced and overcome a much more lethal circumstance when I had to take Jel to the medical center. If I could succeed at that time I could make it through this also. Then I also thought of the strange and wondrous signal that had guided me to the medical center, which I still marveled at and wondered if that marvelous protective element was still there.

March 15, 2396 Corinne and Tom moved back to the farm with me after John passed away. I had adapted to living by myself but it was very right and satisfying that they did so. One year later Corrine had her final deactivation. It was the traditional android ceremony, with Tom and I each holding one of her hands. My children and grandchildren, also Tom's 3 children and 4 of his grandchildren attended, along with 3 other humans and androids. Corinne had an accepting attitude and said she was at peace. I share that attitude for her, but will greatly miss her presence and unfailing support. Tom was emotionally devastated, but worked gradually through that. Tom and I then had five year together by ourselves, which was very precious to both of us.

February 13, 2402 I had chosen this day to be my final deactivation day. I felt this was very correct at this time. As usual before my rejuvenations I knew my responses were slowing down, senses were getting less acute and various body parts were starting to get stiff. So I knew I needn't push life any more as no further rejuvenations were possible. The ceremony was pretty standard for an android's final deactivation, with close family and/or friends holding my hands or resting hands on my legs, chest, or feet. Earl and Dawn held my hands, while Tom, as well as Earl, and Dawn's spouses and my two grandchildren put their hands on my chest and legs.

MAROONED ON CHARON

BRANDON'S TRANSLATION

I was ready and resigned when my final deactivation occurred. Of course I loathed the knowledge immediately after I had taken my last breath that I had lost physical contact with my children and grandchildren, but reassured that all were apparently healthy and having successful lives. My main concern for friends and family was Tom, who was 83 years old. This is a very old age for humans to attain especially in the 25th century as average lifespan has decreased over the last 5 centuries, but Tom is still relatively independent and healthy. I had a wider concern, or perhaps awareness of the inevitability of destruction and possibly extinction of the human race, and how this could impact the human members of my family.

My viewpoint of awareness slowly rose above my physical body, hovering several feet above it. Two of my 3 android colleagues in attendance followed my ascent with their eyes and I knew were still perceiving me. None of the humans seemed in touch with my rising spirit. Tom and my children seemed sad but not teary, while my grandchildren were both tearful. I wished I could comfort them, and tried to reach out but my hands and the rest of my body stayed motionless.

My perception of the funeral then faded and I became aware of another location, what seemed to be a swiftly flowing river with whitecaps and rocky banks. I realized this was the infamous River Styx, and immediately felt a sense of fear of Charon, whom I had no doubt was there even though I couldn't see him. I remember I had encountered him before when I was Joe and transitioned. But then Darwin appeared which surprised me and gave me relief. I had never been as enthusiastic as had Jel regarding Darwin as my spiritual guide, or about having any spiritual guide, but thought I had experienced him once in a meditation. Darwin smiled warmly and told me Jel had asked him to help me transition when it was my time.

He asked if that was OK with me, and I gratefully assented. We then turned away from the river and Charon, if he were there, was no longer a worry. Then my perception became hazy and I felt I was moving on to my next destination. After some indefinite but seemingly eternal period of semi consciousness Amon appeared, warm, supportive and calming. He was handsome, wearing a tunic of indefinite color that reflected various colors of the shimmering fog around us. His skin glowed with a light blue aura, as did mine when I looked down.

Amon said it was time again for a life review, so I could see what I did and didn't accomplish in my life, and decide on my circumstances and goals my next life. My next physical life will be another chance to work on my life karma and the choices I will make to do this will ultimately be my own. Amon explained (which had also done in my previous afterlife) human and all at least advanced animals and also androids possessed the ability to make choices about what part of the multiverse of possibilities that will collapse from the waveform for them.

If successful the life review will expiate karma, or if not, we'd need come back or encounter another situation where were we could again try to apply our action to a positive recognition of the goal. In looking back I recall how in the first ten years of my life I was able to carry on much as Joe had until the events on Charon.

I had avoided strong emotions by staying within my android nature, while Joe had done that by withdrawing into his work. It was with a surprising sense of disgust that I recognized that I came across as rather arrogant at that time to others. I had harbored the false illusion that androids were superior to humans in that we didn't have to cope with human emotions and frailties. I clearly remember that day in the android academy art center when I saw Eva's shocking painting of the crevasse swallowing Megan and Marie's vehicle. I'd never had that kind of shock before in this lifetime and I didn't know where it came from until years later.

I recognize that I still have that fear of vast, open, uninhabited areas of land that I developed while trapped on Charon. I still need to work to overcome that phobia. My relationship with Jel was the jewel that helped me through all those challenges, along with what I'd never had before, my family and children. I realize I've grown incredibly as a sentient being through all this. I recognized that I had incorporated some human perceptions and even emotions into my android cognitive structure. But I have much further to go. I also thank Darwin for his guidance and protection along the way. Amon dropped in on me several times during this period of self-reflection and helped me distill my experiences into growth and insight.

I've wondered a million times about the extraordinary visions and signals I and the others have encountered in this past life and the life before it:

1. the strange and destructive transmissions from Pluto that had catalyzed our mission to Charon at the outset.

2. The destruction of the Thule and loss of 4 crew members on Pluto when they sited the pyramid on Pluto.

3. The vision Marie and Joe had by the pyramid on Charon encountering alien figures, and the warning about the subsequent loss of Marie and Megan in the yawning chasm.

4. The alien image Joe saw outside the base on Charon that gave him comfort and motivation when he was at his worst.

5. The inexplicable blue signal that guided the rescue vehicle to the base on Charon when the base had lost all signaling ability.

6. The shocking imagery and forewarning of the Cataclysm seen in the vision of Jel, Slane, Shara, and myself on Earth in the most recent lifetime,

7. and the marvelous blue signal that guided me to the Medical Center with Jel.

My Akashic (karmic) memory than spread out before me, like a deck of cards, each card containing one incarnation. The cards became progressively more blurred the further back in time, and only about the last 5 were clear enough to read. The deck must have comprised a hundred cards, perhaps many more. For sure I was Joe in the previous life. I was drawn to the fifth card from the end, which was completely mind blowing, and drew an amazing connection to my last 2 lives.

Amon appeared multiple times, usually seemingly popping in right in front of my eyes when I least expected it. We talked at length about the alien presence on Charon that I had so futilely pondered. Indeed, they were from a race of aquatic beings that had lived in many solar systems for many eons, including the Alpha Centauri system. Millions of Earth years ago they had established a colony in Earth's oceans. They were the progenitors of modern whales and dolphins though quite different as well. This brought to me some images, like photos in a book of a series of incarnations I'd had in that race in the far distant past.

Their shape was something like a whale, but with extended tentacles like an octopus, giving them extremely sensitive and dexterous psychomotor functions. This image gave me an immediate sense of familiarity, yet still somewhat hazy and indistinct. The Centaurians were a very long-lived race, declining in numbers and racial vitality, and resigned to their eventual extinction. They were of a benign character, interfering as little as possible in the affairs of other celestial races who might share places in solar systems with them, and if possible, not making their presence known at all. But they did want to reconnect with their ancient relatives in Earth's oceans, perhaps to revitalize their own race. That was the reasons for the powerful transmissions that caused so much destruction on Earth.

When Eva, Marie and Megan appeared in the area of Charon monitored by the Centaurians, the Centaurians recognized the deeply distant ancestral heritage of themselves with me and Marie who had also in the hoary past been Centaurians. They were then able to establish a subconscious, nonverbal, imagery and feeling based communication with the 2 of us. They understood then how their signals to their fellow members of their race in the depths of Earth's oceans had disrupted the electronic functioning of the Earth and of our base, and stopped the transmissions. I didn't fully believe their message at the time. If I had I perhaps could have avoided at least some of the overwhelming guilt and uselessness that persecuted me later.

After they made a connection with Marie and I they were able to occasionally sense when Marie or I were in danger and give a signal or message to help us. Marie had been telepathically sent that feeling of danger and urge to stop her vehicle before her disaster occurred, but most unfortunately had ignored it. The Centaurians had provided that vision and message to me in the base when I was overwhelmed with depression and psychosis, which had given me an inkling of light in the black pit in which I'd fallen. Then the Centaurians provided the light above the base that signaled our presence to the rescue crew.

Having gotten so close to Jel in this life, and Joe to Eva in the life before that, Jel also picked up at least part of the vision. The deep connection catalyzed by the disastrous death of Megan (Slane in the most recent life), allowed her to also pick up part of our vision. Finally, the blue signal I saw over the Medical Center was a direct projection to me from Jel who was unconscious but still aware at that time of our extreme danger.

During my Earth life I had always wondered about unsolved mysteries of the universe. Particularly the modus operandi of the "Big Bang" that started the universe remained as totally inscrutable as it had been since it was first proposed in the twentieth century. I thought Amon could explain that since in my present astral body I still had no inkling about this. I asked Amon and he agreed the knowledge available on the astral plane was much deeper than on the physical plane.

However he surprised me by saying the knowledge of that event of the highest spiritual magnitude was not available to him either. In the higher planes of being, particularly the soul plane, such answers could be found. He, as well as I, would eventually ascend to that level of spiritual being. But until then our limited understanding could not encompass that mysterious event.

After another semiconscious period that seemed eternal I became aware that I was in what appeared to be a valley with snowcapped mountains all around. I felt alive, and I knew my vibratory frequency had increased again. There were trees of an evergreen shape but of various shades of blue and purple. The clearing that I seemed to be in had a pungent and delightful aroma. There was a surprisingly red and plate sized sun overhead but the air seemed pure, cool, and entirely refreshing.

A beautiful and large Husky was by my side. Although I'd never met Rupert I intuitively knew it was Rupert. Rupert seemed to know who I was also, and came right over and jumped up on me in a friendly way of old friends, and I had an unexpected and totally unandroid like feeling of glee. We both then saw Jel about 50 feet away, and we all ran together and mutually embraced for a long time. I was completely overwhelmed with joy at this wondrous reunion.

Rupert couldn't speak in human terms but could make gruff, bark like words for many concepts, perceptions and emotions. It was our job to learn to understand Ruperts language. A more refined mental connection was being formed, similar to but richer than dogs owners develop on Earth.

With the guidance of Elin and Amon the three of us mutually decided to create by visualization a home for ourselves while in the afterlife in the mountains around us. We would make a little community for those individuals close to us. Tom and Corinne were still in the semi trance like state of raising their earthly vibrations to that of the astral plane. When they become grounded in their astral lives we would invite them to our little community, and they could set up temporary part time or full time residence as they chose.

Elin and Amon presented to us the possibility of both reincarnating as human babies. Elin said "An ultimate and vitally important adventure into successful humans, under the tutelage of androids. The habitation of the fetuses by your soul bodies would happen about 6 months into the fetal period. This would be preferable to implantation of soul right at this time of fertilization as the error rate for fetal survival is unknown for that time. The only remnants of the human race are hundreds of frozen eggs and sperm, but the viability of at least some these are not good. There are no more living survivors."

"Other disincarnated human souls will also be given this choice. But the ultimate survival of the human race remains in question, and this may be the last chance for its perpetuation. The choice of course is up to both of you." Jel said "it's true that our great adventure on Charon possibly saved humanity from extinction and it would be an honor to again provide a means of restoring the race." Elin said, "you can eventually marry and become one of the first Adam and Eve's of the resurrected race". I was not ambivalent about this decision, which surprised Jel. So we both agreed to this task without undo anxiety or fear. We talked further about hopes and goals for a radically recreated human race.

I think Elin and especially Amon were somewhat surprised at the quick mutual acceptance of this new role. Amon said, "If we should, one or both of us, decide not to do this task we could be prepared for an alternate future life together further in the future" Then Amon stated that we might like to exchange gender roles, to give us an understanding of being the opposite sex. Jel and I agreed that we needed to talk this over before we decided. Amon said they would visit again in about 20 days.

Twenty days after that Elin and Amon both appeared again. Jel and I confirmed that we were ready for the next physical life, and under the circumstances previously described. Nonetheless I still had some ambivalence at leaving this beautiful and peaceful place, and then being separated for a while before we could reunite. I know Jel was thinking of this too. But this was the right time and there was no point in postponing the inevitable. Plus this seemed like a great challenge and hopefully service to the human race. Tomorrow Elin and Amon will come again and will help us transition to our physical bodies after we go to sleep. I'm sure Darwin will be there too to escort us safely to our next physical realities.

Author's biography

Bruce Maaser has been a clinical psychologist in Ohio for 35 years. His fields of interest are psychological diagnosis, neuropsychology, the psychology of consciousness, rehabilitation and corrections. Dr. Maaser has presented numerous public presentations to mental health professionals in the areas of post traumatic stress disorder, borderline personality disorder, violence in our society, and the nature of consciousness.

www.ingramcontent.com/pod-product-compliance
Lightning Source LLC
Chambersburg PA
CBHW020922090426
42736CB00010B/996